18 TINY DEATHS

18 TINY DEATHS

THE UNTOLD STORY OF FRANCES GLESSNER LEE AND THE INVENTION OF MODERN FORENSICS

BRUCE GOLDFARB

THORNDIKE PRESS
A part of Gale, a Cengage Company

GALE
A Cengage Company

Thorndike Press® Large Print Nonfiction.
The text of this Large Print edition is unabridged.
Other aspects of the book may vary from the original edition.
Set in 16 pt. Plantin.

**LIBRARY OF CONGRESS CIP DATA ON FILE.
CATALOGUING IN PUBLICATION FOR THIS BOOK
IS AVAILABLE FROM THE LIBRARY OF CONGRESS**

ISBN-13: 978-1-4328-8008-8 (hardcover alk. paper)

Published in 2020 by arrangement with Sourcebooks, Inc.

Printed in Mexico
Print Number: 04   Print Year: 2020

For Bridgett, Kaya, and Quinn

The investigator must bear in mind that he has a two-fold responsibility — to clear the innocent as well as to expose the guilty. He is seeking only facts — the Truth in a Nutshell.

— Frances Glessner Lee

CONTENTS

KEY CHARACTERS

The Glessner Family

John Jacob Glessner

Sarah Frances Macbeth Glessner — Wife of John Jacob Glessner, known as Frances Macbeth

John George Macbeth Glessner — Son of John Jacob and Frances Macbeth Glessner, known as George

Frances Glessner Lee — Daughter of John Jacob and Frances Macbeth Glessner, known in childhood as Fanny

Glessner Family Friends

George Burgess Magrath, MD — Harvard classmate of George Glessner, medical examiner for the Northern District of Suffolk County

Isaac Scott — Designer, craftsman, and artist who made furniture and decorative objects for the Glessners

Harvard Medical School

James Bryant Conant — President of Harvard University, 1933–1953

C. Sidney Burwell, MD — Dean of Harvard Medical School, 1935–1949

Alan R. Moritz, MD — Chairman of the Department of Legal Medicine, 1937–1949

Richard Ford, MD — Chairman of the Department of Legal Medicine, 1949–1965

Others

Roger Lee, MD — Prominent Boston internist and personal physician of George Burgess Magrath and Frances Glessner Lee, to whom he was not related

Alan Gregg, MD — Director of the Medical Sciences Division of the Rockefeller Foundation, in charge of funding projects to improve medicine

Erle Stanley Gardner — Bestselling author of Perry Mason novels

12

INTRODUCTION
JUDY MELINEK, MD

I first encountered Frances Glessner Lee's dioramas as a young doctor in 2003, when I traveled to Baltimore to interview for a position at the Maryland Office of the Chief Medical Examiner. The chief, Dr. David Fowler, asked if I had seen the Nutshell Studies. I told him, honestly, that I had no idea what he was talking about. Fowler then escorted me into a dark room and switched on the lights. Pushed into a corner, some hidden under sheets to keep the dust off, were a bunch of little boxes, and inside those, enclosed in plexiglass, I discovered a precious and intricate world of violence and death.

The Nutshell Studies of Unexplained Death are miniature death scenes. I scrutinized them. In one of the tiny rooms, I noticed the dotted pattern on the tiled floor and the incredibly precise floral wallpaper. Another showed a wooden cabin with a

13

kitchen and bunk beds. There were snow-shoes in the attic, a pot on the counter. I played with dollhouses as a girl and would regularly beg my father to drive us to the miniatures store hours away from our home in order to purchase supplies for my own tiny world, but I had never seen dollhouses this sophisticated before. To make plates for my dolls, I would pop out the plastic liner inside bottle caps. The plates in the Nutshell Studies were made of porcelain. *Porcelain!* The labels on the cans stacked on the kitchen shelves and the headlines on the newspapers were legible. I couldn't stop peering at the details.

Among those details, of course, were the blood spatters on the wallpaper, the grotesquely charred remains of a body on a burned bed, a man with a purple head hanging from a noose. These were no ordinary dollhouses. This was not child's play. What was I looking at? Who made these? And the most compelling question: What had happened here, in each of these stories frozen in miniature?

I had come to the interview in Baltimore after two years of training as a forensic pathologist at the New York City Office of the Chief Medical Examiner. Part of my education there included going to death scenes with the medico-legal investigators from the office and learning what to look for at a scene and what I might find at the scene that would help inform my final determination of cause and manner of death in the sudden, unexpected, and violent stories we were tasked by law with investigating. This is how you learn death investigation anywhere — through on-the-job training.

Still, there was always something uncomfortably voyeuristic about entering someone's home unannounced and going through their medicine cabinet, trash cans, and refrigerator as a part of the process of trying to find out why they were lying dead on the floor. The investigators at the New York City OCME were certified professionals, and they told me where to focus my attention and what to look — and smell and listen and feel — for. The medicine cabinet would hold evidence of the decedent's ailments. A big bottle of antacids could mean they suffered from gastrointestinal problems, but they could also be a clue pointing to undiagnosed heart disease. Prescription drug bottles might indicate whether those medicines were being used as directed, underutilized, or abused. The wastebasket might have unpaid bills, eviction notices, or an abandoned draft of a suicide note. The refrigerator could be full of food or empty except for a single vodka bottle. If the food was fresh, so was the body, most likely. If it was rotting . . . then it could help us confirm the degree of decomposition we were observing in the decedent, in an effort to hammer down the time of death. Everything at a death scene is part of the story, and it is the details I would find there that mattered most. I couldn't interview the patient. The surrounding environment was the medical history I would rely upon the next day, in the morgue, when I would perform the forensic autopsy and add those findings to the findings from the scene. As my mentor, the late Dr. Charles Hirsch, long-serving chief medical examiner for the city of New York, taught all of us who were fortunate enough to work for him, the autopsy is only *part* of the death investigation.

It was during my autopsy training in New York that I also learned the scene findings weren't necessarily revealing. They could be irrelevant. They could be misleading. At the scene, the gun in the dead man's hand and the witness who said that he was depressed suggested a suicide; but in the morgue, the absence of powder burns or stippling on his bare skin told me the gun had to have been fired from at least thirty inches away. He was murdered, and the scene staged to look like a suicide. The dead woman in her apartment appeared to have died peacefully in her sleep. The next day, in the morgue, her naked dissected body showed the deep bruises under the unblemished skin of her neck, and the petechial hemorrhages in the whites of her eyes were witness to homicidal strangulation. I learned what you see at the scene can inform what you see in the morgue, but it cannot replace it.

Peering into the unique and incomparable scenes encased in the Nutshell Studies, I was taken back in time to a period in history when death investigation was beginning to emerge as a scientific discipline, and doctors were just starting to challenge the primacy of coroners and police detectives in distinguishing criminal acts from other types of deaths. Here was the work of both a gifted artisan and a medical expert, joining her skills to create something more than science and deeper than art. The exhibits were designed to be functional, educational, and fully decipherable — but the interpretation of each scene could change based on the medical information provided by autopsy findings. There is something about peering into a room from above, at dolls rather than at moving, living people (or their no-longer-moving, no-longer-living bodies) that allows you the time and space to train your eye, that makes you notice the details. I realized the Nutshell Studies were my on-the-job training with the New York OCME death investigators, but in miniature. The skills I learned from those investigators in life-size apartments and homes, businesses and construction sites, could be honed here, too, from many types of scenes at once, and in minute detail. I was awed by the time and effort it must have taken to create such elaborate, complex, and perplexing scenarios, and at how much could be gleaned from close observation of them.

When I first viewed those dioramas, stashed away in the back room of the Baltimore OCME's office, they had been in storage for years, and they were not in the best shape. Their only pupils seemed to be the staff of the medical examiner's office, who occasionally brought in visitors to look at them as historical curiosities. There was no way for the public to see them. As far as I knew, despite their age and condition, they were still being used for training death investigators. Still, it seemed to me a sad fate for such a remarkable body of work.

In subsequent years, and with the dedicated attention of Bruce Goldfarb, an administrator at the Baltimore OCME and the author of this book, Frances Lee's Nutshell Studies of Unexplained Death have been repaired, renovated, and preserved. They were displayed at the Smithsonian Institution in 2017 and 2018, and they have been publicized in books and magazines and on the internet. This book is a culmination of years of historical research using primary sources, including the papers of Frances Glessner Lee herself. It is the story of how one stubborn, intelligent, and creative self-taught woman immersed herself in a passion that had immense repercussions in the fields of both medicine and the law. Goldfarb places Frances Glessner Lee and her intelligence, influence, wealth, and forceful personality in context within the world of medico-legal death investigation. As this absorbing and evocative book will show you, Frances Glessner Lee should be recognized as the matriarch of the modern practice of forensic pathology.

Her 18 Tiny Deaths have made a whole world of a difference.

Judy Melinek, MD,
forensic pathologist and coauthor (with T. J. Mitchell) of the memoir *Working Stiff: Two Years, 262 Bodies, and the Making of a*

1
LEGAL MEDICINE

October 2, 1944
Seventeen pathologists and medical examiners, all dressed in dark suits and neckties, sat around a long table in a wood-paneled conference room on the third floor of Building E-1 of Harvard Medical School. It was the autumn of 1944. Thousands of miles away, war ravaged Europe and the Pacific islands. The men had gathered at Harvard to attend a seminar on legal medicine, a field that would later be known as forensic science — the application of medicine to matters of law and justice.

Dr. Alan R. Moritz broke the grim news to the group. Unfortunately, Captain Frances Glessner Lee, her preferred title since being made an officer in the New Hampshire State Police the previous year, was unable to attend the seminar as planned, he told the men. She had fractured her right tibia in a fall and subsequently suffered two heart attacks.

As trained professionals affiliated with one of America's most prestigious medical institutions, the men well understood the grave prognostic implications for a woman almost sixty-seven years of age with a constellation of health problems. The heart attacks were the latest setback of encroaching infirmity that increasingly limited Lee's ability to function day to day. Now she faced a long period of strict bed rest under the watchful care of a physician.

For Moritz, one of the nation's leading pathologists, Lee's absence was a personal and professional loss. The seminar participants would miss the benefit of Lee's encyclopedic knowledge of legal medicine as well as the civilizing effect of her presence.

Lee's seminar curriculum was intended to provide the men specialized knowledge to probe unexpected and unexplained deaths, including how to estimate the time of death, decomposition and other postmortem changes, blunt and sharp force injuries, and related areas of death investigation. No other medical school in America offered anything like it.

Lee was an improbable figure to assume the mantle of authority in the emerging field of legal medicine. A decorous grandmother with a preference for brimless Queen Mary hats and black dresses she sewed herself, Lee was an independently wealthy scion of Gilded Age Chicago society. Often a difficult woman with impossibly exacting standards of perfection and an almost fanatical sense of purpose, Lee was more than just a guiding presence for Harvard's legal medicine program. By the force of her personality and spending a substantial portion of her personal wealth, Lee was nearly single-handedly responsible for the establishment of legal medicine in the United States.

As a reformer, educator, and advocate, her influence on the field was immeasurable. This genteel matron, herself on the threshold of senescence, was respected as one of legal medicine's leading authorities. But getting to that point had not been an easy path for Lee. "Men are dubious of an elderly woman with a cause," she once said. "My problem is to convince them that I am not trying to butt in or run anything. Also, I have to sell them on the fact that I know what I am talking about."

In the seven years since she had approved hiring Moritz to chair the country's first academic program in legal medicine, Lee and Moritz had become friends as well as collaborators. They had been working on an innovative project that could revolutionize the investigation of unexpected and suspicious deaths: an intensive, week-long seminar on legal medicine for police officers. The ambitious curriculum mapped out by Lee and Moritz was groundbreaking, intended to train police in modern scientific forensic methods.

For the better part of two years, Lee had been working obsessively on a series of intricately detailed scale-model dioramas to teach crime scene observation, the identification of clues that may be important to determining the cause and manner of deaths that are unexpected, sudden, or the result of injury. She called the teaching models the Nutshell Studies of Unexplained Death. Now, because of her illness, their plans seemed doomed.

"The models are none of them finished and none of them can be finished," Lee wrote Moritz while recuperating at The Rocks, her fifteen-hundred-acre estate near Littleton, New Hampshire. "I hope you will agree with me that under these circumstances the Police Seminar should not be held."

In the Building E-1 conference room, the men paused in their somber legal medicine studies curriculum to draft a resolution for Moritz to deliver to Lee:

> Resolved, that Mrs. Frances G. Lee shall have the everlasting gratitude of all those attending the Seminar in Legal Medicine at Harvard Medical School in 1944, and that all those present extend their profound thanks and appreciation for her philanthropy which has made possible the holding of these seminars which, in turn, have done so much to advance the cause of legal medicine throughout the United States; and that it is the sincere hope of all of those present that Mrs. Lee will soon be fully restored to her normal health and activities.

To appreciate Captain Lee's pioneering work in legal medicine, it is necessary to travel back in time and understand how societies have dealt with death, especially unexpected or unexplained death, over the centuries.

A little more than 1.4 million Americans died during the year of 1944 according to the Vital Statistics of the United States. Most of these people died at home or in hospitals. Their deaths were attended by a doctor, nurse, or family member. They were known to have an illness or disease, became progressively worse, and then died.

Historically, about one in five deaths are sudden and unexpected. These are people not known to be ill who died by violence or injury or under unexplained circumstances. Of these 283,000 or so questionable deaths in 1944, no more than one or two percent, a few thousand at most, were investigated by qualified medical examiners — doctors with specialized training to diagnose cause and manner of death. At that time, only a handful of East Coast cities — Boston, New York, Baltimore, and Newark — had competent medical examiners trained in legal medicine and who had properly equipped offices. The vast portion of the United States still used the coroner system, an archaic throwback to medieval England.

Despite its universality as an inevitable fact, the occasion of death has always held a special place in human experience. Intellectually, we know it happens to all of us and everyone we know, but when somebody dies, it's still shocking and upsetting. The need for answers is deeply rooted. What happened? Why did this person die?

The earliest methodical inquiries into the nature of a death were mostly concerned with suicide. Through human history, suicide was viewed an act of defiance against god or authority or a crime against oneself known as *felo de se*. Soldiers of the Roman Empire who took their lives were considered deserters. Some cemeteries prohibited the burial of a person who died by suicide.

The coroner system of death investigation dates from medieval England. As the "keeper of the pleas of the Crown," an official known as the crowner (later corrupted into coroner) served as the royal judicial representative. The coroner had a variety of responsibilities. One of his primary duties was collecting money owed to the monarchy, mainly taxes and fines. The coroner was designated to serve writs from the court — orders and summonses — on the sheriff or, when necessary, arrest a sheriff. He was also authorized to seize royal fishes — sturgeon, porpoise, and other sea life fit only for the palate of a king — and investigate shipwrecks and treasure troves. It was his job to make sure the crown received its share.

The coroner also investigated deaths that were sudden or apparently unnatural, mainly to determine whether the decedent was murdered or a suicide. A murderer who was executed or imprisoned forfeited all his property — home, land, all his possessions. Since suicide was a crime against the crown, the coroner took his property too.

Coroners are responsible for answering two questions: what caused this death and who is responsible for this death. One is a medical question, while the other is a matter of criminal justice. The coroner didn't need any knowledge of medicine or the law. He would hold an inquest, a process that is part investigation and part adjudication. The coroner called together an inquest jury of ten or twelve men, most of whom were illiterate farmers and many of whom likely knew the deceased or were witnesses to the death. Only adult men were allowed to participate in inquests.

The coroner and inquest jury were required to observe the dead body, often at the place where the death occurred or the body was found. The inquest had to be held *super visum corporis* ("upon view of the body"). Failure to view the body voided the inquest. If there was no body to view, an inquest could not be held at all. The jury had to get a good look at the body, not just a quick peek. They were required to examine the body for signs of violence and note the presence of wounds.

Of course, without a foundation of basic medical knowledge, there is little to learn from looking at a dead body. Nonetheless, after viewing the body and hearing from witnesses, the jury rendered a verdict by holding a vote. It wasn't very scientific.

If it was decided that the decedent had been murdered, the inquest was then required to name the killer. The coroner was authorized to charge the accused murderer and arrest him, and it was the duty of the sheriff to hold the accused in jail until trial. The coroner heard confessions when they were offered and confiscated the property of those who were convicted and executed.

When northern Europeans colonized America, they brought English common law along with them. Today's sheriff, justice of the peace, and coroner are lingering vestiges of the Middle Ages.

One of the earliest American coroner's inquests on record took place in New Plymouth during the winter of 1635 when John Deacon, a fur trader's servant in his twenties, was found dead. "Having searched the dead body, we finde not any blows or wounds, or any other bodily hurt," the jury reported. "We finde that bodily weakness caused by long fasting and weariness, by going to and fro, with the extreme cold of the season were the causes of his death."

Maryland had its first coroner three years after the colony was founded. Thomas

Baldridge, a tobacco farmer, was appointed sheriff and coroner of St. Mary's County in 1637. Baldridge was given the rather vague instruction to "Doe all and everything . . . the office of sheriff or coroner of any county in England doe." A more detailed description of the coroner's duties was issued in 1640:

Upon notice or suspicion of any person that hath or shall come to his or her death entirely within the limits of that hundred as you conveniently may to view the dead body and to charge the said persons with an oath truly to inquire and true verdict to grant how the person viewed came upon his or her death according to the evidence.

Two days after being appointed coroner, on January 31, 1637, Baldridge held his first inquest. An inquest jury of twelve freemen, all tobacco farmers, was summoned to view the body of John Bryant, who had been killed while chopping down a tree. Joseph Edlow, also a tobacco farmer, was with Bryant when it happened.

Testifying under oath, Edlow told the inquest jury that he warned Bryant to get out of the way. "John, have a care of your selfe, for the tree is falling," he recalled telling his friend. Edlow said that Bryant stepped back five or six paces. As the tree toppled, it glanced off another tree and rebounded onto Bryant, crushing him beneath its weight. "The said John Bryant spake not one word after," the inquest record noted.

Baldridge and the inquest jury examined Bryant's body and noted "two scratches under his chinne on the left side." They did about as well as could be expected of a group of untrained tobacco farmers, reaching the conclusion that Bryant died because "his bloud bulke broke."

As coroner, it was Baldridge's duty to bury the body as well as to sell off Bryant's property to settle his debts. The record of Bryant's inquest includes a dreary inventory of his earthly possessions: "two suits & an old doublett," stockings and drawers, bowls and spoons, a few scraps of furniture, a canoe, a cock and hen, and his servant, Elias Beach.

The earliest known forensic autopsy in America was performed in St. Mary's County, Maryland, on February 25, 1642. It was performed by George Binx, a "Licentiate in Physicke" who served as foreman on the coroner's inquest investigating the death of a Native American youth shot by a blacksmith by the name of John Dandy.

"We find that this Indian ladd (named Edward) came to his death by a bullet shott by John dandy, which bullet entered the epigastrium neare the navel on the right side, obliquely descending, & piercing the guts, glancing on the last vertebra of the back, and was lodged in the side of Ano [the anus]," the inquest reported.

As for Dandy, he was fined three thousand pounds of tobacco and sentenced to death. The coroner seized all of Dandy's "goods & chattells, & in the meane time to remove his gonnes & ammunition, into some place more secure from surprisall of Indians." Dandy's death sentence was commuted to a seven-year term of service as the public executioner.

The course of human history is overall one of continual progress and advancement. Our lives improved immeasurably by breathtaking advances in agriculture, sanitation, transportation, and medicine. We tamed electricity, built railroads, and invented telephones. But for the better part of three centuries, little changed in how unnatural deaths were investigated in America. For most of the country, the investigation of death remained a peculiar anachronism, a holdover from the thirteenth century related more closely to alchemy than to modern science-based medicine.

The coroner was a local official with a jurisdiction within a county or city. He might have been a sheriff, magistrate, or justice of the peace. He also could have been a woodworker, baker, or butcher. In many places, the local undertaker served as the coroner. The coroner got the job by being elected to office or by being appointed to office by elected officials. As such, the position was inherently political. He didn't get the job on the basis of his diligence and expertise but for his political affiliations and loyalties. Keeping the job depended on remaining in the good graces of voters or political leaders. Since the coroner didn't necessarily know anything about medicine, he had help in determining the cause of death from a doctor, known variously as the coroner's physician, medical referee, or medical examiner.

Some might argue that a coroner's inquest may have been good enough back in the day when America was mostly rural and agrarian. Most sudden deaths were likely to be from accidents or natural causes like heart attack or stroke. On the rare occasions of a suspicious death, the culprit usually didn't have opportunity to travel far from the scene. There were often witnesses. Identifying a body wasn't an issue because there were usually family or neighbors around. Most people didn't travel far from where they were born, so everybody knew everybody and their business. Perhaps twelve uninformed minds using common sense were better than nothing at all.

The deficiencies of the coroner system, however, grew more apparent as the population of urban areas swelled. As people crowded into cities, the opportunities for crime increased. Within a few blocks of a big city, tens of thousands lived in ramshackle tenements. Cities teemed with vulnerable populations: transients, immigrants, people who left the farm to seek work. A perpetrator could quickly distance himself from his deeds by streetcar or train. It was easy to vanish in a city like New York, Philadelphia, Chicago, or Boston, and that made investigating suspicious deaths more difficult.

Additionally, throughout most of the country, the coroner system was notoriously corrupt and incompetent. The coroner was in a position ripe for bribery, kickbacks, and extortion. He could send bodies to undertakers willing to line his pockets. In some jurisdictions, the coroner was authorized to file charges and set bail in cases of homicide or criminal negligence, such as a workplace death — problems that can be resolved with money and influence.

Authorizing coroners to call inquests at their own discretion, for which the coroner and the inquest jurors were paid by the case, essentially gave coroners a free hand in the public treasury. Inquest juries were packed with cronies and associates who could be trusted to rubber stamp whatever conclusion was preferred by police or prosecutors. Rather than being an asset to criminal justice, coroners were often a detriment. They unnecessarily delayed charges in cases of homicide, and due to their ineptitude, they made basic errors in the performance of their duties. Coroners were often terrible witnesses in court, giving testimony that was unreliable and useless to prosecutors.

The men who served as coroner's physicians were often no better, largely incompetent and indifferent. In the 1920s, Columbia University criminal justice professor Raymond Moley conducted a study of coroner cases in Cuyahoga County, Ohio, which includes the city of Cleveland. He found a plethora of nonsensical causes of death, such as "could be suicide or murder," "aunt said she complained of pneumonia, looked like narcotism," "looks suspicious of strychnine poisoning," "found dead," "head severed from body," "could be assault or diabetes," "diabetes, tuberculosis, or nervous indigestion," and "found crushed."

In 1914, a man by the name of Leonard Wallstein, New York City's commissioner of accounts, conducted an investigation of the city's coroner system. The commissioner of accounts is similar to an inspector general, with the authority to issue subpoenas for documents and compel testimony.

Word of the investigation lit a fire under coroners who had been sitting on long-overdue reports. Within a month of Wallstein's investigation being announced, coroners filed reports on 431 potentially criminal deaths, nearly 200 of which were more than a year old and 63 of which were more than three years old.

After hearings with scores of witnesses, including all the city's coroners and coroners' physicians, Wallstein issued a scathing report in January 1915. Of all the men holding office as coroner, "not one was thoroughly qualified by training or experience for the adequate performance of his duties," according to Wallstein's report.

Of the sixty-five men who had served as

coroner since New York City was consolidated in 1898, only nineteen were doctors. The report noted that eight were undertakers, seven were "politicians and chronic office-holders," six were real estate dealers, two were saloon keepers, two were plumbers, and the remainder previously worked in a variety of occupations including printer, auctioneer, butcher, musician, milkman, and wood carver.

George LeBrun, who served as a coroner's secretary for four decades, said in his testimony that New York City's coroners were "outrageous crooks who dispensed 'justice' for cash. Their only interest in each new case was to discover how they could extort money, and they used their office for blackmail purposes."

Coroners' physicians were "drawn from the ranks of mediocrity," Wallstein's report said. Good doctors with thriving practices didn't want to be bothered with examining dead bodies in the middle of the night or be inconvenienced by entanglement in a legal proceeding. Doctors willing to serve as coroners' physicians were motivated by a steady source of easy money. They often did a cursory, superficial examination of a body or none at all. The report documented instances of doctors signing stacks of death certificates at the morgue with barely a glance at the bodies.

The cause of death certified by coroners was often questionable to the point of absurdity. In one example, a man had his cause of death listed as rupture of a thoracic aneurysm, a diagnosis that had somehow been made without benefit of an autopsy. The coroner's report failed to mention that the man was found holding in his right hand a .38-caliber revolver with one spent round and a lethal bullet wound in his mouth.

Wallstein's investigators reviewed eight hundred death certificates and found a "complete lack of evidence to justify the certified cause of death" in 40 percent of the documents. When coroners' physicians were asked why they chose one diagnosis over another with similar signs and symptoms, they often admitted an inability to explain their conclusions. They seemed to pluck diagnoses out of thin air.

"Generally, the coroners' physicians have a preferred cause of death," Wallstein's report said. "Among these are chronic nephritis, chronic endocarditis and, among infants, infantile convulsions . . . A contest between chronic nephritis and endocarditis, for example, would be both close and exciting."

The cause of death certified by coroners was so untrustworthy that health department officials testified that the city's vital statistics would be more accurate if death certificates signed by coroners were excluded altogether.

By contrast, in a medical examiner system, the responsibility to diagnose the cause and manner of death is in the hands of a competent doctor with specialized training in these diagnoses. The criminal justice aspects of the coroner's job are performed by the police, prosecutors, and the courts. Inquests are eliminated altogether.

This is not to say that all coroners were corrupt or incompetent. Certainly, there were decent men with integrity who conducted their duty in good faith. By the same token, some medical examiners were doctors unfit for the task. In their defense, doctors weren't taught much about death in medical school, since the patients they were expected to treat were living. Diagnosing cause and manner of death was not part of medical school curriculum at that time.

Police were also utterly unequipped for scientific homicide investigations until midway through the twentieth century. Few police departments required a college degree for employment, and many police officers didn't even graduate from high school. As with coroners, many police officers were unable to read and write, particularly those in smaller towns and rural areas. Training for the job was minimal. The Cleveland Police Department's eight-week course for new recruits, established sometime in the late 1910s, was considered one of the most rigorous in the nation. Officers weren't hired for their intelligence but for their strength and fearlessness, the ability to break up a brawl or strong-arm a suspect into custody. Critical thinking skills weren't necessary if a suspect's confession could be coerced by third-degree tactics — intimidation, threats, or acts of physical violence.

At the scene of a death, the police were often a hindrance. Through their clumsy efforts, police were likely to destroy evidence — walking through blood, moving the body, handling a weapon, putting their finger through bullet holes in clothing. What the police did during those first moments influenced everything that subsequently happened in the investigation. If the police didn't handle the scene properly — if they overlooked signs of foul play or failed to preserve evidence that was critical for determining the cause and manner of death — the investigation was bungled from the beginning.

In Raymond Moley's report on criminal justice in Cleveland, he reserved particularly harsh criticism for detectives, presumably the senior and more experienced police officers, whom he described as undisciplined, poorly trained, and ill-equipped to work homicides and other serious crimes. "These detectives are supposed to be the cream of the uniformed force," Moley said. "About 25 percent are possessed of inferior intelligence, which means that they have the mentality of boys nine to thirteen. This is attested by numerous examples of poor detective work."

In the mid to late 1800s, the reputation of coroners in Boston was as bad as anywhere. There was no limit to the number of coroners the governor could appoint. The designation of coroner was a valuable plum to hand out as a political favor, practically a license to steal. Before the medical examiner office was established in 1877, Boston had forty-three coroners. The city of New York, with three times the population of Boston, had four coroners for the entire jurisdiction. Suffolk County had more coroners than New York City, Philadelphia, New Orleans, Chicago, San Francisco, Baltimore, and Washington, DC, combined.

"You have in the coroner an officer armed practically with the utmost power of the law," said prominent Boston attorney Theodore Tyndale.

He decides in the first place, upon his discretion, whether an inquest be necessary or not; it is obvious how large are the opportunities for corruption in this direction: that for a man whose cupidity or possibly culpability and fear are stronger than his honor and integrity, it would not be difficult to thwart justice and close the door to all judicial investigation of a crime by corruptly declaring an inquest unnecessary, and even aiding in the removal of suspicion and the concealment of the evidence and traces by authorizing a speedy burial. But if he may thus on the one hand shield the guilty and endanger the public safety, on the other the opportunities for a man prompted by malice or vindictiveness or the desire of cheap notoriety are enough, truly, to make us tremble.

The scandal that precipitated the end of the coroner system in Boston began when the body of a newborn baby was found in a trash can. One of Boston's district coroners convened an inquest, which returned a verdict of "death at the hands of a person unknown." Each member of the inquest jury earned two dollars, and the coroner made ten dollars. But rather than show some decency, coroners saw an opportunity. The body of the baby was dumped in another district for another coroner to hold another inquest and dump the body again. Four times this decomposing baby was exploited until word of this appalling practice got out.

That was the end of coroners in Boston. In 1877, lawmakers abolished coroners and inquests and placed a competent doctor in charge of death investigations.

This, then, was the world Captain Frances Glessner Lee made her mission to change. Before her time, progress in the field of death investigation was slow, lurching toward progress only when scandals shocked the public's sensibilities. It was her goal to bring the United States out of the Middle Ages, to replace coroners with medical examiners and modernize the investigation of sudden and unexplained deaths.

The Chicago Police Department is older than the city of Chicago itself. On January 31, 1835, two years before the city was incorporated, the Illinois General Assembly authorized the town of Chicago to establish its own police force. Seven months later, Orsemus Morrison was elected the town's first constable.

As constable, Morrison carried the "staff of office," a whitewashed wood baton that was more ornament than weapon, to indicate the authority of his elected position. His duties included collecting fines and taxes and serving as coroner of Cook County by leading inquest juries in cases of questionable deaths.

The first death that Morrison investigated was that of a visiting Frenchman found dead in the fall of 1835. He was discovered in the early morning, half-buried in a muddy pit in "the woods," an area densely overgrown with foliage bounded by LaSalle, Washington, and Randolph Streets — the location of present-day city hall. Morrison called an inquest jury. The decedent, they were told, had been staying at a hotel and went out for an evening walk. He had been drinking and apparently got lost and became mired in the mud pit, where he fell victim to the elements. The jury concluded that the man froze to death by misadventure. No evidence suggested otherwise.

At the time of Morrison's tenure as constable, Chicago was a village of fewer than

4,500 inhabitants. Favorably located in proximity to the Great Lakes, railroads, and the Mississippi River, Chicago rapidly grew into a major center of manufacturing and distribution. Agricultural equipment sold through Chicago transformed the country's vast prairies into productive farmland. Cattle and hogs raised on farms throughout the Midwest returned to Chicago for slaughter and from there, along with corn and grain, were shipped throughout the United States. The city became home to some of the country's largest manufacturers and some of the country's wealthiest families.

During the 1800s, the population of Chicago rose at a breathtaking rate. By 1860, Chicago was home to more than one hundred thousand people. In the next decade, the population nearly tripled, approaching three hundred thousand. And among the legion of young people migrating to Chicago during this period of growth were Lee's parents, John Jacob Glessner and Frances Macbeth.

The son of a newspaper publisher, Glessner was born in 1842 and spent his formative years in Zanesville, Ohio, At the age of twenty, he struck out on his own and took a position as bookkeeper at Warder, Child, & Co. in Springfield, an industrial town in the southwest part of the state. Warder, Child, & Co., a maker of reapers, mowers, and planters, was one of the largest farm equipment companies in the country. In Springfield, Glessner rented a room with the Macbeth family, where he met and fell in love with Frances, a young schoolteacher. He rapidly advanced his station in Warder, Child, & Co. Adept in the world of business, Glessner seemed destined for success.

In 1869, the firm's principals decided to open an office in Chicago to increase their share of agricultural markets in the Midwest. Glessner asked to head up the new operation in Chicago, so long as he was given authority to run the business as he saw fit, and he was appointed a vice president of the company. He and Frances were married at her parent's home in Springfield, then after a visit to his parents in Zanesville, they took the train to begin their new lives in Chicago.

On October 2, 1871, one week before Chicago's Great Fire, the Glessners celebrated the birth of their first child, George Macbeth. A daughter, Frances, arrived on March 25, 1878. A plump and healthy baby, she was called Fanny.

As Glessner's career advanced, his personal wealth grew accordingly. As a junior partner, Glessner's share of the company's profits in 1877 was $39,600 or almost $872,000 in present-day value. By the time he was forty years old, Glessner was a millionaire, with a net worth of about $27 million in today's currency. He was among the wealthiest men in Chicago.

Eventually, five major agricultural machinery companies — the McCormick Harvesting Machine Company, Deering Company, Plano Manufacturing Company, Wisconsin Harvester Company, and Warder, Bushnell, & Glessner (the successor of Warder, Child, & Co.) — merged to form the International Harvester Company. At its inception, the company was valued at $150 million. By then the last active principal of Warder, Bushnell, & Glessner, John Jacob Glessner was elected chairman of International Harvester's executive committee. He suddenly owned a piece of the largest manufacturing company in the world, and his family's security was set for generations.

In their personal lives, the Glessners' wealth allowed them to indulge their shared passion for music and the arts. They enjoyed live performances, attending the opera and musical events at venues throughout Chicago, and raised their children, George and Fanny, to appreciate the fine arts their parents patronized. Most of all, the Glessners enjoyed classical symphonic music. Glessner was one of a group of prominent Chicagoans who provided the funding to establish the Chicago Symphony Orchestra in 1891. He was a staunch supporter and benefactor of the orchestra for the rest of his life.

Elected a trustee of the Orchestral Association, Glessner contributed more than $12,000 to the construction of Orchestra Hall, designed by Daniel Burnham. When Orchestra Hall was completed in 1904, Box M, directly behind the conductor's podium, was reserved exclusively for the Glessners. The Glessners were also close friends of Chicago Symphony Orchestra conductor Theodore Thomas, his successor, Frederick Stock, and several members of the orchestra. Ignacy Jan Paderewski, a celebrated concert pianist who served as prime minister of Poland, was another family friend. Music was often performed in their home.

The Glessners were enthusiasts of cultural and intellectual self-improvement. John Jacob was active in the Literary Club, while Frances took lessons in literature, French, Italian, and German. They enjoyed acquiring fine furniture, art, and decorative objects for their home.

During a visit to the Interstate Industrial Exposition in 1875, the Glessners admired black walnut furniture carved by Isaac Scott. Scott was an artist, woodworker, and designer particularly known for art furniture. The Glessners commissioned Scott to build a bookcase for their home. It was the beginning of a close personal friendship the Glessners had with Scott for the remainder of his life. Over a matter of years, Scott designed furniture, pottery, picture frames, embroidered works, pewter, and other decorative items for the Glessners.

Wealth seemed to assure a life of comfort and security for the Glessner children.

2
THE SUNNY STREET OF THE SIFTED FEW

Privilege is no immunity to misfortune. George Glessner developed severe hay fever at around age four. By the time Fanny was born, his doctor advised the Glessners to summer away from the filthy, pollen-filled air of Chicago and take George to the country for respite from his symptoms.

The Glessners heard about an area in the White Mountains of New Hampshire with a claim for being practically pollen-free. They visited in the summer of 1878. Frances had taken ill since Fanny's birth, so she remained in Chicago with the baby while George was sent to New Hampshire with Frances's sisters, Helen and Lizzie.

After a two-day train ride, the group arrived in Littleton, New Hampshire. Littleton was a town of fewer than two thousand people about twenty-five miles west of Mount Washington. Littleton had a well-developed hospitality industry receiving guests from the Midwest and the East Coast. At the time, the White Mountains region boasted numerous large hotels and resorts — the Flume House, the Maplewood, the Mount Pleasant, the Fabyans, and the Crawford House among the best known. George and his aunts booked themselves into the Oak Hill House, but the boy experienced little relief of his symptoms. Helen Macbeth consulted a local doctor, a homeopath, who concluded that George wasn't "far enough into the mountains." The doctor recommended a hotel about fourteen miles away, the Twin Mountain House.

It turned out that the homeopath may have been onto something. "Aunt Helen made the move and George was very much better almost overnight," according to Lee's recollection. At last, George found blessed relief from the misery of hay fever.

Frances Glessner Lee later described the Twin Mountain House as a "great barn of a place." It was an impressively grand three-story wood frame structure, with the upper floor a steeply sloped mansard roof. "Of course there was no plumbing," she said.

Many guests, including the Glessner family, returned to the Twin Mountain House summer after summer. One Twin Mountain regular was Henry Ward Beecher, a celebrated clergyman who was an outspoken abolitionist and suffragist. Beecher had recently been embroiled in scandal, his reputation soiled by an adulterous relationship with his assistant's wife and the high-profile lawsuit brought by the wronged husband that followed.

At Twin Mountain House, five-year-old Fanny befriended Beecher. "He took a fancy to me as I did to him," she recalled. "In the middle of the morning he would go into the bar for a lemonade and often took me with him. I would sit on his knee with a little glass of ice cold lemonade."

One morning, during a visit with his family, John Jacob walked down the stairs and saw Fanny sitting with Beecher, having their lemonades. He stopped in his tracks, disapproving of his young daughter being in the company of unsavory characters. He spoke with his wife. "My dear, a summer hotel is not a good place to bring up children," he told her. "I think if we're going to have to come up here year after year for George's hay fever, that we will have to have a home of our own."

Touring the area in a horse-drawn buggy, the Glessners found a prominent hill that had been cleared of timber, leaving a rough rocky pasture strewn with boulders. The view was spectacular, with Mount Washington to the east and the towns of Bethlehem, Littleton, and Scythefactoryville spread out below. The Glessners purchased one hundred acres of farmland from Oren Streeter for $23,000, which included a farmhouse and a few assorted ramshackle buildings on the property. They called their new summer home The Rocks. The summer home would become one of the most important places in their lives for many decades to come.

Isaac Scott designed a nineteen-room mansion built on a high prominence overlooking the White Mountains. It was completed by the summer of 1883 at a cost of $10–15,000. The Glessners called their summer residence the Big House.

The Glessner's Big House was "the finest summer residence in the mountains," according to the *Littleton Gazette.* The home had "one of the finest and most extensive views of any house in the mountains."

Scott designed a carriage barn with a granite foundation and wood shingle siding, which was completed the following year. He designed many buildings and structures for The Rocks, including an apiary for Frances Macbeth's beekeeping and several gazebo-like summerhouses that dotted the estate, connected by walking trails. For young Fanny, Scott designed something truly special: her own two-room log cabin playhouse, complete with a kitchen with a working wood-burning stove.

In the neighboring villages of Littleton and Bethlehem, there were distinct class differences between townsfolk who had lived in the area for generations and the wealthier newcomers like the Glessners who purchased summer homes at the higher, more picturesque elevations. It was "up the hill" — the seasonal residents — and "down the hill" — people who lived there year-round. Locals couldn't understand why somebody would prefer to build a grand house way up in the mountains, in the middle of nowhere, far from the amenities of town. Sensing their curiosity, Frances Glessner invited local residents to visit The Rocks and meet the family. She made elaborate preparations for her guests, having a huge black fruitcake made by Delmonico's restaurant in New York City and stocking her cellar with fine French wines.

One day, a mountain wagon drawn by four horses brought about sixteen guests from the Twin Mountain House to call on the Glessners. Frances had the wine and fruitcake brought out and served. "Each lady looked at the cake and with turned up nose said, 'No thank you' until one lady braver than the others took both cake and wine and then said, 'Better take some, Mrs. Devoe, it's pretty good,' " Fanny recalled later in life.

The visitors peppered the Glessners with questions. *Don't you get lonely up here? Do you get anything to eat up here?* "We were always so glad to see them go and so annoyed when they came," Fanny said.

For a while, visiting The Rocks became something to do, to go see what the Glessners were up to. Wagonloads of locals and seasonal visitors came around at random intervals, much to the annoyance of the family. Matters came to a head one day when a wagonload of tourists pulled up to the kitchen window and ordered a pitcher of lemonade. The cook, in no subtle terms, refused. Fanny took great pleasure in telling the story to her parents, who had a pair of formal stone gateposts installed — the gate was never closed — and a sign that read THE PUBLIC IS REQUESTED NOT TO ENTER THESE GROUNDS.

There was "much discussion over whether it should be 'the public is' or 'the public are,' " Fanny said.

Around this time, the Glessners began to

think about building a home of their own in Chicago. They wanted a home designed and built for them, one that reflected their tastes and style and in their way contributed to the architectural renaissance of post-fire Chicago.

Having looked at several neighborhoods, the Glessners settled on acquiring a lot on the southwest corner of Prairie Avenue and Eighteenth Street, on the city's near South Side.

Some of the finest homes in Chicago were on Prairie Avenue. The street was lined with magnificent mansions framed by manicured lawns and sculpted gardens, majestically sweeping staircases leading to porches or grand entrances.

John Jacob Glessner wanted an architect of note for the home. He regarded Henry Hobson Richardson highly but had been informed by friends that Richardson only undertook monumental buildings — Boston's Trinity Church, the Buffalo State Asylum for the Insane, and Albany's city hall, among others. He decided to contact Richardson anyway.

Richardson, along with Louis Sullivan and Frank Lloyd Wright, was one of the leading architects of his time. After attending Harvard, he went to Paris in 1860 to attend the famed École des Beaux Arts — only the second American to attend the École's architectural division.

The style that Richardson developed for his designs, like Isaac Scott's with its allusions to medieval elements, was so distinctive that it is known as Richardsonian Romanesque. Characteristics common to Richardson's buildings include thick walls, semicircular stone arches, and clusters of squat columns.

Glessner told Richardson that he'd heard he only did large, institutional buildings and not private residences.

"I'll plan anything a man wants, from a cathedral to a chicken coop," Richardson said. "That's the way I make my living."

Glessner and Richardson took a carriage to visit their Washington Street residence to give Richardson a sense of the Glessners' present circumstances. They sat in the library to discuss Glessner's needs and wants for his family's home. On the mantel was a small photograph of a building at Abingdon Abbey in Oxfordshire, England.

"Do you like that?" Richardson asked, gesturing to the photo.

"Yes," Glessner replied.

"Well, give it to me," Richardson said. "I'll make that the keynote of your house."

Later, driving to view the lot, Richardson sat in silence in the carriage. After several minutes, he blurted out, "Have you the courage to build the house without windows on the street front?"

"Yes," Glessner said without hesitation, knowing that he could tear up the plans if they were not to his satisfaction.

The men agreed to discuss plans for the house during dinner at the Glessners' the following night.

Frances painted a vivid portrait of Richardson in her journal, describing him as "the largest man I have ever seen." Concerned about resting his girth on the Glessners' fine furniture, Richardson insisted on sitting on a piano stool during his visit.

"He parts his hair in the middle," she wrote in her journal. "He stutters and spatters — breathes very heavily — and aside from his profession is not what I would call an interesting man."

After dinner was served, Richardson took a scrap of paper and began sketching in pencil. He drew a large L shape, marked the location of entrances, and filled it with boxes to represent rooms. Within minutes, he had designed the first floor of the house, almost exactly as it was ultimately built.

"He was the most versatile, interesting,

ready, capable and confident of artists, the most genial and agreeable of companions," John Jacob said of Richardson. "He delighted in difficult problems."

Richardson's plan for the Glessner home was a stark departure from typical residential architecture of the time. It was certainly unlike any other home on prestigious Prairie Avenue. Rather than framing a welcoming front yard, the north and east exterior walls of the Glessners' house are almost at the sidewalk property line. Rows of rusticated Wellesley granite blocks in contrasting colors emphasize the home's horizontal lines. With only small square windows at the street level, the public is presented broad, flat, relatively unornamented walls.

The long side of the house on Eighteenth Street has a few narrow windows on the first floor and a service entrance sheltered by a semicircular arch. The main entrance, on Prairie Avenue, is understated, almost plain. No staircase, no veranda, just a modest street-level door of heavy oak. Stylized columns support another semicircular arch, smaller than the service entrance.

From the outside, the Glessners' house looked institutional, like a prison or hospital. What the public couldn't see was that the house wrapped around a large private courtyard. All the landscaped spaces of the home were within the courtyard, away from public view, giving the family their own private oasis in the city.

Stepping through the front door, a twelve-foot-wide staircase leads to a foyer large enough to be a hotel lobby. There's enough room in the eighteen-thousand-square-foot house for a sit-down dinner with more than one hundred guests, which the family eventually did many times.

Richardson placed the main family rooms in the interior of the house, facing the courtyard. Windows on the southern side bathed the family's living spaces with warm light. Most of the rooms have two or more entryways, allowing household staff to move discreetly through the house. A hallway along the north side of the house, used primarily by staff, insulated the family from street noise and Chicago's bitter winter winds.

Reactions to the Glessners' new home were mixed to say the least. Frances Macbeth dutifully made note of comments she heard about the new home:

"How do you get in it?"

"There is not a single pretty thing about it."

"It looks like an old jail."

"I like it. It's about the oddest thing I ever saw."

"It expresses an idea, but I don't like the idea."

"It looks like a fort."

"You have astonished everyone with your strange house."

"It is like themselves, plain and substantial without and sweet and homelike spirit within."

Railroad car maker and immensely wealthy industrialist George Pullman, who lived diagonally across the street on the northeast corner of Prairie and Eighteenth in one of the largest and grandest homes in the neighborhood, said, "I don't know what I have ever done to have that thing staring at me in the face every time I go out of my door."

A newspaper clipping from July 10, 1886, made note of the unusual addition to Prairie Avenue:

Prairie Ave. is a social street and also a gossipy one and it does not suit the neighbors that this newcomer should exclude all possibility of watching his windows and finding out what may be going on within doors . . . that this house is going up in spite of disapproval has thrown the neighborhood into a state of stupefaction.

The Prairie Avenue residence was the last design Richardson completed. Three weeks after finishing the plans, Richardson died of kidney disease at forty-eight years of age. Richardson's assistants completed every project that was underway at the time of his death, including the Glessners' home, and gave the entirety of the $85,000 in commissions to his widow.

"The house responds [to all the demands put upon it]," Glessner wrote in his book about 1800 Prairie Avenue. "It seems available for almost any social function. Large companies have been entertained in it comfortably and easily . . . . Music and dramatic readings have been given to hundreds of persons, and receptions to more than four hundred at one time, without any feeling of crush, confusion or heat. Elaborate course dinners have been served in its rooms to more than one hundred guests at a time, the cooking all done in our own kitchen and by our own cook. Twice the full Chicago Orchestra had dined there, and once the Commercial Club." The expansive house was the clearest manifestation of Glessner's rapid journey to the heights of Chicago society.

On Frances Macbeth Glessner's birthday or other special occasions, orchestra conductor Theodore Thomas would sneak two dozen or more musicians into the house, unbeknownst to her until the soft strains of music floated from the front hall during dinner. For the Glessners' twenty-fifth wedding anniversary, the entire orchestra sneaked through the Eighteenth Street servant's entrance and up the rear stairs to surprise the family with an impromptu concert.

Despite the fatigue and discomfort of chronic health problems, for which she was prescribed "cannabis indicie (Indian hemp)" — a form of medical marijuana — Frances maintained a busy social schedule. She was a board member of the Decorative Arts Society and the highbrow Fortnightly Club. Aside from the lessons in languages and literature, Frances applied her silver-smithing lessons to refine her skills in jewelry making.

Frances was a voracious reader, completing two or three substantial books a week. In 1894, she established a gathering that became one of the most desirable in their social circle, the Monday Morning Reading Class.

Membership in the Monday Morning Reading Class was by Frances's invitation. Every season, Frances created a member roster with up to ninety names. Members were all married women — with the exception of Frances's sister, Helen Macbeth, and the class's paid professional reader, Anne E. Trimingham — many of whom were the wives of the faculty of the newly formed University of Chicago. Almost all of the members lived on the city's South Side.

The classes began at 10:30 a.m. with an hour of serious reading by Trimingham or a lecture by an invited guest, then an hour of lighter, more amusing works or a musical performance by one or more members of the Chicago Symphony Orchestra. On the first Monday of each month, the class was followed by a luncheon.

Many members of the Monday Morning Reading Class sewed or knitted during the readings. During World War I, the women knitted gloves and sweaters for men fighting overseas. After the war, they made blankets and garments for infants at Cook County Hospital. "The ladies' fingers were busy with sewing and other womanly occupation," John Jacob Glessner recalled. "And when the reading stopped doubtless their tongues grew active in womanly conversation."

Invitation to the Monday Morning Reading Class was highly sought. "All of Prairie Avenue was present," the newspaper social

64

page reported, noting a gathering of "smartly arranged women in glossy furs, becoming hats, and the latest importation in work bags over their arms." The classes met weekly in the library of the Glessners' home from November through May for more than three decades, until Frances's poor health forced an end to the club in the 1930s.

The Glessners' wealth ensured that Fanny and George wanted for nothing. The children were provided every advantage: lessons in horseback riding, dance, and art and private tutors. Due to George's severe hay fever, a doctor advised that he not be subjected to "the nervous strain of school where he would meet the competition of others." George and Fanny were educated at home by some of the finest private instructors for hire in Chicago. Richardson designed the Glessners' Prairie Avenue home with a schoolroom immediately off the front door, allowing the children to come and go without walking through other parts of the house.

"Over the thresholds of this house has passed a regular procession of teachers for you — in literature, languages, classical and modern, mathematics, chemistry, art, and the whole gamut of the humanities and the practical, considerably beyond the curricula of the High Schools," John Jacob Glessner wrote in a collection of photographs and remembrances, *The House at 1800 Prairie Avenue.*

"Whether this plan of education was wise or not may be questioned," Glessner said. "Of this I am sure, that it gave to each of you a great fund of general information, a power of observation and of reasoning, an ability and desire for study, and to be thoroughly proficient in what you might undertake. If ever there was a royal road for that, you had it, whatever its defects may have been in other respects."

Fanny was every bit the achiever she had been groomed to be. Like her brother, she was tutored in literature, art, music, and the natural sciences. Both children learned to play the violin and took dance lessons. From the time she could hold a needle and thread in her tiny fingers as a toddler, Fanny was practiced in sewing, knitting, crochet and other forms of needlework. She became fluent in German, French, and Latin. Accustomed to spending most of her time in the company of adults, her father noted that even at a young age, Fanny was a good conversationalist.

George had a chemistry laboratory that

was the envy of his teacher. He had a fire signal repeater installed at his home so he would be notified of fire alarms and a telegraph system with lines running to the homes of seven of his friends. When an alarm came through, George and his "fire brigade" friends chased the fire trucks to the scene. In many cases, George took photographs of fire scenes and the aftermath. He developed into a skilled amateur photographer.

The schoolroom was a "rendezvous for George's friends and teachers alike, for they were all comrades together," John Jacob Glessner said. "Here they had their long, long thoughts of youth, their boyish activities, their fire brigade, their regularly organized telegraph company . . . And similar activities for Frances and her friends — no espionage, no punishment, no need for that; no too hard and fast rules, no too rigid disciplinary regulations."

Every summer, Fanny and George escaped the heat of Chicago and enjoyed the freedom of their time at The Rocks. Every season, servants and the cook were sent ahead to open the Big House and prepare for the arrival of the family. Frances traveled with her children and a governess, often accompanied by her sister Helen and other family members. Anticipation built during the two-day train ride as the children counted off the stations until reaching their destination. A carriage drawn by a pair of bay horses met them at the station for the three-mile ride to The Rocks.

"Never shall I forget the effect when, stepping off our car in Littleton, I drew the first full breath of good clean country air," Fanny wrote in a letter much later in life. "George and I were so happy to be there that we thought we couldn't live till we got home."

"That first night at the Big House was always something never to be forgotten — so cool, so clean, so quiet," she said. "George and I would settle down in our beds so deliciously comfortable we could hardly get to sleep and wake up in the morning to bright sunshine and getting up to be sure that everything was still there."

Fanny used the wood-burning stove in the two-room cabin Scott had built for her to make jams and preserves for the household. On at least one occasion, Fanny used her stove to make a full-course meal.

The children were accompanied by Hero, their Skye terrier, a fierce hunter of woodchucks with at least seven kills to his credit who "does not easily make up with strangers," Frances wrote in her journal.

Days were spent swimming or exploring in the White Mountains or hiking around Franconia Notch, location of the iconic "Old Man of the Mountain" formation that is a State of New Hampshire symbol, and an eight-hundred foot-long natural gorge called the Flume, where granite walls rise to a right of seventy to ninety feet.

Whether in Chicago or The Rocks, evenings were whiled away with cards or word games or elaborate *tableaux vivants* — "living pictures" — using improvised costumes and props to represent works of art or figures from the theatre or classical literature.

At The Rocks, Isaac Scott built a thirty-five-foot tower with a small platform at the top, which the family called an observatory. The elevation of the observatory allowed a grand overview of The Rocks property and the villages of Littleton and Bethlehem below in the distance. George and Scott made a daily ritual to climb the observatory at sunset and light a candle at the top, the flame a faint beacon in the darkness.

Scott was close to both George and Fanny, teaching them drawing and wood carving, but he was bound closer to Fanny. Over the summers at The Rocks, Scott was one of Fanny's constant companions. He often accompanied the family on walks to observe wildlife.

"We have been most interested in the lovely birds," Frances wrote in her journal. "There are hundreds of them and of many varieties — bluebirds, king birds, robins, song swallows, gold finches, swallows, chippies, etc. We do not consider the day complete without finding a nest."

Fanny developed an interest in medicine at an early age. As a child, she was fascinated with mummies and the anatomical drawings of Vesalius. Her interest in medicine took a personal turn at the age of nine in May 1887 when she developed a serious illness while traveling by train from Chicago to The Rocks — fever, sore throat, and vomiting.

While on layover in New York City, Frances Macbeth took her daughter to a doctor, who diagnosed tonsillitis and recommended she consult with a surgeon. An operation was not a matter taken lightly in those days. Before the advent of antibiotics, analgesics, and aseptic surgical methods, even a minor procedure could easily develop into a harrowing, life-threatening ordeal.

The first consultation was with a surgeon by the name of Dr. Vanderfolk. "He said there was nothing to be done but remove her tonsils, that he painted them with cocaine and snipped them off," Frances recorded in her journal.

Fortunately for Fanny, her mother got a second opinion from another surgeon, Dr. Lincoln, who was recommended as one of the best in New York City. Dr. Lincoln said he would do the surgery — and use ether as an anesthetic agent. Frances opted for Dr. Lincoln's approach.

The surgery was done on the afternoon of May 12. Dr. Lincoln, assisted by Dr. Porter administering the ether, performed the operation in the Glessners' hotel room.

Fanny "was very brave and good," her mother reported. "Only once did she hesitate."

She sat in an armchair with a sheet pinned around her neck. Dr. Porter dripped ether onto a cloth-covered mask over Fanny's mouth and nose. The operation proceeded uneventfully. Fanny woke briefly as the ether wore off, suffering great pain in her throat and ears, then slept for hours.

There is no way to know what substances may have been given to a nine-year-old girl in such circumstances at that time. Drugs and patent medicines were unregulated. There was no requirement for a drug to be proven safe or effective. A patent remedy

71

might contain opium, morphine, heroin, or cocaine.

Dr. Lincoln gave the Glessners a prescription for an unspecified drug, but there was no need to have it filled. Fanny recovered slowly, without the benefit of modern medicine, over a period of weeks. In two months' time, she was back to normal.

Once fully recovered, Fanny wrote a poem in gratitude to her doctor:

D is for Doctor Lincoln
Of whom Fanny is constantly thinkoln
If he will come to The Rocks
We will don our best frocks
A white one, a blue one, a pink oln —

My dear doctor
It is very hard to find a rhyme for your
name —
But I had to make a verse for you
So I have done my best all the same
And this is all that I can do.

Your little friend
Fanny

Fanny began to accompany local doctors from Littleton and Bethlehem on their rounds visiting patients convalescing at homes. Watching the doctors' ministrations filled her with awe. They were always wise and knowledgeable, kind and comforting. When necessary, Fanny was recruited to actively assist the doctor with procedures and minor operations. She began to use her cabin kitchen to make remedies — broths, nutritive wine jelly — for the doctors' patients.

"But cooking and surgery were not the only interests in a home where mother and aunt were both domestic and artistic, such activities as fine sewing, embroidery, knitting, crocheting, painting and even working in handmade jewelry were as natural as breathing," Fanny said in an unpublished memoir.

In 1890, George began his undergraduate education at Harvard University with the goal of a law degree in mind. He became fast friends with a medical student, George Burgess Magrath. The two Georges, as Fanny called them, were inseparable. They even shared the same birthday, October 2.

Born in 1870, the only son of Reverend John Thomas and Sarah Jane Magrath, George sang in the choir at his father's church and at an early age became the church organist. Magrath worked his way through medical school as an organist. Through adulthood, he sang with the Handel and Haydn Society, the Boston Cecilia chorus, and the Harvard Alumni Chorus.

One thing seemingly absent from Magrath's attention was a romantic interest in women. He confirmed his bachelor status in an alumni directory published by Harvard College. "I am unmarried and expect to remain so," he reported to former classmates. A newspaper profile published later in his career noted what might be considered Magrath's alternative lifestyle in genteel euphemisms. "Yes, he's a bachelor, not yet old enough to be called 'confirmed,' " a reporter wrote. "He appears to be one of those who 'would rather live in Bohemia than any other place.' "

As students at Harvard, the two Georges were their own fire brigade. When the sound of clanging bells and the clattering of horse hooves barreled down the street, they gave chase to the fire wagons and pumpers on their bicycles. If his camera was handy, George Glessner might take photographs of the fire scene.

During breaks from school, the two Georges visited The Rocks or the Glessner home in Chicago, often with their classmate Frederick Law Olmsted Jr., son of Frederick Law Olmsted.

Before winter sports became a popular

form of recreation, the two Georges and Frederick spent time by themselves at The Rocks, which was shuttered for the season. Despite the brutal winter weather that often occurred, the two Georges and Frederick trudged through the snow to their hideaway. The only building on The Rocks estate that could be heated during the winter was Fanny's cabin. The wood-burning stove generated enough heat to comfortably warm the two rooms, where they drank alcoholic beverages and engaged in the shenanigans of young single men on college break.

June 25, 1893
Fanny, fifteen years old at the time, rode the Ferris wheel with the two Georges at the World's Columbian Exposition. The fair, on 690 acres of Chicago's south side water-front, was an opportunity to display Chicago's recovery from the great fire.

The Glessners visited the World's Columbian Exposition several times. John Jacob served on a steering committee of prominent businessmen that brought the World's Fair to the city. The family had special access to the grounds during construction and for the duration of the fair and attended the grand opening ceremony presided over by President Grover Cleveland.

Fanny toured the fairgrounds with her parents before the grand opening. The Glessners were accompanied on their preview tour by Daniel Burnham, the fair's director of works. At night, Burnham took the Glessners on a tour of the lagoon on an open motorboat. The boat floated past the Women's Building, an impressive two-story neoclassical structure near the Midway Plaisance.

The eighty-thousand-square-foot Italian Renaissance building was designed by twenty-one-year-old Sophia Hayden, the first female graduate of the architecture program at the Massachusetts Institute of Technology. Hayden was the first woman to design a prominent public building in America.

The Women's Building contained the largest and most ambitious exhibition of women's art ever undertaken — before or since. The World's Fair was the first time women created public art. Women were thought unable to use the ladders and scaffolding necessary to work on sculpture and large-scale paintings. Critics and patrons were curious about the art women could produce.

Hayden and her building were intensely scrutinized. Other builders wondered aloud whether a woman could navigate a muddy construction site in a dress and heeled shoes. Critics and the public projected their own biases onto Hayden's design, assigning feminine qualities to her architecture. They said the building was somehow less assertive, more reticent and demure than buildings designed by men.

The clearest difference between Hayden's building and others at the World's Fair was how much the architects were paid. Hayden earned $1,000 for her first commission. Men who designed comparable buildings at the World's Fair commanded $10,000 for their work.

There was also much discussion in the Glessner household about the World's Congress of Representative Women, a weeklong convention held in May in conjunction with the World's Fair. The congress was the largest gathering of prominent women from across the spectrum of advocacy and activism to date. Nearly five hundred women, including representatives from twenty-seven countries, delivered lectures and participated in panel discussions during the congress. More than 150,000 participants attended sessions during the week.

Maud Howe Elliott was a houseguest at the Glessner's Prairie Avenue residence for a fortnight. During the week of the women's congress, she was joined by her mother, Julia Ward Howe.

George Glessner took numerous photographs at the World's Fair. Frances Macbeth's journal notes the evening that fifteen-year-old Fanny and the two Georges rode the Ferris wheel.

In France's pavilion, Fanny and George likely encountered an exhibit from the Paris Police Department and a curious bearded man, Alphonse Bertillon. George would certainly have been intrigued by Bertillon's odd photographic equipment.

A reliable way of identifying criminals was a long-standing problem. Police needed to know who they had in their custody so wanted men couldn't run away from their deeds. Names could be changed and signatures faked. Appearances could be altered.

Even when police departments began using photography, creating rogues' galleries of criminals, the images were often useless for identification. Photos were of poor quality, overexposed or blurred, or just a wide shot of the whole body that made identifiable features hard to see.

The son of a noted French statistician and anthropologist, Bertillon believed that no two people were *exactly* alike. He devised a system to record five primary measurements

— the length and width of the head, the length of the middle finger, the length of the left foot, and the length of the forearm from the elbow to the extended middle finger.

Bertillon created a record that included these measurements and descriptions of physical characteristics such as hair and eye color. His record also included standardized photographs — a clear close-up portrait of the face and a second image of the subject in profile. The profile photograph was particularly important, Bertillon contended, since the profile changed less dramatically with age, weight gain, and facial hair.

Bertillon called his system *anthropometry,* the measurement of humans. The system became known as *bertillonage* and was adopted by police departments throughout Europe and the United States.

In preparation for the World's Fair, Chicago police compiled a massive database of known criminals and recent parolees from throughout the country, the largest collection of bertillonage records in the United States.

One name missing from the rogues' gallery was H. H. Holmes — a physician, an entrepreneur, a devious liar, a skilled swindler and con man, and a sadistic murderer from the stuff of nightmares. Holmes was responsible for dozens of murders in Chicago during the World's Fair, including many young women and children. He built a hotel with false walls and hidden rooms that became known as the "Murder Castle."

By some accounts, Holmes may have lured two hundred victims to their death. Despite being in the hands of police numerous times in cities throughout the United States, authorities were completely unaware of his crimes until long after the World's Fair ended and Holmes left Chicago.

Bertillonage was far from ideal. It could only be applied to adults, since the measurements of children continue to change until they stop growing. More problematic, the system required calipers and other measuring equipment that tended to bend and misalign. Bertillonage was difficult and unreliable and was abandoned when fingerprinting emerged in the early 1900s. All that remains of bertillonage today are the photos — the classic mug shot.

Upon graduation from Harvard in 1894, George Glessner spent the summer at the family's estate in Littleton, New Hampshire, intending to return in the fall to begin law school. "Before summer was out however, I changed my plans, and went to work with my father's company," he reported to Harvard classmates. "I began at the bottom as a filing clerk, and for a time had good prospects of staying there, but owing to a fortunate combination of circumstances have been appointed to the position of assistant manager. I find the work much more interesting than I expected, but also more engrossing."

George remained with Warder, Bushnell, & Glessner through its merger into International Harvester, ultimately rising to the position of manager in the firm's Utility Division. He was involved in a number of organizations popular with businessmen of means, including the Chicago Club and the University Club, and was a member of the board of trustees of the Art Institute of Chicago.

His friend Magrath remained at Harvard as a pathology assistant after graduation from medical school. He taught medical students and was a consulting pathologist for several hospitals in the Boston area.

Fanny came of age in 1896. As befitting her arrival to young adulthood, she was called Frances more often rather than Fanny. The occasion of her birthday was noted in her mother's journal. "On Wednesday, Frances was eighteen years old," Frances Macbeth wrote. "We had eighteen carnations, eighteen lilies of the valley, eighteen candles and a fine cake on the breakfast table. We gave her a lovely watch and chatelaine."

The Glessners celebrated their daughter's milestone by sending her abroad with Frances Macbeth's sister Helen. In May 1896, Frances and Helen departed on the steamer *Etruria* for London, where they stayed for several months. Their excursion included Norway, the Netherlands, Germany, and France. They returned fourteen months later, in July 1897.

Within months of Frances's return, she began keeping company with a thirty-year-old attorney, Blewett Lee. They were introduced by Dwight Lawrence, Blewett's legal partner and a Harvard classmate of George Glessner. Blewett visited the Glessners often during the later months of 1897, having dinner with the family and taking Frances out for carriage rides.

A native of Columbus, Mississippi, Blewett was the only child of Stephen Dill Lee and Regina Lilly Harrison Lee. Stephen Dill Lee was a venerated former Confederate military leader, the youngest lieutenant general of the Civil War. As a twenty-eight-year-old captain in the artillery service of the South Carolina militia, he delivered a formal demand of surrender to Major Robert Anderson at Fort Sumter on April 11, 1861. When Anderson didn't surrender, Stephen Lee gave the order to begin firing artillery at Fort Sumter, launching the Civil War. Subsequently, he fought in the Second Battle of Manassas, the Battle of Antietam — the bloodiest single day of the war — and the defense of Vicksburg.

After the Civil War, Stephen Lee served in the Mississippi state senate and was the first president of the Agricultural and Mechanical College of the State of Mississippi, now known as Mississippi State University. Some regard him as the father of industrial education in the South. He also remained active in Confederate veteran organizations.

Blewett Lee graduated in the first class of the Mississippi Agricultural and Mechanical College, attended the University of Virginia for two years, and received his law degree from Harvard Law School. After clerking for U.S. Supreme Court associate justice Horace Gray for a year, Lee settled in Atlanta to practice law but found the business difficult to break into and not particularly lucrative.

Hungry for work, one day, Lee was visited by a man named Candler who asked the lawyer to draft the paperwork to incorporate a company. The client planned on producing a beverage based on a secret formula. He didn't have much money, so he offered Lee either shares in the new company or $25 in cash. Blewett sipped the beverage, thought it tasted awful, and insisted on payment in cash money.

That man was Asa Candler, and his company was Coca-Cola.

Lee moved to Chicago to teach law at Northwestern University. To supplement his income, he formed a practice partnership with Lawrence, who had flunked out of Harvard Law School but had extensive connections in the business and social worlds. This worked well for Lee, since he knew the law but had no connections in Chicago.

The engagement of Blewett and Frances was announced in late December 1897.

A notion persists that Frances didn't go to university because one or both of her parents forbade it. There is no evidence for this. John Jacob and Frances Macbeth Glessner were loving, supportive parents who doubtless would have helped their daughter fulfill her dreams.

As a young woman of affluence, Frances was not supposed to be concerned about a career or higher education. She wasn't expected to work outside the home. She would never have to earn a living but could look forward to a comfortable life of leisure and wealth.

Later in life, Frances told a reporter that she might have enjoyed being a nurse or going to medical school when she was young, but that sort of thing "just wasn't done." The truth is a little more complicated than that. Frances could have gone to university, even to medical school, if that was what she really wanted.

To be sure, the medical field was an unusual choice for women. It was a common belief that medicine was too indecent for a woman's delicate sensibilities and that women shouldn't know about the inner workings of the human body. By the end of the 1800s, however, there were hundreds of women practicing medicine in the United States and several women's medical schools. Thanks to the efforts of five prominent Baltimore women to raise $500,000 to establish the Johns Hopkins School of Medicine, three of the eighteen students in the first class in 1893 were women.

Sarah Hackett Stevenson, the first woman accepted into membership in the American Medical Association, was a longtime friend of Frances Macbeth and often spent holidays with the family, so the concept of a female medical doctor wasn't unfamiliar to the Glessners.

Frances had options but not the choice that she really desired. There was only one university that she wanted to attend, only one medical degree worth pursuing, and that was irremediably beyond her grasp: Harvard.

She wanted to study at Harvard like her brother, like George Burgess Magrath, Blewett Lee, H. H. Richardson, and almost all the important men in her life. The Glessners were a Harvard family. Frances wanted to experience Harvard and belong to the St. Botolph Club like everybody else. But Harvard Medical School did not accept women as students.

Despite being unable to attend Harvard Medical School, Frances maintained an affinity for the university. After all, it was still Harvard. The best and the brightest. The elite of New England blue bloods. In time, her feelings for Harvard would become more complicated, but it would be several decades before the university became an important part of her life again.

Frances was a month shy of her twentieth birthday when she married Blewett Lee, who was ten years her senior. "We would rather have her a little older," her mother wrote in her journal, "but Mr. Lee is so nearly everything in the world that is good and perfect that we cannot find it in our hearts to interfere with their complete happiness."

The wedding was at 5:00 p.m. on Wednesday, February 9, 1898, in the Glessners' Prairie Avenue residence. Men moved the grand piano to the second floor and removed all the furniture from the parlor and hall. The floors were covered with muslin and the parlor draped with lilies, wild smilax, and white orchids. Frances wore a satin gown with a deep, narrow flounce of double rose Venetian point lace and a tulle veil and carried a bouquet of lilies of the valley.

The ceremony was conducted by Reverend Philip H. Mowry, who had officiated John Jacob and Frances Macbeth's wedding in 1870. The Chicago Symphony Orchestra played the Swedish Wedding March, "Call Me Thine Own" for the procession, and the Mendelssohn Wedding March after the ceremony.

At nine in the evening, Frances changed into her traveling clothes as the carriage waited to take the newlyweds to the train station. "Then they — the two — went out alone together, never to enter the home in the same way again."

3
MARRIAGE AND THE AFTERMATH

The newlywed couple embarked on an excursion by railroad to honeymoon at Blewett Lee's ancestral home in Mississippi, stopping along the way in St. Louis. The marriage seemed blissful. Frances appeared to be the perfect bride, dutifully fulfilling the roles expected of her. Within a month of their wedding, she was pregnant with their first child.

"I have never seen two young people more happily married," Stephen D. Lee wrote to Frances's parents after their visit.

Upon returning from a brief honeymoon, the Lees resided at the swank Metropole Hotel on Michigan Avenue. The Metropole, built in 1891 as luxury accommodations for the World's Columbian Exposition, later achieved notoriety as Al Capone's hangout during his heyday.

After several months at the Metropole, the couple took an apartment at Indiana

Avenue and Twenty-First Street, four blocks distant from her parents' Prairie Avenue home.

Despite the happy outward appearances, friction soon emerged in the marriage. As individuals, Frances and Blewett had quite different constitutions. He was a churchgoing nondenominational Christian, while for most of her life, Frances was not religious. She enjoyed hiking and spending time outdoors, but he preferred reading and other quiet intellectual domestic pursuits. She was a northerner, raised in a progressive and cultured family; he was the son of a revered Confederate figure who espoused the supremacy of white males above all others.

Blewett was unable to feign enthusiasm for his wife's interest in needlework and crafts. Frances was prone to bursts of creative energy, sometimes seizing upon an idea and working all day and into the night. She likely felt unappreciated and unfulfilled in her marriage.

Neither Frances nor Blewett was used to the everyday adaptations and accommodations that are necessary for a successful marriage. He was an only child, while she was an only daughter who had not socialized in a school setting. Both of them had grown set in their ways.

As a Glessner, Frances had a certain style of living to which she had become accustomed and that her parents also expected for their daughter. Blewett's salary could not afford the lifestyle Frances demanded, so it was necessary for the couple to depend upon the continuing financial support of her parents. The Glessners' subsidy was gratefully accepted, but no doubt gnawed at Frances and Blewett for different reasons. Relying on the assistance of his in-laws likely undermined Blewett's masculinity and his confidence as a breadwinner for the family. Frances resented the strings implicit with her parent's money, the insinuation of their presence and control in her life. Anybody who has been a child may understand a parental love that is wanted and yet at times overbearing and smothering. Frances was frustrated that she did not enjoy the independence and autonomy she thought would come with adulthood.

The birth of their first child, John Glessner Lee, on December 5, 1898, was barely ten months into their marriage. "The Doctor said several times that he had never seen a more heroic girl or a quarter piece of stoicism than she showed all day," Frances Macbeth noted in her journal. "She made no outcry or complaint."

Frances did not have an easy time after John's birth. "She has been quite nervous," her mother journaled. "Saturday I was three times at Frances' house. I found her in tears several times. Yesterday she told me she doesn't like her nurse, that she is not obliging or agreeable, neither sympathetic nor gentle. I talked with the nurse and tried to impress her and make things better."

By the time the couple's second child, Frances Lee, was born in 1903, John Jacob Glessner had built matching homes for his children a block away from his own — at 1700 and 1706 Prairie Avenue. The stately three-story homes were symmetrical, with the home where George and his wife, Alice, lived with their children a mirror image of the Lee family home next door.

Shortly after the birth of their daughter, Blewett Lee moved out of the family home. The specific issues leading to the separation were not recorded, but deep temperamental and cultural differences likely drove a wedge between Blewett and Frances. Blewett Lee remained on good terms with his in-laws during the marital separation. The Glessners never wavered in their affection for Blewett and remained sympathetic to the difficulties of having to deal with a headstrong and contemptuous woman.

Blewett rented an apartment at Prairie Avenue and Twenty-Second Street, directly above the apartment of Frances's aunts, Helen and Anna, and visited his children every day. After his workday, he arrived at the residence at 5:00 p.m. on the dot, read the bible or Uncle Remus — the children delighted in his drawling rendition of Br'er Fox and Br'er Rabbit — and left forty minutes later. He often visited and had meals with Helen and Anna.

The Lees reconciled briefly in 1905, during which their third child, Martha, was conceived. Not long after Martha's birth in the autumn of 1906, Blewett moved out for good.

Blewett was hurt by the separation but never spoke ill of his children's mother, his son, John Glessner Lee, recalled later in life. His mother, on the other hand, was "extremely outspoken and partisan" about Blewett.

Meanwhile, attending to the family's interests in New Hampshire placed increasing demands on George Glessner's time, particularly as his parents grew older. The fresh air at The Rocks was a welcome respite from George's severe hay fever, which was worsened by the malodorous smog shrouding the streets of Chicago.

Spending time at The Rocks allowed George to work on civil engineering projects that he enjoyed, such as improving roads built by his father and diverting water from the abandoned Bethlehem Waterworks to fill a reservoir on the family's property. George built the powerhouse providing The Rocks with electricity.

The Rocks had a complete woodworking shop, equipment for milling and forging metal, and any tool that George could want. He had a staff of eighty people at his disposal, many of whom lived in one of the twenty buildings scattered throughout the property. George built his own home on the estate, which was named the Ledge.

George and Alice, along with their three children, relocated from Chicago in 1907 to reside full-time at the Ledge. George acquired majority ownership of the Bethlehem Electrical Company, which provided electrical power to the community, and served as managing director of the affiliated utility Lisbon Light and Power Company.

Glessner served as the Bethlehem town auditor for three years, and in 1912, he was elected to the state House of Representatives, where he served two terms. George was engaged in a variety of civic roles, including serving as a trustee of the Littleton Savings Bank and as president of the Littleton Hospital Association, an organization founded by his father that built a modern fifteen-bed community hospital in 1907.

After Christmas 1903, on December 27, John Jacob Glessner gave $125,000 in International Harvester stock to Frances and $100,000 of stock to her brother in addition to the $25,000 in stock he had received upon graduation from Harvard. Dividends from the stock would provide a comfortable source of income for both of Glessner's children for the rest of their lives.

Three days later, several of Frances's friends and their children were among more than two thousand people in the Iroquois Theater for a performance of *Mr. Blue Beard,* a musical featuring Dan McAvoy and Eddie Foy. Located on West Randolph Street between State and Dearborn, the newly constructed Iroquois was advertised as absolutely fireproof.

Designed with a capacity of sixteen hundred on three levels of seating, the venue was sold out for the December 30 performance. Hundreds more watched from the "standing room" at the back of the theater.

An additional three hundred people were working that day as performers or crew.

At the beginning of the second act, sparks from an arc lamp ignited a nearby muslin curtain. The fire quickly grew, filling the theater with thick smoke as a panic broke out. More than six hundred people died, many of whom were women and children. That evening, Frances visited her parent's home with her children as word of the tragedy filtered through the community. Among the missing, presumed dead, were Mrs. Gartz's two children, Dr. Zeisler's son, Mrs. Hoyt's daughter, Mrs. Fox and her three children, and George Higginson's sister and his son.

"It has all been a most horrible sickening thing, a most terrible disgrace in a civilized city," Frances Glessner wrote.

The exact number of fatalities is unknown, since some victims were carried away from the scene and unaccounted for, and many of the dead were burned beyond recognition and had to be identified by jewelry, clothing, or other personal belongings. The Iroquois Theater fire remains the deadliest single-building fire in United States history.

On the evening of the fire, George Glessner went to the Iroquois Theater to help recover bodies.

At her parents' home, Frances held her children close. Such a wrenching tragedy. It could happen to anybody, she thought. How horrible to lose a child or for a child to lose a parent or sibling, to never see them again. Not even in a casket. Most heartbreaking were the bodies that would never be identified.

In the summer of 1911, Frances read newspaper stories about the brazen theft of a painting from the Louvre. She remembered visiting the landmark Paris museum with her parents during their 1890 European tour.

Without anybody noticing, somebody walked out of the museum with *La Gioconda,* a portrait by Leonardo da Vinci from the early 1500s. *La Gioconda* was an undistinguished work, painted with oil on a plank of white poplar, depicting the wife of a merchant. As a work of art, the painting was pleasing to the eye but not particularly noteworthy.

The theft wasn't noticed until the next day when an artist visiting the museum found four mounting pegs where *La Gioconda* — better known today as the *Mona Lisa* — was usually displayed.

The *Mona Lisa* instantly gained fame as

the theft made headlines around the world. Police scrambled to solve the case, at one point taking Pablo Picasso into custody for questioning as a suspect. But the police never did break the case. More than two years later, the perpetrator, a former museum maintenance worker by the name of Vincenzo Peruggia, was arrested when he tried to sell the painting to an art dealer.

Peruggia's theft elevated the *Mona Lisa* from obscurity, imbuing it with an aura of celebrity that has made it one of the most recognizable and most-discussed works of art in the world.

The theft of the *Mona Lisa* could have been solved soon after it happened. A single fingerprint was left on the frame that held the *Mona Lisa.* The police had Peruggia's fingerprints on file from previous brushes with the law for petty crimes. But the Paris police classified criminal records based on bertillonage measurements, not fingerprints. It was impossible to track down the individual to whom the fingerprint belonged.

Little could Frances have imagined when she heard about the *Mona Lisa* theft that she would one day become an authority on crime scene investigation.

Around the same time, Frances's son, John, about thirteen years of age, was diagnosed as having "tubercular glands," an infection of the lymph nodes of the neck that these days would be cured with a course of antibiotics. In those days, the air of seaside resorts was believed to be the most hygienic environment for the condition.

John had surgery to excise the affected lymph glands, and the Lees were advised to spend the winter in California. For two years, Frances and the children spent the winters in Santa Barbara, California.

During one of these winter visits, the family undertook a touring trip to San Diego to see Charlie Witmer, a former chauffeur from The Rocks who left to learn to fly at Glenn Curtiss's flying school. Frances, the children, a governess, and a chauffeur trundled along the coast in a Rambler, a four-cylinder touring automobile with balloon tires considered the most luxurious vehicle of its time.

The 218-mile trip from Santa Barbara to San Diego and back took a week. Highways didn't exist yet, so a voyage of that duration was an invitation for adventure. The chauffeur had to wrap the tires with rope to climb hilly roads slippery with mud. John recalled that the ball bearings fell out of a front wheel one day, causing a delay. On another occasion, the road was washed out by flooding, and the Rambler was loaded onto a railroad flat car to bypass the obstacle. "I can remember eating lunch in the middle of the river while the chauffeur went to get a team of horses to pull us out," he said.

Back in New Hampshire, Frances purchased a property with a rustic hunter's cabin on Forest Lake about an hour's drive away from The Rocks. She called this property Camp Lee, and it was her refuge from her parents. During the summers, Frances and her children would spend three or four days roughing it at Camp Lee. She cooked over fire while the children went fishing or swimming.

The times spent at Camp Lee "were the happiest times of my childhood," John said. The family made up long adventure stories to tell each other and invented their own games. Frances was cheerful during these sojourns away from The Rocks and when relaxed made for amusing company. "Once she undertook to sing opera, all the parts, with gestures," John said. "Frances and I nearly died of laughter."

No longer inhibited by Blewett, Frances's creative energies flourished. She produced needlepoints, sewed outfits for herself and her three children, and devised elaborate centerpieces for the family dining table. In 1912, she undertook an ambitious project to create the entire Chicago Symphony Orchestra in miniature as a gift for her mother.

The Glessners had continued their close association with the CSO. The couple rarely missed a performance and maintained close relationships with conductor Frederick Stock and many orchestra musicians. Members of the CSO were often entertained at the Glessner home and played music for the family. On more than one occasion, the full symphony orchestra performed in the spacious courtyard of the Prairie Avenue residence.

Frances Macbeth Glessner was so fond of music that she once expressed the fanciful desire to have the orchestra at her house every day. The idea germinated in her daughter's mind to make her mother's wish come true. Frances envisioned a miniature orchestra: all ninety musicians in formal performance clothing and their instruments. Miniature men — the orchestra was exclusively male — and miniature instruments weren't enough to satisfy her obsession with detail. Each figure in the orchestra would be finished to appear as close as possible to his real-ife counterpart.

Frances chose to use a familiar 1:12 scale that is standard for miniature dollhouses, with one inch representing one foot. She sat in her parents' box at the symphony hall during rehearsals, sketching details of each musician in pencil on porcelain bisque heads — hairline and facial hair, the bushiness of eyebrows. Many members of the orchestra posed for her sketches and assisted in the construction of the miniature. In her home workshop, Frances replicated the hair, mustaches, and beards by applying slip, a clay slurry, to the heads and refired them in a kiln. Painting with color-matched enamel completed the transformation.

She bought ninety identical wooden dollhouse straight-back chairs and acquired a complete set of miniature musical instruments. Some instruments were purchased from dealers and specialty stores if they appeared realistic and were in the correct dimensions. Instruments not precisely in scale were unacceptable to Frances. She hired a craftsman to make the brass instruments and carved the reeds herself. The reed instruments, along with the bows of the string section and other parts, were made from wooden candy boxes and other cleverly repurposed household items. Harpist Enrico Tramonti introduced Lee to a company that made her a six-inch harp, complete with a carrying case.

In appreciation for the Glessners' patronage, the CSO's conductor, Frederick Stock, wrote out by hand, working under a magnifying glass, a page of one of Frances Macbeth's favorite works, Arthur J. Mundy's "The Drum Major of Schneider's Band," on sheets of paper the size of postage stamps. Each musician had the correct score for his instrument sitting on his stand.

For the clothing, Frances sewed formal evening dress for each figure. The musicians wore white shirts with pearl buttons, a black single-breasted waistcoat, and matching evening coat. She made detachable paper wing collars for each person. Stock, his arms raised, was dressed in a swallowtail evening coat. As a nod to her mother's practice of sending carnation boutonnieres to the orchestra before performances, each of the figures has a perfectly formed fabric carnation, one-sixth of an inch across, pinned to the right lapel.

Frances hired a stage carpenter to build a tiered platform nearly eight feet long. The miniature Stock was surrounded by musicians on platforms rising up five levels. Six potted palms behind the orchestra decorated the display, along with roses in tasteful pink vases on either side of Stock.

The orchestra was presented to Frances Glessner on January 1, 1913, on the occasion of her sixty-fifth birthday. John Jacob Glessner described the event in his wife's diary:

New Years was Frances' birthday and that afternoon Frances Lee gave her the wonderful "little orchestra" — the full orchestra stage and full 90 men and their instruments, doll size, all worked out in exquisite detail, and most of it done by Frances' own fingers . . . Nothing could be more complete or perfectly done, or more interesting.

Little did anyone in the family — least of all Frances — know that her life's work would culminate in the creation of an entirely different kind of miniatures several decades in the future.

Days later, the entire orchestra was invited to the Glessner home for dinner and to see Frances's finished creation. As was his custom with daily events that occurred in the home, John Jacob Glessner documented the occasion:

Every member of the organization except

three was present, making with the 15 or 16 other guests, 105 or 106 who sat down for dinner that was prepared in this house . . . There was a punch at the close and toasts and songs and the musical program before that was fine and humorous. The men were much interested in the "little orchestra" and in seeing themselves as others see them, and went back again and again to the room over the parlor where it was, and Frances Lee was fully satisfied with their appreciation.

Frances's next artistic endeavor was an homage to the celebrated Flonzaley Quartet. Formed in New York City in 1903, the quartet was founded by Swiss-American banker Edward J. de Coppet as a pickup ensemble to accompany his amateur pianist wife. The group was named after de Coppet's summer villa near Lausanne, Switzerland. Members of the Flonzaley Quartet — Alfred Pochon on second violin, Adolfo Betti on first violin, Ugo Ara on viola, and Iwan d'Archambeau on violoncello — were supported so they would not have to tutor or do any other work and were free to devote their full time to playing music together.

The Flonzaley Quartet rose to prominence

after their first public concert in 1905, which led to performances in major cities in Europe and the United States. It was the finest and best-known string quartet of the time, a critical and commercial success. The Flonzaley Quartet was the first string ensemble to record and issue music under their own name, allowing them to cultivate a following.

Frances's model of the Flonzaley Quartet was constructed in the same 1:12 scale as her miniature orchestra and used the same bisque heads, but these would be better replicas. She took what she had learned working on the miniature orchestra to improve her techniques. All she needed were good, detailed observations about the physical appearance and distinguishing characteristics of each musician in the quartet.

Frances's fifteen-year-old son, John, accompanied her to hear the Flonzaley Quartet perform. "We went to concerts together, and sat on opposite sides of the house," John Lee recorded. "We made elaborate notes on how the men sat and what they wore . . . Mr. Betti's vest . . . how Mr. Pochon put his feet . . . d'Archambeau's gold watch chain and how it hung . . . and last, but by no means least, Ugo Ara, who played the viola, a little Italian man with a magnificent Assyrian beard, how he managed his viola amongst the profusion of shrubbery."

Betti and Pochon were depicted in dark evening coats and pinstriped trousers. D'Archambeau wore gray flannel trousers, vest, and bow tie, the gold chain of his watch slung across his midsection. Each wore white shirts with detachable paper collars and black shoes. Wires running under the clothing held limbs posed in place.

The instruments were perfect miniature replicas, and the tiny four-inch violoncello even worked somewhat. "You could actually play the 'cello," John Lee wrote. "It emitted a faint squeak, but no sound would come from the smaller instruments, despite the care in making the bridge and strings and other parts."

The model was presented to the musicians during their 1914 cross-country U.S. tour. Frances had the Flonzaley Quartet for dinner at her home. She sat at one side of the long, narrow table across from her father, between Pochon and d'Archambeau. John Jacob Glessner was placed between Betti and Ara. Aside from Frances's children, the dinner was attended by Stock and his wife, harpist Enrico Tramonti and his wife, and the orchestra's assistant manager and treasurer, Henry Voegeli, and his wife.

The figures were hidden within a large floral centerpiece in the middle of the table. "After dinner, the flora piece was removed with a flourish, and there, not two feet from their noses, was this model of themselves playing!" John Lee recalled. "The effect was extraordinary. For a moment nobody spoke, and then all four members of the Quartet burst out in voluble language. Nobody listened. But each one of them pointed with delight to the eccentricities of the other three. I still remember Mr. Betti, with a magnifying glass, peering over the shoulder of his own miniature, trying to read the music on the music rack."

Once again, the music was painstakingly handwritten by Stock, the orchestra's conductor, on sheets of paper less than an inch tall. Stock wrote an original composition mimicking the style of Austrian expressionist Arnold Schoenberg. As a subtle musical joke, Stock's composition was not humanly possible to perform.

The quartet asked Frances the favor of a photograph as a remembrance of the occasion. She gave the quartet the models to keep.

Producing exquisite miniatures was no diversion from the continual deterioration of her marriage. It became obvious that the relationship was beyond repair. Frances wanted a divorce. At the time, the only acceptable grounds for divorce was desertion. Had Blewett been asked whether he would return to the family home, he would have responded affirmatively. It was Frances who didn't want him.

In June 1914, after five years of separation, Blewett finally agreed to a divorce. Frances filed for divorce on the grounds of desertion. At the divorce hearing, she said that she had adequate financial means for herself and their three children, who would remain in her custody.

The period after the divorce was "an unhappy time for all," son John recalled. "There was much family bitterness stemming from the divorce."

Frances was never on easy terms with her parents or her brother's family again. She felt that her family was sympathetic to Blewett's side and not supportive of her needs. She believed that she was being blamed for the marriage's failure.

Isolated at home with her children, Frances whiled away her hours. She sewed all of her children's clothing. "During these troubled times FGL produced monumental amounts of needlework and played endless hours of solitaire," John said. He also said that his mother's dark moods were punctuated by flurries of activity. During summers at The Rocks, Frances would recruit her children for a candy-making binge.

"When a candymaking spree was started, the furniture was all pushed against the walls, and two alcohol pressure stoves brought down from the attic," he recalled. "White enamel kettles appeared from elsewhere, along with long candy thermometers, wooden stirring paddles, and a lot of miscellaneous equipment, including several professional candymaker's [recipe] books."

Frances and the children made chocolate creams, caramels, fudge, peanut brittle, and taffy. Her candy-making equipment included a candymaker's hook for pulling taffy and a marble slab she had obtained from a tombstone carver.

Whatever project she was involved in, Frances allowed herself to be consumed by her work. Projects became all-absorbing, as she would often work all day and half of the night for weeks at a time.

A year after the divorce, Blewett Lee married Delia Foreacre Snead, a former teacher and director of the Atlanta Library. He had known her years earlier when he was a young attorney in Atlanta and she was married. Now a widow, she had much in common with Blewett. Snead's father was Colonel Greenberry Jones Foreacre, leader of the Atlanta Confederate Volunteers, who was seriously wounded at the First Battle of Manassas.

Blewett and Delia were married in Atlanta on July 20, 1915, in a two-minute ceremony notable for its brevity and simplicity. One of the most striking aspects of the wedding was the absence of the word *obey* in the bride's vows, which was sufficiently novel to be mentioned in the headline of a brief news story. The omission was "particularly notable because of this being the first use in the south," a reporter observed.

Mr. and Mrs. Lee settled in New York City where Blewett grew a thriving law practice. He may have missed the opportunity to invest in Coca-Cola early in his career, but he was one of the first attorneys to recognize that the new flying technology introduced by Orville and Wilbur Wright had legal implications that had never been previously considered. Drawing upon established precedents within maritime law, Blewett pioneered the field of aviation law.

After the divorce, Frances destroyed every photograph in which she appeared with Blewett. No photos exist of Frances and Blewett together.

When the United States entered World War I in 1917, Frances took an interest in Naval Station Great Lakes, the U.S. Navy's boot camp near North Chicago. During the course of the war, about 125,000 sailors trained at the base.

Frances hosted sailors from Great Lakes at her Prairie Avenue home. In particular, she sought to invite musicians, whether enlisted men or officers. On Sunday evenings, sailors were welcomed to dinner and an evening of entertainment and socializing, with talks and music provided by members of the CSO.

Frances kept detailed notes on each guest: the dates of his visits, a physical description, whether gifts or correspondence was exchanged, hometown, family situation, and preferred beverage. If a sailor was a well-behaved and gracious guest, the boys she liked best, she pasted a gold star by his name.

Two of her favorite sailors, Charles Young and Talmage Wilson, were musicians in John Philip Sousa's band. When the United States joined the war, Sousa was well known as the premier composer and leader of military band music, and at sixty-two years of age, he was at the navy's retirement age. Nonetheless, Sousa was commissioned as a lieutenant in the U.S. Naval Reserve and led the Navy Band at Great Lakes. Independently wealthy by this time, Sousa donated his salary, less a token $1 per month, to the Sailors' and Marines' Relief Fund.

Frances gave servicemen stamped, self-addressed envelopes so they could keep in touch with her when they moved on. Many men wrote her letters and sent photographs. She rewarded the men considerate enough to write letters by sending a package of cookies in return.

One such correspondent was George Wise, a navy musician from a small town in Kansas who served on a battleship. "Dear Mother Lee," his letter begins. Later in his missive, he explained his term of endearment. "I trust you are not offended by my salutation," Wise said, "as you were so kind to me and I look toward you in that respect."

In March 1918, Chicago newspaper society pages announced an unusual performance at the Chicago Art Institute called the Finger Tip Theater. The announcement promised interpretative dancing from around the world, a circus performance, acrobatic stunts, and tricks by trained animals.

"The performance will be given on a stage 2 × 3 feet, with a proscenium arch 19 inches

113

high," the announcement said. "Living performers only; no manikins."

The Finger Tip Theater was scheduled to perform daily at 3:00 p.m. for ten performances over a two-week period. Proceeds from the show were for the Fatherless Children of France fund, to help the children of soldiers killed in the war.

Curiosity was piqued about how living performers could appear on such a small stage. "The auditorium will seat about fifty people, and the stage will be so tiny that everyone is wondering what or who the living performers that are advertised will be," wrote the *Chicago Daily Tribune*'s society columnist. "So whether dwarfs or trained fleas or white mice, one is left to wonder."

Finger Tip Theater premiered on the afternoon of March 19. The sold-out audience included Hattie Pullman, wife of railroad magnate George Pullman, Grace Murray Meeker, wife of the Armour meat-packing company general manager, John Jacob and Frances Glessner, and many of Chicago's elite.

The stage was set up in the doorway between two galleries of the Art Institute. Drapes of black muslin framed the proscenium, giving the audience no clue as to what lay behind the screen. Bronze figures of a huntress goddess and her prey stood on newel posts flanking the sides of the stage.

When the show began, the audience was delighted to find that the performers were "none other than the clever fore and middle fingers of Mrs. Frances Glessner Lee, who originated the new art," the *Chicago Herald* reviewer wrote.

Lee sewed costumes and dance outfits for her fingers, with little fingertip ballet slippers and a ruffled frill around her knuckles. Each act included exquisitely detailed sets and decorations. "If one has an imagination that will shrink and shrink (which we all undoubtedly have), one can see on this miniature stage the most complete panoramas and thrilling dances one could possibly desire."

The program began with "Scourge de Djeverghitleft Ballet Russe," poetically performed by Madame Karsanoma. Charlotte Russe, the Matchless, the Champion Glace Skater of the World, was assisted by Axel Erickson, late Skater-in-Chief to the King of Scandinavia. The program included the dazzling flame dancer Luciola, Mademoiselle Sallpoffska and her Arabian Charger, Perpetuum Mobile, and featured the Smallest Show on Earth, the Amalgamated and Consolidated Circus Company of Kalamazoo and Oshkosh, with Elmer, the smallest trained pachyderm in captivity, and sensational slack wire artist Signor Centrifugo.

"There seemed to be no limit to Mrs. Lee's ingenuity and versatility and the tiny scenes, which were perfect to the smallest detail," said the *Chicago Tribune*'s society and entertainment columnist.

Finger Tip Theater raised about $1,000 for the Fatherless Children of France, equivalent to more than $16,000 in present-day money. On March 30, the *Tribune* printed a letter written by Lee thanking the Art Institute for its generosity in providing the room and paying for the lighting and other Finger Tip Theater expenses, allowing all the proceeds to go to charity. "I am glad to have given my small efforts to this cause, and am grateful to you for your kind notices," Lee's letter said.

Lee wanted to do more than provide dinner and entertainment for sailors or host another benefit for a worthy cause. While working on Finger Tip Theater, she felt the tug of a higher calling. She felt a drive to do something with her life that was more meaningful and permanent, something in the service of others, something that might change lives for the better.

"I didn't do a lick of work to deserve what I have," Lee once told a reporter. "Therefore, I feel I have been left with an obligation to do something that will benefit everybody. I feel that I must justify my reason for being here." The end of World War I would give her that opportunity.

Over the years, she continued to get updates about her old friend Magrath from her brother's frequent visits to Boston. "All this time [my] interest in medicine did not lapse," Lee wrote in an unpublished memoir. "George Glessner accompanied George Magrath countless times on his cases, always bringing home a living detective story, all the more fascinating because it was true."

When the war ended in November 1918, servicemen returned home in droves. Thousands of young men returned from overseas, many still shell-shocked from battle. They found themselves still far from home, unsure of whether they wanted to return to the rural farms and towns they had left as younger and less experienced men, unsure of what to do next with their lives. Servicemen's homes cropped up in major cities, providing a place for returning troops to decompress and reintegrate into society. In

Boston, the Massachusetts Branch for Women of the Special Aid Society for American Preparedness opened a servicemen's house in Beacon Hill called Wendell House.

Wendell House was named in honor of Mrs. Barrett Wendell, president of the Massachusetts Branch for Women, whose husband was chairman of the English faculty at Harvard. The house occupied two adjoining buildings on Mount Vernon Street within blocks of Boston Common.

At forty years of age, Lee took the first job she had in her life. She was hired as resident manager of Wendell House. While her daughters — fifteen and twelve years old at the time — remained under the care of their governess in Chicago, Lee moved to Boston, where twenty-year-old John was attending the Massachusetts Institute of Technology.

The Chicago social pages noted Lee's departure for postwar service in Boston. She attended a concert of the Chicago Symphony Orchestra and "said au revoirs to all friends present 'till the last man's out of uniform.' "

Lee lived at Wendell House full-time, serving as house mother, and supervised the hostesses and service staff. Unlike other servicemen's homes, Wendell House was intended to feel like a private home rather than a dormitory or club. Lee furnished the residence with carefully selected used furniture to give the home a lived-in feel so servicemen would step into a comfortable, familiar domestic environment.

Wendell House had a capacity of about one hundred residents, although men occasionally slept on cots or couches when necessary. A private room cost fifty cents a night, or men could share a dormitory room for thirty-five cents. Wendell House provided showers, laundry, a writing room, a reading room, and gymnasium. Breakfast was provided for a modest cost.

Writing to the Monday Morning Reading Class in Chicago, Lee said that the servicemen appreciated her efforts. "The boys all say 'well ma'am, this is the only place we have ever struck that is just like *home.*' They settle down as contentedly as cats," she wrote.

Within five months, Wendell House had hosted 1,212 different servicemen. Wendell House helped them get back home, find work, or figure out the next chapter of their lives.

The war now over and troops returning to

civilian society, Lee also faced the prospect of figuring out the next chapter of her life.

4
THE CRIME DOCTOR

February 1, 1922

George Burgess Magrath was exasperated. As the law was written in the Commonwealth, medical examiners in Massachusetts did not have independent authority to investigate deaths. They worked at the discretion of district attorneys, although an autopsy could also be ordered in writing by the mayor or the district selectmen — local elected officials.

Medical examiners were limited to investigate "dead bodies of such persons only as are supposed to have come to their death by violence." In other words, the medical examiner was consulted when police or a district attorney believed that violence may have occurred. Neither the law nor the courts ever defined what was meant by *supposed* or *violence.*

The problem was that medical examiners relied upon the ability of police and prosecutors to recognize when a victim was supposed to have died by violence. What was meant by violence? Was poisoning a form of violence? Was drowning violence? Did an infant suffocated in its crib suffer a death by violence?

By the time the signs of violence were recognized, the decedent was often already in the funeral parlor. The indications of violence could be as subtle as the puncture of a hypodermic needle or the pinpoint red spots of petechiae on the inside of the eyelid. There might have been nothing externally visible at all.

It's the nature of murder that perpetrators try to cover up their deeds, attempt to alter facts to throw suspicion off their trail. A murder could be staged to look like an accident or a suicide. The signs of violence could be obscured by leaving a body on railroad tracks for a train to mutilate, setting the body and building on fire, or leaving a body buried in the woods to skeletonize.

Police, coroners, and even many medical examiners were reluctant to examine a body that was in an advanced state of decomposition or burned beyond recognition under the erroneous belief that any meaningful evidence was gone. These were also the most unpleasant cases, an additional incentive to keep at a distance and dispose of the body quickly.

As often as not, police and district attorneys supposed wrong, letting an unknown number of suspicious cases go undetected and calling in the medical examiner when most of the important evidence had already been altered or destroyed.

"We should do our own supposing," Magrath said in a talk to members of the Massachusetts Medico-Legal Society. "Certainly if we wait for outward evidences of injury irrespective of the mode in which it was sustained, if we wait for proof that an individual has been shot, stabbed or run over, from the appearance of the body, we shall miss a good many investigations which ought to be made, when death is due to causes other than natural."

Magrath never cared for the usual practice of clinical medicine. He was more interested in the broader perspectives of public health, serving as an assistant to the state's secretary of health, in charge of epidemiology and vital statistics for the Commonwealth of Massachusetts. In 1907, Governor Curtis Guild Jr. appointed Magrath to a two-year term as medical examiner for Suffolk County, a jurisdiction including Boston.

Boston's medical examiner office, the first in the nation, was established in 1877. Magrath was the second person to hold the job, succeeding medical doctor Francis A. Harris. Magrath was the first medical examiner in the United States with training in pathology — a specialist in the causes and effects of disease. In a very real sense, he was America's first forensic pathologist. Magrath had also been appointed as an instructor at Harvard Medical School, giving weekly one-hour lectures on legal medicine to third-year students as an elective course.

When he assumed the medical examiner job, Magrath inherited an office in shambles. There was no archive of old case files, no systematic organization of records, no memoranda of practices and procedures. His official vehicle was his predecessor's mode of transportation — a horse-drawn carriage. Magrath asked for — and eventually received — a motorized ambulance to transport the bodies of the dead. The county's morgue on North Grove Street, behind the Charles Street Jail, was in poor condition. Even with improvements suggested by Magrath, the facility was barely adequate.

Most seriously, Magrath also discovered that his office lacked funding for basic necessities. The state legislature failed to appropriate money for the medical examiner's office for the first fifteen months of his tenure. It wasn't until 1908 that state lawmakers provided funds for a telephone, printed stationery, and the wages for assistants. Magrath's salary was $3,000 a year.

Suffolk County had four medical examiners in all. Dr. Timothy Leary, a pathologist at Tufts University Medical School, was appointed medical examiner in 1908. By agreement, Magrath and Leary divided the jurisdiction in half, with Magrath in charge of the northern division and Leary in charge of the southern division. The two medical examiners often worked together on cases. Two associate medical examiners assisted Magrath and Leary.

When he was appointed medical examiner, Magrath found scant material on legal medicine. There were a few textbooks and journals but nothing like the literature in Europe, where the field of legal medicine was much more developed.

No medical school in the United States offered the training Magrath believed was necessary preparation for the responsibilities of a medical examiner. Medical school trained him in pathology, the study of diseases and abnormal conditions. But legal medicine, what would later come to be called forensic pathology, was focused on patterns of fatal injuries, poisoning, post-mortem changes, and other subjects that were outside the usual teachings of medical practice.

Before undertaking the job, Magrath spent more than a year in Europe to immerse himself in legal medicine. He spent time in London and Paris observing their systems of death investigation, regarded as the most advanced in the world. Upon his return, Magrath incorporated the principles and practices learned from Europe's brightest legal medicine minds in his work as medical examiner and in Harvard's medical school curriculum. He expressed his view of the responsibilities ahead:

The duties of this office consist chiefly in the investigation of deaths due to injury of any sort and those which are sudden or unexplained; they necessarily include service from time to time in court . . . In doing my work I have sought to apply to the branch of state medicine, which my office represents, the result of the generous type of scientific medical education which it was my good fortune to receive . . . The general standard of medical jurisprudence in this country is none too high and it is my aim to help raise its level by applying to my own work the principles and the methods of modern scientific medicine and by impressing on the student the importance of the responsibility of the physician in all matters wherein medicine is brought into the service of the law.

Magrath carried a leather-bound loose-leaf field book to document cases he investigated as Suffolk County medical examiner. He kept notes on each case in a code understood only by himself and his secretary so that if the field book fell into the wrong hands, no derogatory information would be disclosed about a deceased person.

Inside the cover of his field book, Magrath inscribed a quotation by Paul Brouardel, pathologist and member of the Académie Nationale de Médecine, France's leading legal medicine authority. Brouardel's words became Magrath's fundamental guiding principle:

If the law has made you a witness, remain a man of science; you have no victim to avenge, no guilty person to convict, and no innocent person to save. You must bear testimony within the limits of science.

On duty twenty-four hours a day, Magrath was a well-recognized figure on the streets of Boston, motoring around in the same clattering 1907 Model T that served as his transportation for the duration of his career. The Model T, which Magrath named "Suffolk Sue," was equipped with a fire engine bell to clear traffic and a small, round MEDICAL EXAMINER medallion mounted on the grille.

He was mild mannered and even-tempered, not one known to lose his patience. "He was always cheerful and genial, kindly and tolerant," Lee said. "He never sat in judgement on anyone. I never saw him angry or impatient." Magrath was just like Suffolk Sue's license plate — 181 — which read the same backward or forward or upside down. "Like his car license, 'always the same,' " Lee said.

Physically, Magrath was a striking figure — tall, with broad shoulders muscled from years of rowing on the Charles River and an unruly shock of flaming red hair. He favored flowing ties and a dark-green waist-coat, wide-brimmed hats, and an ever-present curve-stemmed tobacco pipe. Magrath intentionally cultivated an air of eccentricity, for example, by letting it be known that he only ate one ample meal a day, at midnight.

Magrath told his Harvard colleague, the toxicologist William F. Boos, that being conspicuous was a large part of professional advancement. "You ought to set about to impress yourself on 'em more," Magrath said to Boos. "It helps."

At the scene of a death, any semblance of showmanship disappeared. Magrath's investigations were meticulous and thorough, applying keen scientific judgment to the tasks at hand. He often pointed out clues overlooked by police and suggested productive lines of investigation.

In the autopsy room, Magrath fell into a mood of deep concentration the moment the decedent was wheeled in on a gurney. Frank Leon Smith, a young reporter, sometimes spent nights with his friend, a morgue assistant, when he missed the last train to Melrose. Smith often watched Magrath at work. The medical examiner had "the controlled frenzy of the explorer," he said. "More than most men, he had the chance and the genius to explore the mysteries which each of us carries within the envelope of the skin," Smith said. "He gave the same careful attention to a repelling 'floater' taken from the harbor, as the well preserved man of distinction who'd happen to drop dead on Tremont Street."

On the witness stand, Magrath was confident and unshakable. With a baritone voice burnished by choral practice, he answered questions in a clipped, direct manner, hewing to facts that he knew to a reasonable degree of medical certainty, based on scientific evidence, and not drifting into speculation or conjecture. "His statements were the model of precision," Boos said.

In courtroom sketches of Magrath, he is drawn with his face cast downward, eyes closed or obscured behind spectacles. He looks like he might be sleeping but is deep in thought, listening to a question or formulating his response. Framed by a wild mane of hair, on the witness stand, Magrath was "like a lion resting," one observer said.

Outside court, Magrath declined to talk with reporters about cases still unresolved or under investigation. The proper place for matters of legal medicine was the courtroom, he believed, not in the pages of newspapers. Magrath sometimes talked about closed cases years after the fact, spinning yarns about some of his infamous investigations for crime reporters, but never before a case concluded with a conviction or acquittal.

If he had one fatal flaw, it was his weakness for alcohol. Magrath relied upon the medicative effects of distilled spirits. He never drank to the point of stuporous belligerence but consumed on a daily basis to maintain a steady state of intoxication. He drank to calm his nerves at the end of the day. He drank to erase the unspeakable horrors to which his occupation forced him to bear witness. He drank to chase the demons that lurked in the recesses of his mind.

Although the man dissected human bodies for a living, he "went into something approaching eclipse at the death of those close to him," a contemporary of Magrath said. Death is not something one gets entirely accustomed to, particularly when the decedent is somebody known personally or by reputation.

Some of Magrath's duties must have been deeply upsetting, such as the requirement that he witness the execution of condemned prisoners and pronounce their deaths. Friends would meet Magrath outside the state prison after executions to "get three drinks into him quickly."

Those who knew Magrath said it was his superior intellect, integrity, and a fastidious eye for detail that made him particularly well suited for legal medicine. For every measurement he took, he measured twice. So as to not influence an investigation with misbegotten hunches, Magrath forced himself to keep an open mind until he knew all the facts and considered all the circumstances and then applied judgment and common sense in a relentless pursuit of the truth.

"As a Medical Examiner he was preeminent, finding in that profession the niche into which he exactly fitted," Lee said of her friend. "His meticulous accuracy, his exact adherence to the truth, and his immeasurable patience and skill in determining what was the truth, made his advice and judgement much sought after."

At the time of his appointment as medical examiner, Magrath lived in a renovated dwelling at 274 Boylston Street, overlooking the swan boats in the Boston Public Garden. With no other suitable office space available, Magrath based the medical examiner's office on Boylston Street, which was its official address for the next thirty years.

The room behind his medical examiner's office was Magrath's living space, the walls lined with shelves groaning with books. He had a seven-foot-long ship's bunk with a reading light at one end, a steamer chair by a fireplace, and a telephone at the bedside so he could respond quickly in an emergency. To the rear of this room was a combined bathroom and kitchenette, with cabinets and a gas stove.

He ate most of his meals at St. Botolph Club, a gentleman's club conveniently around the corner in a mansion at 7 Newberry Street, to the west of the Public Garden. St. Botolph Club was a gathering place for men who appreciated the arts, sciences, and humanities. Magrath's old school friend George Glessner was a member of St. Botolph, as were H. H. Richardson and many other Harvard men of substance. Magrath was at St. Botolph so often, he used the club as his residential mailing address.

Magrath was on duty twenty-four hours a day, seven days a week. If he wanted to take a vacation, which he rarely did, it was his responsibility to pay for a medical examiner to serve in his place. He was never far from a telephone, never out of touch with his secretary, always immediately available to go to the scene of a death. By necessity, his hours were irregular. He once rowed in an eight-man crew in a regatta after staying awake for forty-eight hours — and won the race.

On a typical day, after working at the morgue or the scene of a death, late in the evening, Magrath telephoned the chef at St. Botolph just as he was about to close down for the night and gave his order for dinner — clams and spaghetti or beef steak barely charred and served bloody rare. Magrath would show up at midnight for his meal, socialize and tell stories for a while, and return home to read until the wee hours of the morning.

Magrath made a name for himself by applying the rigorous methods of medical science to the investigation of death. Newspaper stories about his high-profile cases added to his prestige as a Sherlockian "crime doctor." In time, he was asked to consult on cases by police departments throughout Massachusetts and nearby New England states.

And always, every day and every night as he did his work, Magrath used science to learn as much about the facts of a death as humanly possible. He believed that death merited the most rigorous critical analysis and that the archaic coroner system should be abandoned for one that allowed a rational basis for determining causes of death.

One of the prominent cases that cemented the value of the medical examiner system was the death of Avis Linnell. Linnell was a nineteen-year-old choir singer from Hyannis living at Boston's Young Women's Christian Association. Shortly after 7:00 p.m. on the evening of October 14, 1911, residents of the YWCA heard sounds of distress from within the shared bathroom, which was locked from the inside. They forced open the bathroom door to find Linnell sitting in a chair, her feet immersed in a tub half filled with warm water, gasping for breath and groaning in great agony. The YWCA matron sent for a female doctor immediately. Linnell was moved to a bed, but by the time the doctor arrived, she was dead.

The YWCA matron had the presence of mind to close the bathroom door and leave the room as it was until the police and Leary, the medical examiner, arrived on the scene. Magrath was out of town on a rare vacation, so Leary responded to the scene to inspect the bathroom and Linnell's body. Linnell was taken to the morgue for an autopsy.

During the minutes before she died, Linnell told witnesses at the YWCA that she had lunch that day with her fiancé, Reverend Clarence Richeson, a pastor in Cambridge. The matron asked one of the girls to call Richeson by telephone and notify him of her death. At first, he denied knowing Linnell. Then he said, "Why are you telling me this?"

Leary's autopsy revealed that Linnell was pregnant and had been for about three months. The lining of her stomach had a deep red discoloration with streaks of red radiating over the gastric mucosa, indicating a poisoning by cyanide. Leary retained Linnell's organs for examination by Magrath upon his return.

Magrath agreed with Leary's diagnosis and prepared specimens of Linnell's gastric mucosa for examination under the microscope and laboratory testing for the presence of cyanide. The tests confirmed their suspicion.

The police were ready to close the case as a suicide. Obviously, they said, she took the cyanide herself. Nobody was in the bathroom with her, and the door was locked from the inside. Perhaps the shame of her delicate condition led her to end her life.

Leary disagreed. For one thing, Linnell had a change of clothing in the bathroom to wear after her bath. She also had a harness and sanitary napkin even though she was pregnant and hadn't menstruated in months. It appeared as though she expected to begin menstruating, and she may have been attempting to induce an abortion.

Leary was certain that Linnell expected to leave that bathroom alive and insisted that the police keep digging.

Police interviewed Richeson but were unable to connect him to the cyanide that killed Linnell. The thirty-five-year-old Richeson was a serial philanderer who had left a trail of fraud and broken hearts stretching from Boston to Kansas City. He may have been a cad, but did that make him a killer?

Newspapers latched onto the tragic death of the young singer. Reading about the case, the owner of a drugstore in Newton Center, William Hahn, contacted police to inform them that Richeson had been in his business four days prior to Linnell's death. Hahn knew Richeson, a regular customer. He said that on October 10, Richeson told him that he had a dog at home that was going to have puppies. "She is whining around the house and is a nuisance," Hahn said Richeson told him. "I want to get rid of her."

Hahn sold Richeson potassium cyanide — enough to kill ten people. "It is as quick as lightning, but it is very dangerous," he warned his customer.

Richeson didn't own a dog.

When confronted with Hahn's statements, Richeson confessed to poisoning Linnell.

He wanted to leave Linnell and marry a wealthy socialite, but her pregnancy threw a wrench into his plans. Richeson gave Linnell the cyanide, telling her that it was a medicine that would induce an abortion.

Two weeks before he was to stand trial for her murder, Richeson stood before a judge and admitted that he intentionally killed Linnell. He was sentenced to death. Magrath was a witness when Richeson was executed on May 21, 1912. Were it not for the insistence of Leary, Richeson might well have gotten away with murder.

"There was no primary suspicion of foul play," Magrath pointed out. "It was only when the post mortem examination disclosed a condition in the stomach suggesting poisoning by potassium cyanide that death from causes other than natural was suggested."

"The further discovery of a physical condition compatible with suicide strongly suggested this motive of death," he said. "Only the care and diligence of the Medical Examiner Leary, who had charge of the case, led to a further investigation by the police resulting in the conviction of Richeson."

If Boston had been operating under a coroner system and without the benefit of standardized practices such autopsies, Magrath knew, Richeson more than likely would have gotten away with murder.

Newspapermen believed history may have repeated itself a year later when another young woman was found dead under suspicious circumstances. Marjorie Powers, a twenty-eight-year-old stenographer, was discovered facedown in a half-filled bathtub in a West End hotel room on November 15, 1912. Police found a tumbler of gin in the bathroom and what appeared to be mustard powder sprinkled in the bathwater.

Twenty-four hours earlier, Powers had checked into the hotel with her employer, Albert Cummings, a prominent Faneuil Hall produce dealer. They registered at the hotel as "O. P. Davis and wife, Lynn." Cummings was seen leaving the hotel shortly before Powers's body was found. Police went to Faneuil Hall and arrested Cummings to hold in custody pending the results of Magrath's postmortem examination.

Reporters wasted no time in framing the death as another murder. "Another Boston Girl Thought Victim of Man — Parallel to the Death of Avis Linnell Is Seen in the Case of Stenographer whose Death Is Being Investigated" one newspaper headline said. "Police Hint at Second Avis Linnell

139

Tragedy" read a subhead in the *United Press* story.

Under questioning by police, Cummings admitted being with Powers for about four hours. Then he left and went home. The next morning, when Powers didn't show up for work, Cummings telephoned the hotel and was informed that the occupant could not be roused. He went to the hotel, found her dead, and left in a panic. Cummings denied any responsibility for Powers's death. Police reported that Cummings was on the verge of collapse during questioning.

In speaking with Powers's family, Magrath learned that she had not been in the best of health. The young woman had been suffering fainting spells of late but had no other significant medical history. No marks of violence were observed during the postmortem examination, nothing to indicate asphyxiation or poisoning. During the autopsy, Magrath discovered that Powers had a severely dilated heart. Her death was entirely due to natural causes.

Cummings had no culpability in Powers's death but through a coincidence of circumstances was caught in an embarrassing situation. Police released Cummings from custody, and he went home to his wife. The details of their reunion were not recorded for posterity.

Two similar cases followed: One death, almost mistaken for a suicide, resulted in a man being sent to the electric chair. The other seemed highly suspicious, but Magrath's investigation showed nothing was amiss. Either case could easily have turned out very differently. In another era, in another place, one person may have been prosecuted for a crime he did not commit while another got away with murder. Scientific investigations in each case helped clear the innocent and convict the guilty.

Not a political creature by nature, Magrath did his work and kept his mouth shut. His unwillingness to compromise and single-minded adherence to the facts as established within the bounds of science occasionally made things difficult for others. It comes as no surprise that the medical examiner made enemies along the way. Police couldn't count on him to see things their way. Lawyers were unable to get him to say what they wanted in court. Magrath wasn't on one team or another. His only loyalties were to the decedents who passed through his office.

Magrath had one key ally: Joseph C. Pelletier, Suffolk County district attorney, who was elected to office in 1906 and served until 1922. Pelletier relied upon Magrath's judgment and trusted him to testify truthfully in simple terms easy for a jury to understand.

Some parties in the Boston political machinery wanted to replace Magrath with a medical examiner who might be more malleable to their interests. Magrath's first seven-year term of office was scheduled to expire in January 1914. As the end of his term approached, Magrath became the target of concerted attacks on his work and his character in an attempt to thwart his reappointment by the governor. His opponents hoped to install a crony who could be relied upon to play ball with local politicians.

In February 1913, a politically connected attorney filed a lawsuit on behalf of a woman who claimed that the medical examiner had mutilated her husband by performing an autopsy without her permission. The husband, John A. Brimfield, had been a patient in the psychopathic department of Boston State Hospital for an unspecified brain disease when he died on January 7. According to the lawsuit filed by Berenice Brimfield, in which she sought $10,000 in damages, her husband died from natural causes. When she had been asked about an autopsy, Mrs. Brimfield refused to give permission.

The body, she alleged, was delivered to the medical examiner without her consent. She claimed that Magrath "sacrilegiously cut, hacked, hewed and mutilated the body" of Mr. Brimfield, removing and keeping his brain and leaving the dead man's tongue in his abdomen. "She alleges the condition of the body would offend a stranger, to say nothing of an afflicted and bereaved wife," read one news account.

Months later, as the Brimfield lawsuit inched along, the stakes were raised when a group of morgue employees ill-advisedly plotted to frame Magrath with larceny. On June 17, 1913, Thomas O'Brien dropped dead while painting the Bay State Trust Company building. His body was taken to the North Grove Street morgue where assistant superintendent George Miller and autopsy assistant Frederick Green found more than $350 in O'Brien's vest pocket. Another worker, Thomas Kingston, and the undertaker's assistant who brought the body to the morgue also saw the money.

Three hundred and fifty dollars was a substantial sum of money, a decent month's salary at the time. Miller and Green kept about $230, then sealed the rest of the money and O'Brien's other personal effects in a regulation manila office envelope — essentially an evidence envelope that also serves as a receipt to prove that objects have a continuous chain of custody. Green, Miller, and Kingston agreed to pin the theft on Magrath. It would be the word of three people against one, after all. How could the plan fail?

A couple of days later, O'Brien's nephew, a police officer, went to the morgue to identify the body and collect his uncle's personal effects. It didn't take long for the nephew to notice a discrepancy between the amount of money in the envelope and the amount that the undertaker's assistant told him had been removed from the body. When notified that money was missing, Magrath called the police and referred the matter to the district attorney.

By coincidence, Governor David I. Walsh began receiving letters complaining of shocking goings-on at the North Grove Street morgue — thefts from the dead, a medical examiner who mutilated bodies, all sorts of horrible things. Walsh announced that he would not reappoint Magrath or name a successor while these issues remained a cloud over the medical examiner's office.

Fifteen police reporters representing every newspaper in Boston urged Walsh to reappoint Magrath. Coming together on their own, the reporters told the governor that they acted out of a sense of duty to warn that failure to reappoint Magrath would be a serious blow to the best interests of the people of Massachusetts.

After Magrath's appointment expired in January 1914, his position was in limbo. Although not officially on the job, he was determined to continue working as medical examiner until he was reappointed or replaced and went on with his duties as usual.

Magrath was represented in the Brimfield lawsuit by Pelletier, the district attorney. Testifying in his own defense, Magrath explained that the postmortem examination he had performed on John A. Brimfield was a standard procedure, the same that was followed in every full autopsy. He insisted that the investigation was done in pursuance of written authority from the district attorney and in accordance with the law.

Magrath explained that an examination of the brain was necessary to determine whether Brimfield's death or the condition for which he was institutionalized was related to an injury in any way, either recently or in the past. It wasn't uncommon for patients in facilities to experience falls that resulted in head injury or even to be struck by other patients. The brain was retained, as was routine in these cases, for fixation of the tissue and examination of slides under a microscope.

Yes, Magrath said, Mr. Brimfield died of natural causes. But that couldn't have been known for sure until the postmortem examination was completed. In his closing argument, Pelletier told the jury that if Magrath was guilty, then he was too, because the medical examiner was working under his direction. The jury returned a verdict in Magrath's favor.

Weeks later, the plot by Green, Miller, and Kingston to frame Magrath with theft fell apart and backfired in spectacular fashion.

As it turned out, Magrath was busy on June 17, the day O'Brien died and Magrath was supposedly stealing money from his body. He had attended the Harvard-Yale baseball game, sitting in the front row to be accessible in case of an emergency. After the baseball game, on his way to the morgue, his attention was drawn to a large fire in East Boston. He drove to the fire in case there were fatalities and he was needed.

Later, he attended a dinner with Harvard alumni, and it was three in the morning by the time he arrived at the North Grove Street morgue.

When Magrath arrived to examine O'Brien, he learned that the body had already been searched and O'Brien's property sealed in an envelope. This was a violation of procedures and was noted as unusual by others, including Magrath's secretary. Magrath's rule was that bodies were not to be searched until he issued the order. The medical examiner should always inspect the untouched body first, before a search for valuables and property, to avoid affecting the body in any way and to ensure that the collection of personal effects was witnessed.

Green was forced to admit that he made entries in the log book, searched the body, and sealed the evidence envelope before Magrath arrived at the morgue. Magrath could not possibly have taken money from O'Brien's body. The last person to touch O'Brien's money was, in fact, Green himself. His own handwriting sealed his fate.

Green, Miller, and Kingston were arrested and charged with larceny and conspiracy. They were sentenced to fifteen months in prison. Magrath was reappointed by Governor Walsh to another seven-year term of medical examiner for Suffolk County.

A year after his reappointment as medical examiner, Magrath was asked to help New York City reform its notorious coroner system, which was hopelessly corrupt, a detriment to public health, and a hindrance to the administration of criminal justice.

New York City's coroners were the worst of all worlds. "The coroner is not a medical man and is thus incompetent to determine causes of death," the *New York Globe* noted in a 1914 editorial. "He is not a lawyer and thus does not know how to gather evidence and to examine witnesses; he has had no experience in criminal investigation and is an injury rather than a help to following up clues."

Reform of New York City's coroner system was inspired by the sudden collapse and death of an elderly citizen at the Century Association, one of Manhattan's exclusive clubs. Even though the death was clearly due to natural causes, the coroner refused to sign off on the death certificate unless the body was taken to the funeral parlor he recommended (and from which he was presumably receiving kickbacks). Members of the Century Association were outraged and demanded action from Mayor John

Purroy Mitchel, who appointed his commissioner of accounts, Leonard Wallstein, to investigate.

Magrath told Wallstein's committee he was certain that in at least one case, a coroner's physician had covered up a murder — either on purpose or unwittingly though incompetence. A man by the name of Eugene Hochette was found dead at New York City's Hotel Delaware in March 1913 with a single gunshot wound to the head. Dr. Timothy Lehane, the coroner's physician, certified the death as suicide and permitted the cremation of the body the next day without an autopsy. Two pathologists had an opportunity to examine Hochette — Dr. Charles Norris, director of laboratories at Bellevue Hospital, and Dr. Douglas Symmers, pathologist of Bellevue Medical College. Norris and Symmers noted the absence of powder burns around the gunshot wound in Hochette's head. When a gun is fired, burning gunpowder produces stippling and soot on the skin up to a distance of about two or three feet. This wound was caused by a gun held at a greater distance and could not have been fired by the decedent.

Magrath agreed with Norris and Symmers. "I should say," he said, "that the diagnosis of the coroner's physician was not supported by evidence."

Magrath urged state lawmakers to abolish the office of coroner and replace it with a medical examiner system. Testifying before members of the state legislature, Magrath said that a properly written law would be "a practically perfect instrument, and that under its provisions New York City would be provided with an opportunity to not only protect its citizens but to contribute incalculably to the advancement of medicine as applied to crime and casualty."

State lawmakers drafted a bill to establish a medical examiner office in New York City. The statute eliminated the office of coroner, prohibited inquests, and took away the legal and judicial aspects of death investigation. The legal part of the coroner's job, placing charges in cases of homicides and criminal negligence, would be taken over by prosecutors, while magistrates would assume the judicial duty of setting bail.

Under the new law, the chief medical examiner was authorized to conduct an autopsy in cases of sudden, unnatural, or suspicious deaths without the need for an order from a prosecutor. He was independent of the district attorney and the police, elevated as an equal to provide the medical expertise in forensic investigation. The chief medical examiner was required to be a competent physician expert in legal medicine. He would be chosen based on the civil service exam and not part of any political process. His only duty would be to the decedent.

When passed in 1915, the law included a provision for enactment on January 1, 1918, allowing the terms of the existing coroners to expire and giving time to select a chief medical examiner. Magrath was asked to apply for the position, but he was disinclined to leave Boston. Dr. Charles Norris was appointed as the first permanent chief. Trained in pathology and anatomy in Europe, the independently wealthy Norris was well qualified and ideally suited for the position. Norris immediately began improving forensic investigation in New York City, including hiring key personnel such as Alexander Gettler, who established a chemistry laboratory to perform tests for poisons and drugs. In time, New York City's chief medical examiner's office became a model of a modern forensic medical center, working some of the most sensational cases of the twentieth century and becoming the birthplace of American forensic toxicology.

Election day. President Woodrow Wilson was in a tight race for reelection against the Republican candidate, Supreme Court Justice Charles Evans Hughes. At 5:30 p.m. on that unseasonably warm evening, Bostonians were hurrying home or to Newspaper Row, the stretch of Washington Street that was home to several of the city's newspapers and the place where many people got up-to-the-minute news.

Streetcar #393 was headed inbound down Summer Street, fully loaded with fifty to sixty passengers. As the streetcar barreled down the street, motorman Gerald Walsh realized — too late — that the drawbridge over the Fort Point Channel was open. Walsh pulled the brake, locking the wheels as the streetcar crashed through iron gates blocking the street and slid twenty-five feet down the tracks to the edge of the canal where it teetered, seeming to hang momentarily. The car's rear platform lifted into the air until it plunged over the side and sank into thirty feet of water.

"The rear end seemed to catch on the edge for an instant so the car tilted almost straight up and down. Then it shot downward toward the water," said tugboat captain William G. Williams, who witnessed the incident. "The crash was followed by a death-like stillness. I expected to hear shrieks and shouts, but not a sound of human voice did I hear. Everything was very quiet."

Fifteen people who had been standing on the rear platform of #393 were able to jump off before the car dropped into the water. An unknown number remained in the packed streetcar sinking toward the bottom of the channel.

The incident was a calamity unlike anything ever seen, a disaster of unprecedented scale and complexity, compounded by large crowds gathering on Summer Street to watch the unfolding tragedy. By 9:00 p.m. thousands of people thronged along the canal at the approach to the bridge. Police repeatedly charged at the crowd with batons drawn to push them back from the edge of the water.

Magrath was responsible for identifying and examining bodies recovered from the canal. Mayor James Curley ordered that the bodies be recovered out of view of the public, determined to deny gawkers and press photographers the ghastly and undignified sight of bodies being fished from the water. The bodies were moved underwater by a team of six divers: four commercial

153

divers and two divers from a submarine at the Charlestown Navy Yard. The divers tied ropes to the bodies, which were dragged underwater to the police boat *Guardian* moored a distance away from the scene. Without arousing public attention, the bodies were lifted aboard the police boat and taken to the aft cabin where Magrath set up a temporary morgue. After a preliminary assessment, the bodies were transferred to the police boat *Watchman,* ferried to Constitution Wharf, and taken from there by ambulance to the North Grove Street morgue for identification and postmortem examination by Magrath and his assistant medical examiners.

The first body was pulled from the water about ninety minutes after the streetcar sank. In the decedent's pocket was a receipt with the name of George Wencus. Magrath assigned the body the next number in his field book: 8298. By the time Magrath was done, forty-six bodies had been recovered from the submerged streetcar. It was the deadliest disaster in Boston history. Magrath's thoughts about the incident were never recorded, but the scale of the tragedy was unlike anything he had ever seen and likely left him stunned and exhausted.

Less than three years later, in January

1919, Boston was struck again by an unusual disaster. At the city's North End, an old waterfront neighborhood where the Charles River emptied into the Boston Harbor, stood a tank of molasses on the Purity Distilling Company wharf. The tank, five stories tall and ninety feet across, held 2.3 million gallons of molasses destined to be fermented into ethanol. The tank was located on Commercial Street near a turn in the elevated train line, next to the North End Paving Yard. Across the street was the three-story Engine 31 firehouse and the freight shed of the Bay Street Railway Company.

What the neighbors didn't know was that the tank, only three years old, was defective. It had been poorly designed, was never pressure tested, and was constructed with substandard materials. The tank was so badly built that children ate chunks of hardened molasses that leaked through the seams.

At 12:30 on the afternoon of January 15, the 150 paving yard employees were taking their lunch break when they felt a low rumbling. Suddenly, rivets popped like gunfire, and the tank blew apart, releasing 26 million pounds of molasses in a twenty-five-foot-tall wave moving at thirty-five miles per hour, destroying everything in its path. A section of the tank blew out two supports of the elevated train line to the south, causing it to collapse to the ground and nearly derailing a streetcar.

The freight shed and paving yard were instantly reduced to kindling, covering workers with molasses and debris before they had a chance to escape. Trucks, motor cars, and horse-drawn wagons were swept along the relentless tsunami of molasses. The firehouse was pushed off its foundation, killing one fireman and injuring two. Another fireman was knocked into Boston Harbor; he managed to survive. A ten-year-old boy pinned beneath an overturned railroad car was not so lucky. More than a dozen injured horses were mired in molasses and eventually had to be shot to end their suffering.

Magrath was one of the first to respond to the scene. He helped set up a field hospital and temporary morgue in a nearby building. Wearing hip-high rubber wading boots, he surveyed a scene of unimaginable devastation. Every structure within four hundred feet of where the molasses tank had stood was demolished. Buildings were splintered, and steel beams and sheet metal lay in twisted piles. More than two blocks, hundreds of thousands of square yards of a busy city neighborhood, were coated with molasses up to several inches thick.

Bodies recovered at the scene looked "as though covered in heavy oil skins," Magrath said. "Their faces, of course, were covered with molasses, eyes and ears, mouths and noses filled." He examined the bodies as quickly as they arrived at the morgue. "The task of finding out who they were and what had happened to them began by washing the clothing and bodies with sodium bicarbonate and hot water."

Autopsies showed that several of the victims had been crushed or fatally injured by debris. Some were horribly mutilated, their chests caved in and limbs twisted. Many victims suffocated to death, molasses filling their airway and lungs. They had drowned in molasses. Twenty-one people died in Boston's molasses disaster, and about 150 people were injured. Despite all his training and the thousands of cases he had examined up to that point, nothing prepared Magrath for the devastation wrought by a common storage tank.

Magrath became involved in the most controversial case of his career on April 15, 1920. Two employees of the Slater-Morrill

Shoe Company in South Braintree, Massachusetts, were robbed and shot to death while carrying the company's $15,700 payroll into the factory.

Magrath performed the autopsies on Alessandro Berardelli, a thirty-four-year-old security guard, and forty-four-year-old Frederick A. Parmenter, an unarmed paymaster. The men were fathers with two children each. Berardelli was shot four times and Parmenter twice. Magrath measured the path of each wound, using his fingers to retrieve the projectiles, never grasping with metal instruments that might scratch the bullet and obscure rifling marks.

As each .32-caliber projectile was recovered, Magrath used a surgical needle to scratch a Roman numeral on the base of the bullet — the one surface without significant markings. The bullets were numbered individually, in sequence, so Magrath could verify his mark and describe the damage caused by the projectile in court.

Police charged Italian-American anarchists Nicola Sacco and Bartolomeo Vanzetti with the homicides of Berardelli and Parmenter. The men were swept up in postwar hostility against foreigners and radicals, and the prosecution of Sacco and Vanzetti became a cause célèbre throughout the country.

Sacco, a shoemaker and security guard, and Vanzetti, a fish peddler, denied involvement in the crime. Neither of them had a criminal history. Both men were carrying handguns when they were picked up for questioning by police. Sacco had a Colt automatic pistol he said was necessary for his job as security guard. Vanzetti's gun was a .38-caliber Harrington & Richardson revolver he said he carried to protect himself while carrying cash he earned selling fish.

The case against Sacco and Vanzetti was built on a profusion of confusing witness statements and ambiguous ballistic evidence. Both men had alibis for the day of the crime. Vanzetti had peddled fish to customers that whole day. Sacco also accounted for his whereabouts. Still, five eyewitnesses placed Sacco and Vanzetti at the scene of the crime.

Prosecutors claimed that the revolver found on Vanzetti had been taken from Berardelli, the slain guard, but Vanzetti's gun was never positively linked to Berardelli. Others have suggested that Berardelli didn't even have his gun with him on the day of the robbery.

Witnesses said that Berardelli was shot twice, then two more times while lying prone on the ground. The .32-caliber bullets Magrath recovered from Berardelli's body were consistent with the witness statements, with two wounds in the back fired by a person standing over the body. Magrath described one projectile, which he had etched with the Roman numeral III, as the fatal bullet. This bullet pierced Berardelli's right lung, severing the pulmonary artery.

To Magrath's eye, nearly all the bullets recovered from Berardelli looked the same, and none of them could have been fired by the .38-caliber weapon found in Vanzetti's possession. But bullet III was different from the others. The other five projectiles had markings with a right twist produced as the bullet spins down the gun barrel. Bullet III, the fatal bullet, had a left twist, consistent with Sacco's automatic pistol.

The ballistic evidence was less than conclusive but still sufficient for a jury whose prejudices had been inflamed by the depiction by prosecutors of Sacco and Vanzetti as disloyal radical aliens. Additionally, Sacco and Vanzetti did themselves grievous harm when they lied to police during their initial questioning, believing they were being detained for their political beliefs. Police questioned them about their political activities and loyalty to the United States. Months earlier, the U.S. Department of Justice had initiated a program of mass arrests and deportation of aliens suspected of being communists or sympathetic to the cause. Sacco and Vanzetti knew of two friends who had been deported so far and thought they were about to be next.

The lies they told police about their politics came back to haunt them at trial. Prosecutors argued that the lies were evidence of "consciousness of guilt." Innocent men, they told the jury, had no reason to lie.

Sacco and Vanzetti were found guilty and sentenced to death. After several years of appeals, they were executed at Charlestown State Prison on August 21, 1927. Magrath was present to witness the execution and declare Sacco and Vanzetti dead.

The prosecution of Sacco and Vanzetti remains one of the most contentious and controversial criminal cases of the twentieth century. Evidence in the case is still debated and contested. Some believe the men were guilty as charged. Others contend that the execution of Sacco and Vanzetti is among the great miscarriages of the American criminal justice system.

5
KINDRED SPIRITS

During the early 1900s, Prairie Avenue began to decline as the character of the neighborhood around it changed. The area's proximity to the city's business and transportation hubs, once so desirable to Chicago's elite, became more valuable to commercial interests. One by one, the grand mansions of Prairie Avenue and nearby streets were razed for large commercial buildings, apartments, and parking lots. Wealthy residents fled to more pastoral environs in suburban communities farther from the city center.

About two dozen Prairie Avenue homes were converted to furnished rooms for rent, some housing as many as forty-five people. Marshall Field Jr.'s mansion at 1919 South Prairie was converted into the Gatlin Institute, a hospital for the treatment of alcohol and drug addiction. No longer an exclusive address of Chicago's elite, Prairie Avenue became overrun with transients and the unfortunate.

By 1920, the elderly Glessners were among only twenty-six original Prairie Avenue settlers who still lived on the street.

At this time, Frances Glessner Lee was spending most of her time in Boston and at The Rocks and had little need for the Chicago home her parents had purchased for her after her marriage to Blewett Lee. The residence at 1700 Prairie Avenue was sold in 1921.

For several years, likely starting around 1920 or 1921, Lee operated an antique shop in Littleton along with her older daughter, Frances, who was then in her early twenties. The antique shop was located in a former one-room schoolhouse and was called the White Schoolhouse. Lee and Frances visited dealers and antique shops throughout New England, touring through New Hampshire, Vermont, and Boston and going as far as New York City. Having grown up in a family steeped in crafts and fine furnishings, Lee had an experienced eye for antiques. The women looked for undervalued bargains or items that could be cleaned up and sold at a reasonable profit.

Lee kept detailed written notes on her competition, making a list that described the offerings, reliability, and prices of each dealer. The antique shops along Boston's Charles Street, Lee said, were "very fishy." She noted if a shop had "city prices" — charging a premium — and which dealers were dishonest. "Highway robber," she said of G. F. Mylkes of Burlington, Vermont. About the Old English Antique Shop of New York City, she just said "Fakes."

When the women found a good dealer — reliable, with a good selection and reasonable prices — Lee assigned it a code word, presumably so that she and Frances could talk business in the presence of other dealers and shop owners. E. H. Guerin of Pembroke, Massachusetts, was described as "average — probably honest" and code named Catholique in Lee's notes. The New England Antique Shop in Boston was code named Paintbrush. The White Schoolhouse remained in business until Frances married Chicago attorney and entrepreneur Marion Thurston "Bud" Martin, an entrepreneur and aspiring businessman, in 1928.

In September 1926, Lee's uncle, George B. Glessner, died at eighty-one years of age. John Jacob's only surviving brother, he had been an officer in Warder, Bushnell, & Glessner and subsequently International Harvester. The childless millionaire left in his will the amount of $250,000 in cash and securities — comparable to about $3.5 million in present-day money — to his only niece, Frances Glessner Lee.

Lee's son, John, did undergraduate work at Massachusetts Institute of Technology and received his master's degree in mechanical engineering from MIT in 1922. He went to work in the aviation industry, designing airplanes. In 1926, John Lee married MIT classmate Percy Maxim of Hartford, Connecticut. John and Percy made their home in Connecticut where John worked for the United Aircraft Corporation.

The following year, in June 1927, twenty-one-year-old Martha Lee married Charles Foster Batchelder, a Harvard-educated engineer who had been hired by George Glessner to divert an unused water reservoir he had acquired for use on The Rocks estate. The Batchelders set up residence in Augusta, Maine.

With her children successfully launched into their own lives, Lee needed a place to stay in Chicago for those occasions when visiting with her parents or taking care of business in the city. In 1928, she purchased a twelve-room apartment in a high-end building at 1448 Lake Shore Drive for $55,000, about $800,000 in today's money.

In the first days of January 1929, George Glessner, Lee's brother, began feeling ill at his home on The Rocks estate — pain in the lower abdomen, fever, and a general malaise. He was diagnosed with acute appendicitis and admitted to a hospital in Concord. Surgery to remove the inflamed appendix was successful. However, during his recovery, George developed pneumonia and died. He was fifty-seven years old.

The period after her brother's death was a low point for Lee. She was as distant as ever from her extended family. Her children were grown and having children of their own. She had little to occupy her time since closing the White Schoolhouse. The death of somebody close often leads to reflections upon mortality, looking inward to take full measure of the legacy that remains when we leave this mortal coil. Lee felt melancholy, alone, and unmoored.

To compound matters, Lee had to go to Boston for medical care at Massachusetts General Hospital. The nature of her condition is unknown but evidently involved a surgical procedure that required a lengthy convalescence in Phillips House, the hospital's deluxe private care facility. An eight-story building located on Charles Street near Boston's Beacon Hill, Phillips House was an innovative concept when it opened in 1917. Wealthy people avoided the open wards typical of hospitals at the time, preferring to have procedures done in their home, a private home offering nursing care, or in a hotel room as it was when Lee had her tonsils removed. Medical care had come a long way since then. Patients who were able to afford it no longer needed to have surgical instruments disinfected on the kitchen stove but could receive care with the latest in anesthesia, aseptic surgery, and modern technology. Phillips House offered tastefully furnished private rooms. A fenced-in rooftop and verandas on the north end of the building allowed patients plenty of sunshine and fresh air during their stay.

Lee, fifty-one years old at the time, was a patient at Phillips House for an extended period of 1929. By coincidence, her old friend George Burgess Magrath was hospitalized at Phillips House during some of this time. She could not have foreseen how the time spent recuperating with Magrath at Phillips House would become a pivotal episode in her life and lead to the work that stands as her legacy.

The medical examiner had a severe infection and inflammation affecting both of his hands, a consequence of circulatory problems caused by his failing liver and repeated exposure to formaldehyde and strong disinfectants. It was his third time being admitted for care at Phillips House for his crippled hands. The condition was very serious and could lead to amputation.

Lee and Magrath rekindled their friendship during their sojourn at Phillips House. They whiled away the endless hours visiting and talking, often sitting together on rocking chairs on the veranda overlooking the Charles River. They reminisced about long-ago days; life at The Rocks, the 1893 World's Fair, youthful memories. They talked about music, art, and literature. And they talked about Magrath's career as medical examiner. Lee found Magrath's work endlessly fascinating. Magrath's stories were so much more interesting than the usual conversations among women in Lee's social circles. Magrath was concerned with weighty subjects that mattered: life and death, crime and justice. The world was an unpredictable and often violent place, Lee knew. Magrath helped make order out of chaos, satisfying the most basic human drive to understand why death happened.

"He used to tell me many of his most interesting cases, but never until they were settled and finished and 'through the court,' as he said he was a Public Servant whose job was to find the truth and steadfastly adhere to that truth when found, and also at the same time keep his mouth shut," Lee recalled. "He didn't give out information to the Press while a case was still under investigation, or pending in the Courts, but I never heard of this making an enemy for him amongst the newspaper people."

Magrath told vivid, engaging stories filled with drama, pathos, and occasional morbidly dark humor. There was the case of an elderly man found dead in his sixth-floor room of a Boston hotel, sitting in a Morris chair beside an open window. He was discovered when hotel staff checked on guests after a fire on the fourth floor. It was a small fire, confined to one room, and didn't create enough smoke to asphyxiate the old man. Near the body was a small metal container with the residue of an unknown substance.

Magrath learned that the man was a retired chemist. He had a morbid fear of fire, having nearly been burned to death as a youth. To avoid that fate, he always carried a small vial of aconite — a fast-acting poison derived from wolf's bane — in case of an emergency. When he smelled the smoke and saw flame licking out the window, he was certain his end had come. He consumed the aconite, preferring to die by poison than by flames or smoke inhalation, although he was never at risk from the fire.

Another of Magrath's oft-told stories was about the murder of Florence Small. Her husband, Frederick Small, thought that he devised the perfect crime. And he almost did.

"I consider this one of the most remarkable of all my cases," said Magrath, who was called in to help the New Hampshire State Police with the investigation.

On September 28, 1916, the body of thirty-seven-year-old Florence Small was found in the debris of a fire that destroyed her Ossipee, New Hampshire, home. She had been burned beyond recognition, some of her bones exposed to such intense heat that they were calcified and crumbling.

Frederick Small was not at home when the fire erupted but miles away attending the movies in Boston with friends. A hired driver who took Small to the train station said he saw him say goodbye through the open door when leaving his house but did not see Mrs. Small or hear her reply. The fire broke out seven hours later. Certain things about Small's behavior aroused the suspicion of police. The couple had recently taken out a life insurance policy, paying the surviving spouse $20,000. Only one premium payment had been made.

When Magrath asked Small his preference for a funeral parlor to receive his wife's body after the postmortem examination, he said to the medical examiner, "Is there enough left of the body to require a casket?"

Frederick Small's skinflint ways ultimately proved to be his undoing. The Smalls' cottage was not maintained well. The cellar was prone to flooding and at the time of the fire was filled with several feet of standing water. The bed on which Florence Small had been lying burned through the bedroom floor, dropping her body into the cellar and preserving her body.

During Magrath's postmortem examination, he found that Florence Small had a cord tightly wrapped around her neck. Her skull was fractured, and she had also been shot in the head with a .32-caliber bullet. More evidence was sifted from the ruins left from the fire — a .38-caliber revolver, a spark plug, some wire, and a charred alarm clock. Magrath noted something curious: a cast-iron stove with bits of fused metallic material on its surface.

The small defects "showed the stove had been subjected to a shower of molten steel,"

Magrath said. "Neither cast iron nor steel fuses in the heat of an ordinary house fire."

Magrath looked around for something that could cause such intense heat and found evidence of thermite — a gray flammable powder used to weld steel. He theorized that somebody scattered thermite all over Florence Small's body, the bed, and the bedroom floor and rigged an alarm clock to ignite the material.

Small denied responsibility for his wife's murder. He claimed that she was alive when he left the house. She was assaulted by a lumberjack, he said. Few believed his version of events, and Small was charged with murder.

During the trial, prosecutors pulled a dramatic stunt. Without Frederick Small's knowledge, the district attorney had obtained a court order directing Magrath to decapitate Florence Small and preserve her dissected head as evidence. Before the head was introduced as an exhibit in court, the judge suggested that women leave the courtroom. Some did, but eight women remained among the spectators craning to see the grisly evidence. Frederick Small sat in the courtroom sobbing, his face in his hands, while Magrath described the injuries inflicted upon his wife.

Magrath testified that Florence Small had been struck in the head at least seven times, but the skull fractures that resulted were not severe enough to be lethal. She had been shot through the forehead while lying supine by somebody standing over her. That injury would have been fatal, the medical examiner said, but she had already been strangled to death by the cord around her neck.

It was difficult to discern recognizable features of the disfigured, burned flesh that remained of Florence Small's head. Magrath explained to the jury how he reached his conclusions by pointing out evidence on the skull and specimens of the victim's tissue preserved in formaldehyde. Magrath showed the jury a piece of Florence Small's airway, a pink rectangle of tissue. When a person inhales air thick with smoke, soot is deposited on the airway. Small's airway was clean and perfectly normal, proving she was not breathing when the fire started.

He pointed out injuries to the trachea, horseshoe-shaped hyoid bone, and strap muscles that are evidence of strangulation. Enough of her mucous membrane inside her eyelids survived the fire to identify petechiae, tiny pinpoint hemorrhages that are also characteristic of strangulation. He explained how the beveling of the bullet hole in her forehead and the pattern of stippling on her skin produced by the burning gunpowder indicated the position and distance of the person who had fired the shot. Everybody knows that when you cut your skin, blood flows immediately. The bullet wound through the skin of her forehead did not bleed like the skull fractures did, so that injury occurred after death.

The medical evidence showed that events happened in this order: Florence Small was beaten, fatally strangled, shot, then set on fire.

Next, the prosecution introduced more evidence — the frame of the bed on which Florence Small died and the cast-iron stove — that had been shrouded behind a curtain and revealed with dramatic effect. Everybody in the courtroom turned to look except one person: Frederick Small. He kept his face covered with a handkerchief.

"An innocent man would have been curious what was about to be shown," Magrath said. "But Small was guilty and he knew."

Frederick Small was convicted of murder and executed on January 15, 1918. Magrath attended his execution.

Magrath also told Lee about a time he was asked to consult on a case by Charles

Norris, the medical examiner in New York City. A young man was charged with murder, being accused of throwing his wife from a fifth-floor window. Based on Magrath's findings, Norris ruled her death a suicide, but the district attorney had witnesses who heard a fight and threats from the accused.

Magrath had examined the body of the young wife. She had sustained fractures of the skull that certainly would be fatal. More importantly, she had fractures of both heel bones. The decedent landed on both feet, which is consistent with jumping or dropping straight down from a window, not being thrown. The odds of being thrown from a window and landing on both feet are very remote indeed. The young man was acquitted.

With each story, Lee gained a deeper appreciation for Magrath's pursuit of the truth to clear the innocent and convict the guilty. One day during their convalescence, Magrath discussed the difficulty of explaining evidence to a jury. Trying to describe the place of a death was challenging. Since the scene itself no longer existed, jurors developed an image in their mind that may or may not be correct.

"I'm still trying to find something better than a diagram and a photograph to show a jury, the exact spot where the body was found in proper relation to the stairs, the stove, or the window," he said. "That's the hardest thing in the world to get across."

Lee thought a moment, remembering the miniature orchestra and quartet she had made years earlier. "What if you had a small model of a room, drawn in the correct scale, and a doll or dummy dressed exactly like the victim and all the other details in the correct place?" she said. "Would that help?"

Magrath tapped his pipe. "A model?" he said. "Could I use it in court? Half the time, they won't even let me introduce photographs. Let me think about it a while."

Lee was awestruck by Magrath's boundless energy and enthusiasm for preaching the gospel of the medical examiner system. Despite his age and increasing infirmity — in addition to the acute sepsis of his hands, he was also losing his vision to glaucoma — Magrath was a perennially popular speaker for civic groups and other organizations throughout New England.

"He was a brilliant raconteur and was in great demand as a speaker before all sorts of organizations, from church societies through Boy Scouts on up to state medical societies and bar associations," Lee said.

As Magrath saw it, the legal medicine

education he had received in Europe was a great gift that he had a duty to use. He felt obligated to the profession and also obligated to decedents — not just to those who died in his bailiwick but to all. Every person, he felt, was entitled to a thorough, scientific, and impartial death investigation, should it be necessary.

Magrath considered it part of his mission to promote awareness of medical examiners, the duties they fulfilled, and how they differed from coroners. People needed to know how deaths were handled wherever they lived, he argued. Progress wouldn't occur unless people knew that there were better ways of doing things. Not just the general public, although that was probably the most important, but also lawmakers, police, prosecutors, and the courts.

Magrath argued that legislators needed to understand the importance of reforming state law to abolish coroner systems, institute medical examiner systems, and make them work more effectively. Lawyers and judges needed to be educated about the nature of medical evidence. District attorneys needed to give medical examiners a freer hand to decide which cases required an open autopsy.

Additionally, the police needed to know

what to do — and what not to do — at the scene of a violent or suspicious death. Most police officers were clumsy oafs, Magrath thought, poorly trained and in many cases unable to read and write. They were not equipped to be thrown into a situation in which scientific and medical evidence was paramount. What they did in those first critical moments could make or break a case. Who knew how many people had slipped away from justice due to poor police work or were convicted based on a confession obtained by third-degree coercion while scientific evidence went unexamined, Magrath wondered.

And the public? If people knew the sorts of things that went on behind the scenes, they would demand change. Newspapermen were always hungry for the titillating details of a murder for a story but only had vague ideas about the role of medical examiners. Greater education for the public would lead to a deeper understanding of the need for a thorough and proper inquiry into deaths.

By 1929, when Magrath was recuperating in Phillips House with Lee, in the more than half a century since Boston introduced the medical examiner system in 1877, only two other major cities had followed suit — New York in 1917 and Newark, New Jersey, in

1927. Magrath's hope was to convince jurisdictions of the weaknesses of coroners and the need to switch to a medical examiner system. It shouldn't take a scandal so egregious that the public was shocked to implement reform, he thought, but that seemed to be the only thing that got the job done in many cases.

Essex County, New Jersey, serving the greater Newark area, established a medical examiner's office in the wake of the botched investigation of the murders of Episcopalian priest Edward Wheeler Hall and Eleanor Reinhardt Mills, a singer in his choir and also his mistress. The scene was unsecured for several hours. Onlookers trampled the crime scene and touched the bodies, ruining any evidence that may have existed. Newspaper photos of the scene showed a crowd of men standing around the bodies, stripping a nearby crabapple tree of bark to keep as souvenirs.

Hall's wife, two of her brothers, and their cousin were charged with the murders but subsequently found not guilty in a trial. The case is officially unsolved to this day.

During their time at Phillips House, Magrath gave Lee a printed copy of a landmark study published by the National Research

Council in 1928 titled *The Coroner and the Medical Examiner.* The study had been funded by the Rockefeller Foundation, an organization with a long-standing interest in improving medical education and the criminal justice system.

The study compared the two cities with medical examiners at the time — Boston and New York City — to three cities with coroners: Chicago, San Francisco, and New Orleans. The NRC report was unsparing in its criticism of the coroner system. Aside from the familiar litany of malfeasance attributed to coroners, the study found that medical examiners were more reliable and less expensive than coroners. The report called the coroner system "an anachronistic institution which has conclusively demonstrated its incapacity to perform the functions customarily required of it" and said that it should be abolished.

The report recommended that the medical duties of the coroner be vested in a medical examiner and the nonmedical duties taken over by the appropriate prosecuting and judicial officers. Medical schools were singled out for their failure to adequately train students in the area of legal medicine. Few doctors were prepared to work competently as medical examiners.

"In not a single school is there a course in which the student may be systematically instructed in those duties in which he may be called upon to perform in connection with conditions which may arise as the result of crime or accident," the report said. "There must be a demand for properly trained men, there must be opportunities which would make the medical graduate wish to elect a career as medical examiner, and there must be facilities for obtaining the thorough training which would fit him for such a career."

One day, during those long, dull hours at Phillips House, Magrath's outlook turned dark.

"You know, I won't be around here much longer, and when I die all this dies with me," he said to Lee, referring to the documents that comprised his life's work. "I suppose as soon as I'm gone, all my notes and slides and books and stuff will go to the junk pile."

Lee looked at Magrath. "What would you like to have done with all your material?" she asked.

"If I had my way, I'd have it used as the foundation of a Department of Legal Medicine," he said. "You know, there isn't any such thing in the whole United States. A complete academic department, engaged in education, research, training . . ."

"Wait, I'll get some paper and we will make a rough outline," Lee said.

"I'd have first a new modern research laboratory," Magrath said, "then a library, with my books and notes as a starter, and a complete file of lantern slides and motion picture films for use in instruction. We should need a competent staff of instructors to lecture on the medical angle of the law to doctors, lawyers, dentists, insurance men, coroners, medical examiners, undertakers, and the police."

Lee wrote page after page of notes.

When he was finished, Magrath puffed his pipe thoughtfully. "It's just a dream," he said. "I've thought about it for years, but there's no way it can be done."

During their stay at Phillips House, Magrath said something that changed the course of Lee's life. He made an innocuous offhand remark, a trifling observation that resonated with Lee in unexpected and unpredictable ways.

"I have always contended that the organs of the human body were the most decorative things in the world, and would make wonderfully effective murals for a medical school or doctor's club," Magrath said.

The beauty of human organs? "The idea appealed to me at once," Lee later wrote.

Lee's thoughts began to whir. It was as though a switch had been flipped in her mind. Those extemporaneous thoughts of Magrath's were a seed, an idea that took root and gained a life of its own. His words dispatched Lee on a quest, on a years-long mission to prove him right, that the organs of the human body are indeed beautiful. Perhaps one or two panels depicting a "mix and tangle of bones and glands and organs" that could be hung over a mantel or doorway. Or perhaps something . . . different.

As ideas began to formulate in her mind, she said to Magrath, "I want to look for myself. Soon, when we get out of here, I want you to show me the beauty of human internal organs."

6
THE MEDICAL SCHOOL

Draped in a cotton surgical gown, Lee stood next to Magrath at the side of the autopsy table in the North Grove Street morgue. The autopsy room was as clean and stark white as a hospital operating room. To the right were steeply banked seats of the amphitheater where medical students usually sat. That day, the seats were empty. On the left were a bank of windows and cabinets of instruments. At the far end of the room were the double doors of the elevator leading to the refrigerating room downstairs.

In the middle of the room, beneath a bright overhead light, the body of a man found dead in his bedclothes lay supine on a stainless-steel table. The man looked awkwardly posed, arms raised aloft in rigor, like a department store manikin. A jarring stench permeated the room, redolent of rotting seafood combined with manure. Lee held a perfumed handkerchief to her face.

Magrath pointed out a purplish mottling of the skin on the posterior side of the dead man's forearm. He explained its significance to Lee as he had many times in lectures. It was livor mortis or lividity. This discoloration of the skin results when blood is no longer circulating under pressure. When the heart stops beating, blood pools by the force of gravity in the interstitial space of dependent areas of the body. Lividity appears on whatever surface of the body is lowest except for where the capillary beds are compressed, such as where the body is resting on the ground.

Magrath pulled up the decedent's shirt sleeve to show a patch of paleness in the discoloration at the elbow. "You can see where the skin was under some pressure, at the points of the hips and shoulder blades on which the body rests its weight. You can see how the arms and legs were folded, the imprint of a belt around the waist. You can see where something was pressed against the skin. Many times, I've seen the outline of a weapon.

"Lividity becomes apparent around two hours after death," Magrath said. "The size of the patches increase over a period of hours and reach maximum intensity around eight to twelve hours after death. For the first six hours after death, lividity can be redistributed. That is, if the lividity is on a person's anterior body and you roll them over, it can shift to the posterior side. For the first twelve hours, the lividity will blanch; if you press on it, the skin turns pale. After twelve hours or so, lividity is fixed. It won't blanch, and it won't redistribute. The intensity of livor mortis gradually fades in time.

"Livor mortis is a scientific fact as certain as the sun will rise in the east tomorrow morning. It is a simple matter of physics. If a person if found dead on his back with lividity on his anterior body, he could not have died that way. That is a scientific impossibility. There has to be an explanation. Either somebody placed the victim there or rolled him over.

"Now, another person might look at lividity and not see any particular significance to it," Magrath acknowledged. "Even medical doctors. They don't teach a lot about postmortem changes to medical students. They think it's just a diffuse discoloration without any specific meaning. But nothing could be further from the truth. Proper assessment of lividity can provide a wealth of information — an approximation of how long they have been dead, the position in which a

186

person died, whether the body was moved after death, whether any objects were touching the body, and so on."

Once a body had been taken to the emergency ward or undertaker, all those facts were lost forever. Examining a body the day after death was one day too late. This was one of the reasons why Magrath insisted it was so important for the medical examiner to observe the body in situ. The medical examiner should be involved before the police, for lack of knowing any better, spoiled the evidence that might be present at the scene of a death.

With the assistance of his diener, the decedent's clothing was removed and a cotton towel draped across his hips to maintain modesty. Magrath proceeded with his external examination, looking closely at the decedent's skin and scalp from head to toe. Any defect of the skin — a wound or contusion, any sort of mark — was noted, and a yardstick was used to measure the distance from the midline and from the head or heel. Magrath dictated his findings to his secretary, sitting off to one side taking notes. Lee looked on, fascinated.

The external examination completed, Magrath placed a wooden block beneath the decedent's neck to elevate the chest and extend his head backward. Beginning his incision near the acromion of the shoulder, Magrath drew a scalpel blade diagonally across the dead man's chest to the tip of the sternum. He sliced from the other shoulder, then down the midline from the sternum to the pubic bone, the deep incisions forming a Y on the decedent's torso.

Lee watched as Magrath dissected through the layers of skin and muscle, caught off guard by the absence of bleeding and the orange-yellow color of human adipose tissue, so different in appearance to the fat of beef or pork or even chicken. The medical examiner used a small saw to cut the rib cage from the sternum, lifting the flat breastbone from its place.

With the abdominal and thoracic cavities exposed, Lee looked in wonder at the organs, many of them familiar from illustrations she had seen in medical books and the drawings of Vesalius. The lungs, their surface smooth and glistening, cradled the heart, perfectly nestled together. Viscera, some pale and some starkly colored, snaked around the abdomen. Everything was pristine, as carefully arranged as a floral centerpiece. It was . . . breathtakingly beautiful.

This person was once a living machine of infinite complexity. Each one of these parts

188

worked together, flawlessly, for years until something deranged this human machinery beyond the limit of viability. With his specialized knowledge and the laboratory tools at his disposal, Dr. Magrath would find out what happened.

Lee recalled the words of William Shakespeare, from the prince's soliloquy in Hamlet: "What a piece of work is a man."

Reaching into the decedent's thoracic cavity, Magrath began to dissect the tissues of the neck, the carotid arteries and jugular veins, severing the esophagus, removing the trachea with the tongue still attached above the epiglottis. Working his way downward, the medical examiner cut the diaphragm and the few vessels and suspending ligaments holding the organs in place. In the lower abdomen, Magrath sliced the urethra and rectum.

Grasping the organ block in his arms, Magrath lifted the organs en mass and placed them on the dissecting table. Lee peered into the hollowed-out body, looked at the smooth, shiny lining of the chest and thick bones of the vertebral column.

Magrath felt for the mastoid process — the bump behind the ear — and drew his scalpel in an arc over the top of the head to the other side. He used the scalpel to work the scalp away from the skull, pulling the skin and hair far forward over the face until the calvarium, or skull-cap, was completely exposed.

Using a bone saw with a broad, flat blade, Magrath scored around the circumference of the skull. He then used a chisel, tapped with a hammer, to separate the bowl-like calvarium. Once removed, the brain sat encased in its milky meningeal membranes. Magrath worked the tip of his scalpel around the skull opening to cut the cranial nerves, lifting the frontal lobes to access the optic nerves and finally to sever the brain stem from the spinal cord.

The organs, spread out on the dissecting table, were examined individually. Magrath dictated a description of the appearance of each organ as he felt it between his fingers. Each organ was measured and weighed, then sliced like a loaf of bread to inspect the tissues inside and out. Magrath set aside a specimen from each organ, dropping it in a jar of formaldehyde for later examination under a microscope.

When Magrath had completed the post-mortem examination, the tissues and organs were returned to the decedent's abdomi-nothoracic cavity. The diener put the skull back together, pulled the scalp back into place, and closed the Y incision with a rough baseball stitch using heavy cord thread.

Lee watched as the gurney was rolled toward the elevator that would take the decedent back to the refrigerator room.

At home at The Rocks, Lee read the National Research Council report, *The Coroner and the Medical Examiner.* Ruminating on the recommendations in the report and everything she had learned from Magrath, Lee identified three areas that needed development in order for American society to truly throw off the vestiges of the Middle Ages and embrace modernity in its investigations of unexpected death. Medicine, the law, and the police all desperately needed reform in order to establish a functioning discipline of legal medicine.

"Legal Medicine may be likened to a three-legged stool, the three legs being medicine, the law and the police," she once said. "If any one of these is weak, the stool will collapse."

For medical examiners to replace coroners throughout the country, hundreds more men like Magrath would need to be trained. State lawmakers needed to be persuaded to abolish inquests and the office of coroner and adopt a medical examiner system. And states with medical examiners needed laws reformed to give them greater autonomy and independent authority, to put them in charge and protect them from political and public pressure.

The police were another essential component, Lee knew. A police officer was often the first to arrive at the scene of a death and sometimes the only person present. Those first few minutes at the scene could make or break an investigation, and law enforcement officers needed to be trained on how to avoid compromising a crime scene.

This, Lee decided, was the path she would take through the door Magrath had opened for her. She would spend the rest of her life developing the three-legged stool of legal medicine. But she would need to figure out a way to do so that would be acceptable for a woman of her social status and drawing upon the connections and resources that her upbringing had afforded. However it needed to happen, Lee, with her unbridled curiosity and exacting personality, would get it done.

April 30, 1931
During his early years as an instructor at Harvard Medical School, Magrath had been

given a stipend of $250 annually from the university. During the Great War, for reasons that were never explained, that stipend ceased. Magrath continued with his lectures to medical students from Harvard, Tufts, and Boston University on an unpaid basis in addition to performing his duties as a medical examiner.

In 1918, Magrath wrote a letter to Harvard's medical school dean, Dr. Edward Bradford. Magrath pointed out that he had been teaching pathology at Harvard for twenty years, and the task of doing so had only increased in complexity and workload in recent years with the addition of legal medicine as an emerging discipline. Magrath had developed an entire systematic course on legal medicine for third-year students that had been well-attended in its inaugural year, which he planned to follow up with instruction in the morgue in the fourth year of medical school.

"The subject of legal medicine as I attempt to present it includes many matters relative to various branches of medicine for which one reason or another escape attention in the courses of instruction given therein," Magrath wrote to Bradford, "matters of importance to the practitioner of medicine concerning which it should be certain that every man who received a degree from Harvard University should have some instruction."

All of Magrath's time and the material he acquired to teach medical students was coming out of his own pocket. "I . . . feel sure that you believe me entitled to some advance in academic rank and to compensation for my services," he said.

Among his colleagues, Magrath wasn't considered a typical medical school faculty member. He gave lectures and provided practical experience for medical students at the morgue, but he didn't do research and had never published a paper for a scientific journal about his cases during his tenure as medical examiner.

There is no record that Magrath's request for compensation was acted upon at the time, but he continued teaching and developing a curriculum to teach legal medicine in addition to his established pathology courses.

After becoming interested in legal medicine, Lee saw an opportunity to support Magrath and Harvard Medical School, both things close to her heart. Harvard, after all, was the alma mater of her brother and many other men close to her. Lee still felt affection for the university even though it had been beyond her grasp as a young woman.

In March 1931, Lee approached Harvard University president A. Lawrence Lowell with a proposal to commemorate Magrath's twenty-fifth year as medical examiner. Lee wanted to give Harvard $4,500 a year, $3,000 of which was earmarked for the salary of a professor of legal medicine and the remaining $1,500 for honoraria and travel expenses for outside lecturers on the subject. "It is my desire that Dr. George Burgess Magrath shall occupy this professorship with the title of full professor, which I believe I am correct in assuming to be your intention in this matter," she wrote to Lowell.

Lee said that she intended to leave Harvard $250,000 in her will to support her initiative in perpetuity. "My intentions are to create a Department or Chair of Legal Medicine which will bear the name of Dr. George Burgess Magrath when it is proper," she wrote. Lee's gift included one key condition — that she serve as Magrath's teaching assistant.

The university president responded to Lee's proposal in a letter dated May 4, 1931. "Your wishes will be carried out and I look for there being a great benefit both to our Medical School and to the country,"

Lowell wrote. "They touch the public interest at many points — medical, legal and social."

Lee asked for Lowell's complicity in a ruse to convince Magrath to take a much-needed break with a European trip. Except for the times he was forced to seek treatment at Phillips House, it had been years since Magrath had been away from work for an extended period of time. A change in scenery might help curtail his drinking, too, which continued to be a problem. She asked Lowell to tell Magrath that through a fortuitous oversight, there were fellowship funds available to send the medical examiner to Europe for a period of unstructured study. Lee told Lowell that if Magrath accepted the offer, she would provide Harvard $3,000 to pay for his trip.

Magrath didn't take the bait. "He really does not feel that he can get away until midsummer," Lowell reported back to Lee. "He has not, or pretends to have, any suspicion where the gift comes from."

The subterfuge to send Magrath on a trip to Europe was one of the many ways Lee took an interest in the well-being of her friend. In an era without the medical privacy concerns of today, Lee was kept informed about Magrath's health and drinking habits by his personal physician, their mutual friend Dr. Roger I. Lee (no relation to Frances Glessner Lee), a prominent Boston internist who later served as president of the American Medical Association. She also set up a joint bank account with Magrath and kept the balance flush with thousands of dollars at his disposal should he ever need it.

Friends and acquaintances openly speculated on the close relationship between Lee and Magrath. At times Lee bordered on the coquettish, referring to herself in unpublished writing for Magrath as "Ye Saucy Scrybe," and yet in correspondence between the two, they never used terms of endearment. Lee always called him Dr. Magrath, and to him, she was Mrs. Frances G. Lee.

The relationship between Lee and Magrath was based on mutual respect and common interests, particularly music and art and now legal medicine. While there was clearly great affection between Magrath and Lee, there is no evidence that their relationship was intimate. If Lee did carry a torch for Magrath, it certainly was unrequited. She may never have expressed the depth of the love she felt.

Her children grown, married, and with lives

of their own, Lee divided her time between her cottage at The Rocks and Chicago. She visited the city frequently, traveling by train along with her secretary and a servant, to spend time with her aging parents. When in Chicago, Lee often stayed at the Palmer House hotel, a familiar locale once owned by an old family friend.

After a long illness, Lee's mother, Frances Macbeth, died at eighty-four years of age in October 1932. John Jacob Glessner remained living in the Prairie Avenue home alone.

Around this time, Magrath introduced Lee to Ludvig Hektoen and Oscar Schultz, both of whom had been involved in the National Research Council report comparing coroner systems to medical examiner systems. The men were also active members in the Institute of Medicine of Chicago, a private organization dedicated to improving medical science and public health. The Institute of Medicine was engaged in efforts to abolish the coroner system in Chicago and replace it with medical examiners. Progress moved at a glacial pace, partly because of a requirement to amend the state constitution from which the coroner's authority was drawn.

"I am not sure that our objective should

be a change limited to Cook County, or to counties with a certain population, or to the entire state," Schultz wrote in a letter to Lee. "Personally, I would prefer to advocate a state-wide examiner system."

Suggesting a change to the investigation of sudden and suspicious deaths invariably stirred controversy. Politicians were reluctant to give up what traditionally had been a local authority to the state. Undertakers, coroner physicians, and others with a stake in death investigation held their own opinions.

"Our fight is going to be a long and uphill one, because in most of the counties of the state the office [of coroner] is held to be of so little importance that the inertia against change is difficult to overcome," Schultz wrote to Lee. "In Cook County the office has sufficient spoils to make the politicians desire to hold on to it. And the politicians, after all, are the ones who tell us what we shall or shall not have."

It became clear that winning over hearts and minds regarding the superiority of the medical examiner system would be a very slow process. Everybody wanted something, and their vested interests were often at odds. Creating change would require diplomacy and tact and a great deal of time.

Diplomacy and tact, Lee thought to herself. *I've been doing that my whole life.*

Lee was appointed to an advisory membership in the Institute of Medicine's Committee on Medicolegal Problems. She asked Schultz for advice on arranging for an exhibit of the Massachusetts Medical Examiner's Society at the annual meeting of the American Medical Association, which was based in Chicago. They shared a mission to bring awareness of medical examiners to wider audiences.

Under the sponsorship of the Institute of Medicine, Schultz created a large exhibit for the Century of Progress International Exposition, the Chicago World's Fair of 1933–34. Through text and images, the forty-foot display explained the curious history of the coroner system and challenged viewers to consider whether scenarios depicted in the images might be homicide, suicide, or accident. "Death demands scientific investigation," the exhibit stated in block letters. Schultz's exhibit marked the first time the discipline that would come to be known as forensic medicine was presented to a public audience.

Meanwhile, Lee's self-directed education in legal medicine resulted in a massive collection of literature — books and medical

200

journals from the historical to contemporary works and esoterica. Among her acquisitions were rare and valuable works, including the 1473 text of *De Venenis* by thirteenth-century Italian physician Petrus de Abano and the only complete set in the world of the nine-volume treatise completed in 1779 by German public health pioneer Johann Peter Frank. Lee's collection included a 1512 printing of *De Proprietatibus Rerum* by Bartholomaeus Anglicus and a 1498 edition of *Stultifera Navis* by Sebastian Brant, both of which contained exceptional illustrations of postmortem examinations. She also sought crime-related curiosities, such as the original memoirs of Charles Guiteau, written in his own hand while awaiting execution for the assassination of President James Garfield.

By 1934, she had acquired a collection of about a thousand volumes. She intended to donate the entire collection to establish the George Burgess Magrath Library of Legal Medicine at Harvard Medical School, but Harvard had to create an appropriate place for the library first, and time was of the essence. Lee wanted several rooms on the third floor of Building E-1 allocated for the Department of Legal Medicine, with one room renovated with bookcases and furniture — and painted a color selected by Lee — for the library. She wanted everything finished in time for the dedication of the library and before she had surgery for an unknown ailment — possibly for breast cancer.

Fearing that her death may be imminent, Lee wanted to make sure that arrangements were in place to support the work she and Magrath had done. "I have this morning executed a new Will in which I have given to Harvard, one million dollars for the continuation of the Department of Legal Medicine," she wrote to university president James Bryant Conant. "I think you indicated that I confess it is my hope that in my lifetime I may yet provide a bit more."

After much negotiation between the medical school dean and department chairmen — and the relocation of mice used for experimentation — four adjacent rooms on the third floor of Building E-1 were reserved for the Department of Legal Medicine. One room would be the library, another outfitted into a laboratory, and two rooms would be used for office space.

Dr. David Edsall, who was medical school dean at the time, wrote a letter to Dr. J. Howard Mueller, chairman of the Department of Bacteriology, explaining why rooms were being commandeered for the Department of Legal Medicine.

"The donor of money for Legal Medicine threatens to give more money — all told, quite a large amount — but more particularly wished to have definite arrangements made in a hurry as to what we should be willing to do before she went into a hospital for a major operation which she thought possibly might terminate her life," Edsall said.

Lee's gift was predicated on her serving as curator for library — if she survived the operation — so she could continue to add to the collection as she saw appropriate. The orders from Conant on down were to defer to Lee in every way possible.

The new library contained all Lee's rare volumes, as well as one of three complete sets in existence of the journal of the Massachusetts Medico-Legal Society and complete bound volumes of all European criminology and legal medicine periodicals. The Magrath Library of Legal Medicine was the largest of its kind in the world.

Conant was among the luminaries present when the library was dedicated on May 24, 1934. Magrath, hobbled by illness, was unable to attend.

"By his vigorous personality and the skillful discharge of his duties [Magrath] has played an important part in demonstrating the superiority of the system of medical examiners as compared with the old coroner system," Conant said at the dedication.

The ancient office of coroner involved such a combination of legal and medical duties as to make it unsuitable for complex, modern conditions . . . The problems which confront the coroner or medical examiner are of such a nature as to require that all the resources of modern science be brought to bear upon them. The examination should be made by a skilled pathologist who can call to his assistance other experts in allied fields, if necessary. This is possible only if the medical aspects of the old coroner's duties are put on a professional basis, as they have been under the Massachusetts system. Dr. Magrath, as one of the few men devoting all his time . . . and energy to this important work, has contributed much to building up a high standard for the profession. He has established traditions which affect not only the system in this state, but will serve to influence the practice throughout the country as the old coroner system is gradually superseded by the system of medical examiners.

Lee also spoke at the dedication. "For many years I have hoped that I might do something in my lifetime that should be of significant value to the community," she said.

I was sincerely glad to find that my opportunity to serve lay here at Harvard Medical School. You are possibly all familiar with the objective in mind. My wish is to build up here a Department of Legal Medicine second to none other, but I firmly believe that its growth must be gradual in order to be sure. The plan is destined to be a manifold development, only a small part of which is as yet under way . . . I am grateful for this opportunity to pay a tribute to your colleague, my old-time friend Dr. Magrath, a man who practically created this profession, and whose life has been devoted to perfecting it.

January 26, 1935
Magrath introduced Lee by letter to Dr. Alan Gregg, director of the Medical Sciences Division of the Rockefeller Foundation. Gregg oversaw a broad portfolio of

research and pilot projects in the areas of public health, psychiatry, basic sciences, and medical education. He had been involved in the construction of the Institute of Pathology at Western Reserve University, an early modern European-model pathology facility in the United States. The Institute of Pathology, which served all the affiliated hospitals in the Cleveland area and the university's School of Dentistry, developed into prominence under the directorship of groundbreaking experimental pathologist Dr. Howard T. Karsner.

Lee asked Gregg about developments in legal medicine since the Rockefeller Foundation funded Schultz's survey almost a decade earlier for the National Research Council. How much progress had been made in the recommendations listed in the report?

None at all, Gregg admitted. The report was gathering dust in a file drawer. Not a single major jurisdiction in the country had adopted the medical examiner system since then.

Lee sought Gregg's assistance in developing a fellowship program to train doctors to specialize in legal medicine, much as the Rockefeller Foundation had done with fellowship programs in psychiatry and other areas of medicine.

If medical examiner systems were to be adopted more broadly across the country, there had to be many more young medical men trained in legal medicine, Lee told Gregg. But no medical school on this side of the Atlantic had a fellowship program in legal medicine. With the support of the Rockefeller Foundation, Harvard's Department of Legal Medicine would address this urgent lack of manpower. Wisconsin, Michigan, and Ohio were eager for the development of legal medicine and would change from the coroner system if there were adequately trained personnel available, Lee told Gregg.

Lee shared a proposal she had written, titled "Skeleton Plan for Department of Legal Medicine." An entire field of study was fully formed in her nine typed pages — faculty to lecture to third-year medical students, a fellowship program to train specialists in legal medicine, and courses for coroners, coroners' physicians, and medical examiners. It outlined a complete academic department involved in education, research, and public service — well beyond the scope of the resources that had so far been established for legal medicine at Harvard. The department would have a toxicologist with a well-furnished laboratory, a photography and X-ray unit, and a library with an extensive collection of books, photographs, and instructional material.

"It is sketched on rather broad lines, but in some places I have been able to go into detail, while in others I am still fairly indefinite," Lee wrote Gregg of her plan. "Of course, as I learn more, some changes will occur." Lee said that she was willing to endow $250,000 to Harvard to establish a Department of Legal Medicine — a factory to produce forensic pathologists to work as medical examiners.

What Lee was suggesting was nothing less than creating an entirely new field of medical practice from the ground up. The ultimate goal of Lee's vision was to develop the department into an Institute of Legal Medicine to conduct all forensic death investigations in Massachusetts and serve as a resource for police departments across the country.

"Told her we were interested in doing something in this field and said that we laid particular emphasis on getting good young men to go into the field as a career and getting training for it," Gregg dictated for his diary.

Lee said that she could "induce Dr. Magrath to take such a beginner," a young doctor with an inclination toward legal medicine to train in a fellowship program, according to Gregg, and that she could present any difficult task to Magrath and, if given time, could convince him of it. She intended to develop a program and work with Magrath as long as he was able to serve.

Gregg added another brief note to his diary after his initial meeting with Lee: "Would like a bibliography of legal medicine." Lee would, in fact, turn out to be a relentless and obsessive book collector, constantly asking friends and acquaintances and even the FBI for lists of books on criminology, medicine, forensics, ballistics, and other related subjects.

Lee was a force to be reckoned with, and Gregg was impressed by her determination. "Mrs. Lee bids fair to be the Lucretia Mott of legal medicine," he wrote in a memo to his assistant after a visit. "The next time she comes I want you to see her to get the full flavor of her practical and pertinacious mind."

In 1932, New York University announced the formation of a new Department of Legal Medicine in the medical school catalog. Dr.

Charles Norris, the head of laboratories at Bellevue and chief medical examiner for New York City, served as chairman of the department until his death from heart failure in 1935. Other faculty included the renowned toxicologist Alexander Gettler, Milton Helpern, and Harrison Stanford Martland, the medical examiner from Newark. Members of the NYU faculty provided undergraduate courses to medical students and postgraduate courses in forensic medicine, pathology, toxicology, and serology.

The Rockefeller Foundation could have chosen to develop a fellowship program at the Department of Legal Medicine at New York University, but the foundation believed in investing its resources based on where the funds would have the best chance of success and the widest impact. Largely because of Lee's financial support and personal involvement, the Rockefeller Foundation chose Harvard over New York University. Ultimately, NYU developed its legal medicine program anyway, but Lee's influence ensured that the earliest incarnation of the field came out of Harvard.

Around the time she was discussing the establishment of the Department of Legal Medicine at Harvard, Lee made gifts to her daughters, Frances Martin and Martha Batchelder, of 350 shares each of International Harvester preferred stock in 1934. The stock dividends would provide the women an income of about $2,450 annually, worth about $44,000 today. Lee had been providing her daughters the same amount in cash for many years but thought that giving them capital would provide greater financial security. Recalling her own divorce, Lee understood the importance of women having an independent source of income.

"Many years ago in my young married life, my father made your Uncle George and me similar gifts," Lee wrote to her daughters, "and while the income which you will receive will be no more than you have been having, I know from experience the comfort it is to possess your capital yourself. It is with pride and happiness and love that I transfer to you this part of my capital."

In 1934, Martin and her husband adopted a baby girl, Suzanne. Within months, the thirty-two-year-old Frances Martin contracted pneumonia and died on June 19, 1935.

By the time Magrath was named a professor of legal medicine in 1932, his liver had become cirrhotic, scarred from repeated insults. Whether the cirrhosis was a consequence of alcoholism, occupational infection with a hepatitis virus, or chronic exposure to formaldehyde is debatable. One of the important functions of the liver is removing impurities from the blood. When the liver fails, ammonia and other waste products build up in the bloodstream. People suffering from liver failure often feel fatigued and may become confused or disoriented. Since the liver is also involved in the production of blood-clotting factors, cirrhosis increases the risk of bruising and bleeding.

Others noted a change in Magrath's physical appearance. In his early sixties, he appeared a much older man. He walked with an unsteady gait, his skin seeming to hang on his body. Dr. Roger Lee, the internist, kept Lee informed about Magrath's health.

"George seemed very pleasant. After the first, this sort of false heartiness disappeared and we had a very pleasant talk," he wrote to Lee. "At present he makes a very good appearance, but I think there is a good deal of weakness behind that appearance."

The doctor was trying to manage Magrath's irregular schedule and frequent use of alcohol, prescribing him the barbiturate amytal to help him sleep at night. "Our reports about George are that he still maintains his nocturnal habits and he does not seem very different," he told Lee on another occasion.

Lee's financial generosity to her family extended to Magrath, even eclipsing the joint back account she had opened and kept stocked with funds for him. After Magrath's retirement, Lee bought him a Packard, a substantially larger and more comfortable automobile than the Model T, Suffolk Sue, that had served him so many years. She also paid the fees to store Magrath's automobile in a garage.

In the fall of 1935, deteriorating health forced Magrath to resign as medical examiner. He continued with his teaching activities at Harvard as long as he was able and remained involved in choral groups and rowing organizations.

Magrath's pension from the Commonwealth of Massachusetts provided him $2,250 a year, while the pension available to him from Harvard for his years of service amounted to less than $150 a year. Lee told the medical school dean, Dr. Sidney Burwell, that $2,400 a year was not enough for Magrath to live on. Burwell spoke with Magrath and agreed that Magrath needed another $100 a month to support his customary lifestyle. Lee proposed that she would provide $600 a year if Harvard matched it, with her portion paid to Magrath through the university "without bringing her into the picture," Burwell wrote in a memorandum of the conversation. "I think some action should be taken in the case of a man who has really devoted a lot of time to the University since he was first taken on as a teacher in 1898 and who has received a substantial salary for only a few years," Burwell wrote. Harvard agreed to the unusual pension arrangement, with Lee secretly helping to support Magrath.

With Magrath spending more time at Harvard, Lee's Department of Legal Medicine needed more office space. She had her eye on several offices on the third floor of Building E-1, rooms that were being used by the Department of Pharmacology, chaired by the distinguished physician Dr. Reid Hunt, one of the pioneers of American pharmacology.

In particular, Lee wanted room 307, which she said would be an entirely satisfactory study for Magrath and leave room for his laboratory work next door in room 306. Lee asked the medical school dean if arrangements could be made for her to have it. Hunt wasn't having any of it and wasn't about to give up any of his space for such a dubious endeavor.

"A Medico-legal Library is somewhat of a joke unless it is desired to make a collection of old books to show what absurd views have been held as to poisons," Hunt wrote to the dean. "I have no doubt that Dr. Magrath has an interesting collection of case records, some of which would probably be of considerable interest; but he does not seem to have published anything on them. I do not remember of seeing any publications from him for about 25 years and he gives only six lectures a year to the students."

Room 307, in particular, was out of the question. Hunt refused to give it up. That room held records related to the U.S. Pharmacopeia and some laboratory equipment used for cannabis testing, which had to be done in a quiet, isolated place.

That answer did not sit well with Lee, who took her appeal to James Bryant Conant, the president of Harvard University. "I am loath to ask for (room 307) because you have been so very kind about granting my previous requests," she wrote to Conant, "but we really need the room."

Conant wrote Lee a letter informing her

215

that room 307 was regretfully not available. Lee let Conant's response stew for almost three months, then composed a short note:

"Since receiving your letter . . . which was naturally in the nature of a disappointment, I have been thinking very hard about your decision not to grant the use of room 307 to the Department of Legal Medicine," she said. "The more I think about it the more inclined I am to wonder if you would not care to reconsider."

Lee pointed out that Hunt reached the mandatory retirement age in two years, so the space would become available soon anyway. In the meantime, there were empty rooms across the hall Hunt could use to store the material he presently had in room 307.

"Therefore," Lee concluded, "I do not feel that I can let our decision pass without a protest, and a request that you give this problem a little further study."

Lee got room 307 for the Department of Legal Medicine. Once again, she used her wealth and influence to achieve her goal of advancing the study of legal medicine.

May 16, 1935
Lee paid a social call on John Edgar Hoover, the youthful director of the recently re-

named Federal Bureau of Investigation, in order to bring the discipline of legal medicine to his attention.

The FBI is a descendant of the National Bureau of Criminal Identification, a centralized collection of photographs and bertillonage data established in 1896. Initially based in Chicago, the NBCI, also known as the National Bureau of Identification, was relocated to Washington, DC, in 1902. The database didn't include fingerprints until the NCBI was absorbed by the Bureau of Investigation, a unit of the U.S. Department of Justice, in 1924.

For most of J. Edgar Hoover's tenure, the FBI was primarily involved in enforcing Prohibition laws, eradicating organized crime, and investigating bank robberies. The agency's mission changed dramatically in March 1932 when the twenty-month-old son of aviator Charles Lindbergh and his wife, Anne Morrow Lindbergh, was kidnapped from their New Jersey home. Lindbergh, who had flown solo across the Atlantic, was one of the most famous men in America.

In response to the abduction and murder of Charles Augustus Lindbergh Jr., Congress passed the Federal Kidnapping Act, giving the Bureau of Investigation authority over the investigation of kidnappings. Forensic evidence discovered by the FBI — tool marks on a plank of wood used in a homemade ladder found at the crime scene — was instrumental in convicting the alleged kidnapper, Bruno Richard Hauptmann.

The scientific expertise acquired in the investigation of the Lindbergh baby abduction and murder was the basis for the agency's Technical Laboratory, established about six months after the kidnapping. Now officially known as the FBI Scientific Crime Detection Laboratory, it was not the first crime lab in the country. That distinction belongs to the Los Angeles Police Department, where a crime lab was formed in 1923.

Bearing a letter of introduction from Magrath, Lee charmed her way into a meeting with Hoover on the afternoon of May 16, 1935. At the time of Lee's visit, Hoover was involved in starting up a national police training center, the forerunner of the FBI National Academy. Hoover was not particularly receptive to the opinions of women. When he became director of the Bureau of Investigation in 1924, he fired all the female agents and prohibited hiring them for those positions.

Nonetheless, Hoover met with Lee after

she toured the building and had her finger-prints taken for the agency's civil identification files. According to a memorandum written by H. H. Clegg, assistant director for the investigations division, Lee described her plans for a Department of Legal Medicine at Harvard and encouraged Hoover to train FBI special agents in forensic medicine, correctly pointing out that the agency's expertise was lacking in the area of the medical aspects of investigations. She mentioned the National Research Council report and said that the agency could fill a role as a national resource for legal medicine.

Lee pointed out that the FBI lacked expertise in legal medicine, which could be critical in investigations involving a suspicious or violent death. In an effort to establish a collaborative relationship, Lee let Hoover know that legal medicine expertise was available in Boston to assist the FBI with investigations involving fatalities. "She indicated that she would desire some help and advice from time to time," Clegg wrote.

L. C. Schilder, in charge of the agency's fingerprint division, wrote a memorandum for what would become a file the FBI maintained on Lee. "This lady is interested in the establishment of a Department of

219

Legal Medicine in connection with the Harvard Medical School," Schilder wrote in his memo. "She impressed me as being most intelligent, alert, and aggressive and I believe that she will apply herself to her plans very energetically."

Lee's father, John Jacob Glessner, died one week short of his ninety-third birthday on January 20, 1936.

The Glessners were one of the last residential holdouts as their beloved Prairie Avenue neighborhood was enveloped by commercial buildings. In 1924, the couple deeded their home to the American Institute of Architects, with the condition that the Glessners could remain in the house for the remainder of their lives. The deed also included a stipulation that a photograph of H. H. Richardson remain permanently in the library of the house.

On April 7, 1936, Lee and her sister-in-law, Alice Glessner, hosted a reunion of the Monday Morning Reading Class for one last visit to the landmark residence before its ownership was transferred to the American Institute of Architects. The *Chicago Tribune*'s society page noted the passing of a group that, a generation earlier, "was considered one of the most exclusive and fashionable in Chicago."

Within months of receiving the Glessner home, the American Institute of Architects learned that remodeling the house for the organization's purposes would cost $10,000 to $25,000. The sum could not be raised, and the architects voted to return the property to the Glessner estate. Eventually, the women donated the residence to the Armour Institute of Technology for use as a vocational aptitude testing center.

After his retirement as medical examiner, Magrath wanted to turn his attention to the papers and records he had collected over the course of the three decades of his career as medical examiner, including high-profile cases such as the Sacco and Vanzetti investigation. Perhaps, at last, he would have time to publish about his work. He hoped to write a book. The obstacle in his way was Dr. William Brickley, Magrath's successor as medical examiner for the Northern District of Suffolk County. Brickley was of the opinion that the official records belonged to the medical examiner's office and were not Magrath's personal property.

Lee resolved the impasse. She proposed to Burwell that Brickley be appointed an instructor in the Department of Legal

Medicine. Brickley would be called upon to give two or three lectures a year and would have students to assist with postmortem examinations. Lee would provide a reasonable compensation out of her own pocket. However, she said, the appointment of Brickley should not be made unless all case records, lantern slides, negatives, photographs, microscope slides, and all other material accumulated during Magrath's career were deposited in the Department of Legal Medicine.

"If Dr. Magrath is to write his book, which is the ardent hope of his friends, it will be imperative that he have this, the sum of his life's work, ready at his hand in his medical school quarters," Lee said to Burwell.

Brickley agreed. From then on, Brickley and Dr. Timothy Leary, the medical examiner for the Southern District of Suffolk County, had appointments as legal medicine faculty at Harvard, with their salaries paid by Lee.

7

THE THREE-LEGGED STOOL

May 23, 1936

Lee sent a formal proposal for a Department of Legal Medicine to Burwell, the medical school dean. It would be a full, well-equipped academic department, involved in teaching and research and producing a supply of qualified medical examiners.

Lee intended to give Harvard a total of $250,000 in the form of 1,050 shares of International Harvester preferred stock, a smaller amount of other stocks and bonds, and $12,319.44 in cash. By her figuring, dividends from the stock would produce about $15,000 a year to support the department, supplemented by funds provided by Harvard. Lee indicated that she would also leave Harvard an additional $250,000 in her will for ongoing support of the department. Privately, her plans were grander. A contemporaneous will — drafted but not executed — allocated $1 million for Harvard.

In her proposal, Lee offered to pay Magrath's personal salary until his retirement as well as continue paying for a part-time secretary and a librarian. Lee's gift had two stipulations: "First, that it shall remain anonymous until I release you from this provision, and second, that the name of Dr. George Burgess Magrath shall be attached to [the department] in perpetuity, in whatever manner your good taste shall dictate."

The proposal included Lee's request that she remain actively involved in the Department of Legal Medicine. "It would give me pleasure to reserve unto myself the privilege of adding more volumes to the Library, from time to time, and possibly giving some item of necessary equipment when a specific need for such shall arise," she wrote.

Lee's senior by seven years and approaching his sixty-fifth year of life, Magrath was suffering from rapidly declining health. He had increasing difficulty with mobility and his mental faculties and had been hospitalized repeatedly at Phillips House. Lee knew the amount of productive time her friend had left was running out. She told Burwell and Gregg that no more money would be forthcoming for Harvard unless the medical school made a good-faith effort and invested the resources necessary to develop the Department of Legal Medicine.

The ultimatum worked. Medical school dean Sidney Burwell convened a committee to consider the prospect of legal medicine at Harvard, chaired by Dr. S. Burt Wolbach, the medical school's chief of the Department of Pathology. At their first meeting, the committee unanimously agreed that there were opportunities for pioneering work in legal medicine. The scale of the task seemed overwhelming, requiring recruiting of specialized faculty, creating new laboratories, and finding enough space for everything in the existing medical school buildings. If it developed in accordance with Lee's plans, the Department of Legal Medicine would probably eventually need its own building on the Harvard campus.

Wolbach wrote to Gregg at the Rockefeller Foundation, soliciting support for his mission. "It is my unfortunate luck to be the Chairman of a committee to consider the future of legal medicine in Harvard University," Wolbach wrote. "You, of course, know the reason, which is a very good chance of securing considerable endowment from Mrs. Lee, possibly even as much as a million dollars. The problem of the committee, however, is to satisfy Mrs. Lee and construct and arrive at an organization suitable for a University."

A department or institute of legal medicine at Harvard could provide a public service to communities across Massachusetts and influence the field throughout the nation. However great the potential, Wolbach expressed doubts about the scale of the work involved in developing a new practice of medicine. "Even with a million dollar endowment, the problem seems hopeless," he said.

At the committee's second meeting, on December 11, 1936, the panel concluded that their efforts to search for a successor to Magrath "gave no promise of securing a person with all the necessary qualifications," according to minutes of the meeting. "In all probability it will be necessary to select a young person and provide him with the means for travel and study abroad."

In 1937, Alan Richards Moritz was a bright and ambitious young pathologist looking to make a name for himself. A native of Nebraska, Moritz spent a year studying in Vienna before going to Cleveland for his residency in pathology at Lakeside Hospital. By age thirty-eight, Moritz was pathologist-in-charge at University Hospitals of Cleveland and associate professor of pathology at Western Reserve University's illustrious Pathology Institute, working as the right-hand man for director Dr. Howard Karsner.

Moritz felt that his career had hit a wall of sorts. His dream job — director of the Pathology Institute — seemed out of reach. Karsner didn't show any signs of retiring soon, and the institute's deputy director, Dr. Harry Goldblatt, was young enough to serve for many years as Karsner's successor. "I was third man on the totem pole," Moritz said. "It would be a long time before I got the job I wanted, which is the one that Dr. Karsner had."

Moritz's name appeared on a short list of candidates to develop a Department of Legal Medicine at Harvard Medical School. No pathologist in the United States at the time had the background and expertise necessary for the task, so Burwell and his advisory committee decided to find the best pathologist available and have him trained in legal medicine.

A background in pathology was a good foundation for a medical examiner, but legal medicine required specialized knowledge that wasn't taught in other areas of medical

227

practice. Training in the effects of trauma — blunt-force injuries, stabs and bullet wounds, crushing injuries, drownings and fire victims, asphyxia and poisonings — was a key element of the legal medicine discipline that was often brushed over in the traditional medical school path. To a doctor, a laceration was a wound to stitch up and heal. He didn't need to know how to identify the direction in which it was made. Medical school curricula didn't include how to tell whether a gunshot wound was self-inflicted, postmortem changes, stages of decomposition, or examining skeletal remains.

Moritz was intrigued by the prospect of a career pivot into legal medicine. It was still a fairly new field and presented the opportunity to plow new ground. With the resources of Lee backing the program, Harvard could do something no other medical school had done before.

"There were several schools where it was called a Department of Legal Medicine, but there was just a man who had occasional lectures and had some part-time interest," Moritz said. Harvard "was the only medical school in America that was really giving legal medicine the attention it deserved."

Moritz visited Harvard in February 1937

to meet with Burwell and Lee. "I knew little or nothing about the legal aspects of the frontiers between law and medicine," he said. "Harvard was aware of this, and so was the Rockefeller Foundation." Nonetheless, Moritz was offered the job.

The prospect of creating a Department of Legal Medicine at Harvard was tempting. "The more I have considered it, the more attractive such a development has appeared," Moritz wrote to Burwell after their meeting. "I know of no better place in America to undertake pioneer work in medicine than at Harvard where so much of the progress of American medicine has received its impetus." Still, he had to think about making such a major decision. Without some assurances from Harvard, moving his family to another city in order to start a new department from scratch was a huge risk. "I have some accomplishment and a large investment of time and work in the field of Pathology and I would be gambling with my future to leave the field of General Pathology, to give up a good position in a good medical school, to spend two years study abroad and then be faced with the insecure tenure of an Associate Professorship, an income considerably lower than my present one and no assurance of a budget adequate to build up a department," Moritz wrote to Burwell. "In short, I believe that such an offer indicates a lack of confidence in me or the lack of a means or desire to establish a new department as I feel that it should be established and under these circumstances I cannot consider the offer."

With a full professorship and a pledge to provide adequate financial support to develop the Department of Legal Medicine, an agreement was struck for Moritz to take the job.

Lee's first impression of Moritz was tepid, although his competence as a pathologist was not in question. Moritz was an accomplished researcher, most recently involved in studies of vascular disease. Most who met Moritz were impressed by his knowledge of pathology and his engaging personal qualities, but Lee felt Moritz lacked a political sensibility. She wondered how he would hold up in the crucible of public pressure in which medical examiners often found themselves.

In short order, however, Lee warmed up to the new chairman of Harvard Medical School's Department of Legal Medicine, and they would soon come to form an enduring partnership.

Moritz was appointed professor of legal medicine and chairman of the department at Harvard. He departed almost immediately for a two-year traveling fellowship to survey legal medicine practices in the major cities of Europe. For the two-year sojourn, during intensified conflict leading to World War II, Moritz was accompanied by his wife, Velma, and their two young daughters. In his absence, the activities of the department were halted. No doctors were being trained as Magrath's crippled hands limited his ability to teach. Moritz faced the task of recreating a department from scratch.

Moritz's fellowship began with six months of study with Dr. John Glaister, professor of forensic medicine and public health at the Glasgow Royal Infirmary Medical School, and Dr. Sydney Smith, professor of forensic medicine at the University of Edinburgh. Both highly regarded forensic scientists, Smith and Glaister were involved in the investigation of Dr. Buck Ruxton, a British doctor convicted of the 1935 murders of his common-law wife, Isabella, and her housemaid, Mary Jane Rogerson. The bodies of Isabella Ruxton and Rogerson had been dismembered and mutilated to remove fingerprints and facial characteristics to hinder their identification. It was the first time forensic photography was used as evidence in a murder trial.

It didn't take long for Moritz to arrive at some fundamental conclusions about his new field of study. "Last summer I had a hazy idea about the organization and function of a department of legal medicine," he wrote to Burwell. "Although I have been studying for less than two months and that entire period here in Glasgow I have come to some conclusions which I do not believe will be modified by additional experience."

One obvious conclusion was that a department of legal medicine would need a steady supply of material — dead bodies. It would be difficult to teach postmortem examination without a body to examine. Neither Moritz nor Harvard had any official affiliation with a medical examiner office, so some sort of relationship needed to be made with existing agencies that could provide such material.

Another thing Moritz found was a lack of consensus on the scope of medicolegal practice. In some places, legal medicine encompassed industrial hygiene, which today would be regarded as workplace safety or occupational medicine. Some authorities in Europe and the United States as well considered legal medicine to include the study of the psychological and behavioral aspects of crime. These days, questions about insanity and criminal responsibility are within the purview of forensic psychiatry, not forensic medicine.

Some departments of legal medicine were involved in all scientific aspects of criminal investigation. They performed autopsies and had toxicology and blood typing laboratories and also did fingerprinting, ballistics, and analysis of trace evidence.

"I have forced myself to dig into many of the heterogeneous activities that constitute the practice of Legal Medicine," Moritz wrote to Wolbach, the chairman of pathology at Harvard Medical School. "These have ranged from finger print classification on thru to juvenile delinquency. The result of this is that I am more firmly convinced than ever that the centralization of the practice of Legal Medicine robs the practitioner of his usefulness by making him a jack-of-all-trades."

So what exactly was or should be the practice of legal medicine in the United States? Moritz began to formulate his thoughts.

"My greatest problem to date has been to arrive at some more or less definite idea as to what a department of legal medicine at Harvard University should be," Moritz wrote to Lee.

It is pathology because the determination of the cause of death is of fundamental importance. It differs from the ordinary practice of pathology in that in addition to facts of medical importance all medical evidence likely to be of importance to the law must be ascertained . . . The pathological diagnoses of multiple wounds to the scalp, a comminuted, compound fracture of the skull and laceration of the brain would meet the ordinary medical requirements in a given case. The medico-legal expert might add to such a diagnosis the opinion that the decedent was under the influence of alcohol at the time of his death, that he had been dead for between four and twelve hours, that he had not died where his body was found, that his death represented homicide rather than suicide, that he was killed by being struck by a heavy blunt instrument and that the assailant was a woman whose hair was dyed black and whose skin had been deeply scratched by the decedent.

The medical legal expert should function as a medical examiner representing the

234

state and as such should investigate all cases of violent, suspicious or sudden death as completely as the circumstances warrant. He should be responsible for the examination of medical exhibits for the police and he should investigate all cases of death in which the state may be responsible for compensation of the estate of the decedent. He should be the adviser to and the witness for the court in the medical aspects of litigation before it.

A warm rapport blossomed through the correspondence between Lee and Moritz while Moritz was in Europe. They exchanged letters several times a week, sharing news and updates about developments in the Department of Legal Medicine. Lee had big plans to push forward in his absence. While Moritz was overseas, Lee was busy on the home front getting things in order for his return. Having recovered from her medical scare, she oversaw the cleaning and renovations of the offices and continued to aggressively acquire books for the Magrath Library.

Lee sent letters to book dealers across the East Coast with purchase orders and requests. She wanted any text or periodical that might be remotely relevant to criminology or forensic medicine. Moritz suggested contemporary books for the library. Lee also arranged for books that were only available in foreign languages to be translated into English. On more than one occasion, the medical school library expressed the desire to incorporate the Magrath Library into its larger collection so all reference materials would be available in one building on the Harvard campus. Lee was adamantly opposed to her collection being subsumed by the medical library.

"I had a letter from Miss Holt, Librarian at the Harvard Medical School," she wrote to Moritz. "Miss Holt is anxious to take our departmental library completely in charge, even to move it over to her own quarters and I am, of course, against that . . . Be forewarned so that our library will not be taken away from us."

Lee had strong feelings about the books she had invested so much money and effort to collect. She didn't even want any of her books to be borrowed from the Magrath Library. Her collection included many rare and valuable volumes and irreplaceable original documents. Having spent so much time to accumulate the collection, the incompleteness of a missing volume was intolerable. "Without wishing to be arbitrary, I greatly prefer that no books should go out from the premises of the Library to any other premises, or to any other person, under any circumstances or at any time," she told Burwell.

As a compromise with Miss Holt and the medical school library, three complete sets of catalog cards were created — one for the Magrath Library, one for the main medical library, and one for Lee to keep at home at The Rocks. Lee reimbursed Harvard $66 for the cost of duplicating the card catalog for her.

Burwell wrote a memorandum about his conversation with Lee regarding the Magrath Library. "She approved of the idea of linking it more closely with the general Library, but expressed quite clearly her reasons for desiring not at the moment to be joined to the main Library," he said. "She proposes to write me a letter putting on record her request that the Magrath Library shall always remain a unit, although at some time in the future it may be placed in a special part of the main Library. I consented to this because of the fact that this is a group of books on relatively unified subject matter."

Burwell's final comment in this memorandum was an update on Lee's status as a donor. "She led me to believe that from time to time she would be available to do small things in the near future and that within a year or two there would be a sizable gift to the endowment."

In the fall of 1938, Lee's thoughts turned to the upcoming World's Fair planned for New York City from 1939 to 1940. She saw the upcoming fair as a chance to educate the public about the modern medical examiner system. Lee reached out to Dr. Thomas Gonzales, who had succeeded Norris as chief medical examiner for New York City, to learn whether his agency planned on having an exhibit at the World's Fair.

Gonzales told Lee that an exhibit in the New York City Building was planned to portray the work of the medical examiner's office. Another exhibit, which was still in the formative stage, was planned for the Public Health and Medicine Building to depict various aspects of crime prevention and crime detection. Lee relayed the information about the World's Fair to Moritz in Edinburgh. "I am anxious that the great advertising possibilities in the New York Fair be taken advantage of for the benefit of legal medicine," he replied.

Moritz suggested that the exhibit planned

for the Public Health and Medicine Building could include a series of panels illustrating common situations in which a medical examiner's expertise was needed. Each panel would have a drawing — "calculated to be dramatic without being shocking," Moritz said — and a short description of the hypothetical case, including:

1. An automobile accident involving two cars, the driver of one of which dies during the accident. Did the accident occur because of some incapacity on the part of the dead driver? Did that driver die because of disease or because of the accident?
2. Death from gunshot wound. Was it suicide or homicide?
3. Death from carbon monoxide poisoning. Was it suicide or accident predisposed by some disease or intoxication?
4. Found dead in the water. Was it accident or homicide?
5. Death in suspicious circumstances. Was it due to natural causes, poison, or unrecognized mechanical injury?
6. Unaccounted-for death. Was death predisposed to or caused by some

accident or special type of injury sustained during employment?

There was little Moritz could do from overseas to help with the project. He asked Lee to look into an exhibit for the World's Fair. "If you think that nothing will be done unless we do it, I think that we had better get busy despite the handicap of my being on this side of the Atlantic," he told Lee.

Lee knew that public support was essential to changing laws and other improvements to bring about medical examiners throughout the country, and she recommended making outreach efforts to interest writers in legal medicine.

"She suggests various methods of events in the lay appreciation of the importance of the field of legal medicine, including getting the support of Courtney Riley Cooper, a professional writer, who might prepare an article for the *Saturday Evening Post* or some other journal in this field," Burwell noted after a conversation with Lee.

On a December afternoon in 1938, Magrath happened upon an old friend, Robert Fulton Blake, a fellow oarsman and 1899 graduate of Harvard. Blake informed Magrath that an elderly mutual friend of theirs had recently died of a sudden heart attack. Magrath was saddened but philosophical.

"That's the way to go, when the time comes," he said. "I wonder who will be next?"

Within twenty-four hours, on December 11, 1938, Magrath died. He was sixty-eight years old.

Lee described the circumstances of his death to Moritz, who had only met with Magrath briefly before his departure for Europe. "Since you saw him, his health has been failing but he had not ceased his ordinary activities," she wrote. "On the day of his death he was planning to go, as usual, to one of his musical rehearsals, and was stricken while in the bathtub," Lee said. "Help came to him promptly. He complained of a violent headache over his eyes, soon lapsed into unconsciousness from which he did not rouse. It was only a matter of some eight hours. The post mortem findings proved cause of death to be cerebral hemorrhage."

Lee felt a deep loss by the death of Magrath, her mentor and dear friend. Magrath may have died not knowing the extent to which his comment about the beauty of the internal organs, all those years ago at Phillips House, inspired Lee. That trivial remark sparked a years-long peregrination, sending her on a mission to libraries and museums to study subjects from medicine to the esoteric and obscure.

"I read voraciously for weeks — nay, *years* — in more than a dozen libraries, besides accumulating a small but peculiarly effective library of my own," she said. "I have worked in museums, have employed special photographers, have gathered material wherever it was to be found. It was necessary to study a little of everything — anatomy and physiology (neither one entirely strange to me), the history of medicine, many volumes on book making and book binding, on illuminated manuscripts and lettering, lives of the saints — books on art, on precious stones, on color, on symbolism, on music, on botany, on fish — accounts of savages, their beliefs and customs, histories of ancient religions and cultures — Egyptian, Assyrian, Chaldean, Babylonian, Greek, Roman — on up through the Middle Ages in Europe and the Indian civilizations in the Americas to the present time and place."

Over a period of several years, at the same time as she was establishing the Department of Legal Medicine, Lee also wrote a book. She produced an extraordinary four-hundred-page manuscript intended as a gift for Magrath — written, illustrated, and lettered in her own hand — titled *An Anatomography in Picture, Verse and Music.*

Anatomography, Lee explained in an accompanying letter, was "a coined word of home minting, therefore presumably counterfeit" intended to mean "a graphic anatomy." Her book was a tribute to the beauty of the human body, as expressed in verse and images.

The book told a story through an epic poem, a series of quatrains in the meter of *The Rubáiyát of Omar Khayyám,* about "an Indian deity, without rhyme or reason, sent from the far West to punish the Indian God of the East Wind in Boston, where, meeting with treachery, he is murdered in the Public Garden and his body is taken to your Northern Mortuary," she said in her letter. "His son comes to identify and claim the remains which are buried in due Indian style. They disappear, only to reappear again in part in the tanks at the Harvard Medical School, where they were gathered and described."

Lee's book was meant to be read in a particular way, not like an ordinary book. Each two-page spread was intended to be regarded together. The ideal method of reading her manuscript was to read the heading on the right-hand page, if there was one, then Shakespearean quotations on the left page. Next, the reader was directed to a marginal note and a corresponding quatrain. In her letter to Magrath, Lee said such marginal notes had been employed as a sort of index in ancient texts.

Just open up the abdomen and find Contortions of Intestines, velvet lined By sheathing, fan-shaped mesentery moored In systematic chaos intertwined — Ye Knotty Problem

Dear lovely Lungs, all spotted blue and black, Your dingy substance wrapped in pleural sac, I could not live without you, and I strive To guard you from pneumoniac attack — Ye Aire Castles

The Tibia and Fibula take part In lifting up the human head and heart. Without them continuity is lost, The head and feet would simply come apart — Ye Connecting Links

The Skin, of which we   Ye Tactile
  humans have so much Is full   Tactics
  of pores sebaceous glands
  and such, Seductive, silken-
  smooth and softly sweet —
  Oh man, confess! *some Skin*
  you love to touch!

Every organ and tissue in the human body was represented in *Anatomography* except for some vertebrae, the patella, the parathyroid gland, the adrenal glands, and the genitalia. The art Lee selected for her book was rich with symbolism, classical references, and images with particular significance to Magrath and herself.

"What training in draughtsmanship and design I have had came in childhood from our dear mutual friend Isaac Ellwood Scott, one of the gentlest and most loveable natures I have ever known," she wrote. "I am sure you will recognize lines throughout these pages that could have been inspired only by him."

She hired photographers to document aspects of Magrath's life, such as the Union Boat Club on the Charles River, St. Botolph, and the refrigerator cabinets in the North Grove Street morgue to include in the book. Layers of meaning were hidden within every image. She chose certain foliage, flowers, and animals in her design elements, particularly fish, which she used as her "signature." The seaweed illustrated on one page of her book, for example, is *Chorda filum,* commonly known as dead man's rope. The oak leaves recurring through the manuscript represent strength and independence. Charon, the ferryman who transports the newly deceased across the rivers Styx and Acheron, is depicted, Lee said, because he was one of the earliest oarsmen. Disguised as flowers ornamenting one page are fingerprints — Magrath's and her own.

The book's end pages, beginning with the egg case of the Port Jackson shark (because Magrath was born in Jackson, Michigan) and a fish skeleton on the final end page, she explained, were meant to represent the beginning and the end, birth and death. On the whole, Lee's manuscript is a reflection on the great mysteries of life and death, immortality, and the passage of the soul.

"Like everything else I have ever done, this was blundered into," Lee wrote in her letter to Magrath explaining her manuscript. "It has been all-absorbing and intensely interesting work, and has led me down many heretofore untrodden paths."

Lee's mission — *Anatomography,* the Department of Legal Medicine, the rest of her life — was all a consequence of Magrath's remark about the beauty of the human internal organs. "Perhaps it is well to say right here that this thought of yours, so casually expressed and so casually accepted, has been the little germ from which has grown your Department of Legal Medicine at the Harvard Medical School and the George Burgess Magrath Library of Legal Medicine," she wrote.

Working on *Anatomography* had been therapeutic for Lee. She had been at a low point in her life. As though a veil were lifted, a light illuminated a path forward. Where it would lead, she had no way of knowing. But she had found a subject in which to sink her intellectual teeth and a renewed sense of purpose.

I think this book has been a regeneration in itself. It has brought health and happiness, a wider outlook and a broader comprehension, an increased ability to think and study. It has brought serenity and peace of mind to its maker. Do you not believe that your idea was truly a miraculous one? I know it was. And so let me acknowledge my debt of gratitude to you, first for the idea, second for bringing me, through it, many agreeable and happy contacts both new and renewed, and lastly and principally for the joy and inspiration that your spiritual presence has given me with every stroke of pen or brush. I confess it is with much trepidation that I lay before you my bit of nonsense — you with your accurate knowledge, perfect taste and meticulous attention to detail, yet there is no one who will give my work kinder treatment or who will be more indulgent in his judgement than you. But since it is the outgrowth of your own chance remark, and with the realization that the execution is far less worthy than the idea, I dare offer it to you in all humbleness and reverence, knowing you will enjoy the jest with me, and subscribe myself, with sincere esteem and genuine affection.

There is no evidence that Lee ever gave the *Anatomography* manuscript or the letter to Magrath. Maybe she felt the book was immoderate, or maybe she never finished working on it.

Lee persuaded Moritz to retain Parker Glass, a Massachusetts native who had been Magrath's part-time secretary at the medical examiner's office, to serve as his assistant at Harvard. To keep him employed during Moritz's fellowship, Lee arranged for Glass to receive training at the Hickox Secretarial School, where he honed his skills in dictation, filing, and medical shorthand.

Glass felt a responsibility to continue Magrath's work after his death. "Although our work for Doctor [Magrath], and what he started, will never be finished, what we took over last December will have been carried out to the best of our ability," he wrote to Lee. "Even from my little share in the task, I find satisfaction. How much more you must find after all the years of protection you have given him."

Glass cleaned out Magrath's old office at 274 Boylston Street. It was his idea to retain Magrath's 181 license plate for Moritz's automobile. Aside from being a desirable low number, the license plate held symbolic meaning for Lee, who had to use her influence to prevent the plate from going back into circulation.

"This was the official number and in his day all traffic stopped for it — not by instruction, but by courtesy," Lee told Moritz. "Because of Dr. Magrath's name and standing, I could get this number for you if you wish it. Miss Magrath, his sister, would like you to have it as her brother's successor at the Medical School."

With the installation of a properly trained forensic pathologist in Moritz, Lee saw an opportunity to reform and modernize death investigation in Massachusetts by changing the law to give medical examiners independent authority. She summarized her thoughts in a letter to Sidney Burwell shortly after Magrath's death. "It is a good time to start to revamp the Medical Examiner system in Massachusetts," she wrote. "Massachusetts has always led in Medicolegal matters, but New York and Essex County, New Jersey are ahead of her now and even some of the mid-western states are coming to the front."

Lee suggested the creation of a state-wide system with a centralized medical examiner's office in Boston where autopsies would be performed. The headquarters would also have a centralized toxicology and ballistic laboratory to serve investigations throughout the state. Lee declared that the medical examiner's office should be located at Harvard and one person — ideally Moritz — appointed as chief medical examiner for the state, with two assistants and two associates.

Having the medical examiner's office in

close affiliation with Harvard Medical School would solve the problem of providing a supply of bodies for students and fellows in the Department of Legal Medicine as well. Duties of the existing part-time medical examiners in various districts around the state would be unaltered. Their pay and activities would remain the same, but they would have free access to expertise in Boston.

It was perhaps not a perfect system, but it was a move in the right direction. More importantly, Lee's plan navigated a path that minimized the ruffling of political feathers. "This need not be any more expensive than it is now, would occasion no loss of prestige, nor would it reduce the number of appointive offices for political purposes," she said to Burwell.

Lee urged Burwell to join her in visiting Governor Leverett Saltonstall and Paul Dever, the attorney general, to push for a modern, state-wide medical examiner system. "Since legislation is required, it must be started now," Lee said.

Burwell was disinclined to join the fight at that moment, and nothing resulted from Lee's visionary proposal. Massachusetts didn't adopt a statewide medical examiner system until 1983.

Moritz's fellowship tour included visits to England, Denmark, Germany, Austria, Switzerland, France, and Egypt. He gained firsthand legal medicine experience in Edinburgh, Glasgow, London, Paris, Marseille, Berlin, Hamburg, Bonn, Munich, Vienna, and Graz. Moritz was pleasantly surprised by what he learned at the Federal Institute in Cairo, Egypt. He expected to find poorly trained staff working under primitive conditions. Instead, he found a well-equipped centralized facility that conducted all the postmortem examinations in the kingdom. The facility was kept busy; Cairo was experiencing up to twenty-five homicides a day at the time.

"Poisoning is very common in Egypt," he wrote in a report of his fellowship for the Rockefeller Foundation. "It is doubtful that there is any place in the world where as much toxicology is done as in this Institute."

Moritz summarized his experience at Cairo's Federal Institute in a letter to Sidney Burwell. "I had a very interesting time in Egypt, and saw more things of the 'believe it-or-not' variety than I thought possible," he said. "Crime is a flourishing

252

industry along the Nile, and they have many original ideas as to its performance. With the exception of Denmark I know of no place where all branches of medico-legal activity are so highly organized and centralized in a federal department. The medico-legal experts are well trained, and their work compares favourably with the best I have seen."

Overall, from his survey of systems across Europe and Africa, Moritz discovered a wide range in quality of medicolegal practice. Some cities were quite good. Most systems were not.

"My experience to date, particularly that part of it acquired on the continent, is of value, not because of the good things that I have learned, but rather because I have learned of so many practices to be avoided," Moritz wrote to Wolbach. "I feel that I have made a long journey and spent an inordinate amount of time to study organizations and methods that are fundamentally bad."

Lee managed the introduction of Moritz to her department at Harvard like a stage mother. She arranged for Moritz to deliver a series of lectures on legal medicine at Harvard almost immediately upon his return from Europe in September of 1939. She also urged a series of visits with Governor Saltonstall, Massachusetts State Police Commissioner Paul Kirk, and the head of the FBI laboratory in Washington, DC. Lee also held a dinner for Moritz at The Rocks in late September. She wanted him to speak on legal medicine for thirty to forty minutes after dinner. "I would like to have you make a little talk on legal medicine in general — what it is and why, what you have been doing in your two years abroad, what the needs in this country are, and what the prospects are at Harvard for fulfilling them," she told Moritz. "There will be many doctors, some lawyers and probably some of the New Hampshire medical referees, and we have asked the local undertaker, deputy sheriff and chief of police," she said. "It will be a chance for some missionary work, but as you know it mustn't be too technical, nor, shall I say, too 'gory.' "

Lee's friend Ludvig Hektoen invited Moritz to give a lecture to the Institute of Medicine of Chicago — his first talk outside the Boston area. The University of Chicago wanted Moritz to speak to their students too. Lee had one piece of business advice for Moritz: if you want to be taken seriously, make them pay. "I am firmly convinced that you should ask for or accept an honorarium for your lecture," she told Moritz. "In my opinion it is poor policy to give anything free and the way you start is the way you will have to finish. Don't hold yourself or your information and experience too cheap!"

Lee also suggested that Moritz consider writing an article about legal medicine for the Chicago newspapers, with the rationale that it would be a good idea to inform the public about medical examiners and what their purpose was.

In January 1940, Moritz approached Lee with an unusual proposal. Would she accept the editorship of the *American Journal of Medical Jurisprudence*? It would be advantageous to have the journal associated with the Department of Legal Medicine and control over its editorial policy, but Moritz did not have the time to commit to the work. "I know of no equally competent person in the country for this task," Moritz said, adding that Lee would have a free hand over editorial policy.

The mere notion of Lee as editor of a professional journal is astounding. To be sure, she had unparalleled knowledge of the medico-legal literature, but she didn't have a college degree. Editorships were reserved for the leaders of a profession. Lee's only official credential was honorary membership of the Massachusetts Medico-Legal Society and a founding membership in the New Hampshire Medico-Legal Society. A lay person, however sophisticated, at the helm of a journal was highly unusual to say the least — particularly a woman.

Although flattered by the suggestion, Lee declined the assignment. She said she was too old to put that much work into editing a journal.

A short time later, in February 1940, the Department of Legal Medicine became operational. Harvard honored Lee befittingly on the occasion of the opening of the department's laboratory, with an afternoon tea on February 9. The guest list for the afternoon tea included department heads from Harvard, deans from the schools of law and medicine, the university president and trustees, deans and department heads from Tufts and Boston University, Attorney General Paul Dever, and Governor Saltonstall.

A few days later, Lee wrote Burwell a thank-you note of appreciation. "I'm still thinking of our grand party of last Friday and still wishing to say a nicer thank you for it," she said. "It was a lucky day for legal medicine, for Alan Moritz and for me when you became Dean of Harvard Medical."

The department was funded by the proceeds from Lee's endowment, which generated an income of about $15,000 a year in dividends. This sum covered the salaries of Moritz, assistants, and support staff. The Rockefeller Foundation provided $5,000 for two three-year fellowships to train doctors for careers as medical examiners. Harvard contributed $10,000 for remodeling the departmental quarters and $5,000 for equipment.

Two young pathologists, both of whom planned on careers in legal medicine, were selected as the department's first fellows — Dr. Herbert Lund, a graduate of the University of Pennsylvania School of Medicine, and Dr. Edwin Hill, who received a degree in chemical engineering from MIT and his medical education at Tufts Medical College.

One persistent problem still to resolve was the need for a steady supply of "clinical material" — dead bodies. Lee's plan for a medical examiner's office near Harvard wasn't going to materialize anytime soon.

"I can see one absolutely essential requirement for the development of any real department at Harvard and that is some active responsibility for medical legal work," Moritz wrote to Burwell. "I would as well contemplate teaching surgery without a surgical practice or obstetrics without delivering a baby as to think of developing a university department of legal medicine without an inflow of clinical material."

Despite his appointment as an instructor in legal medicine, Dr. Timothy Leary, one of the Suffolk County medical examiners, was territorial about his office. Leary had been medical examiner for thirty years before Moritz arrived on the scene and was reluctant to allow outsiders, including Lee, whom he saw as a wealthy grandmother with no formal education despite her close relationship with his former colleague, Magrath, to usurp the authority of his office. Lee and Burwell persuaded Governor Saltonstall to appoint Moritz as an assistant to Leary, leaving the veteran medical examiner explicitly in charge.

Moritz was also appointed medicolegal consultant to the Massachusetts State Police. Medical examiners and district attorneys were notified that Moritz would respond to any part of the state to consult or assist with forensic autopsies at no cost to the county.

The calls did not come.

It soon became clear that Moritz and his team of investigators at Harvard were unwanted. Local police didn't appreciate outsider college boys telling them what to do. When Moritz arrived uninvited at one crime scene, he found a man busy washing blood off the walls. The local sheriff said he didn't want his men to get blood on their uniforms. At that point, cleaning up evidence made little difference, since the residence where the death happened was packed with dozens of curious locals, contaminating the scene and leaving their fingerprints everywhere. When Moritz complained about the contaminated crime scene, the sheriff told him to shut up or leave.

For two years, the department had few deaths to investigate. Then, on the afternoon of July 31, 1940, Moritz received a teletype message from the state police headquarters: "DR. ROSEN, MEDICAL EXAMINER, NEW BEDFORD. REQUESTS ASSISTANCE OF DR. MORITZ IN EXAMINATION OF BODY OF UNIDENTIFIED PERSON FOUND IN DARTMOUTH."

Five Works Progress Administration workers picking blueberries on their lunch break had discovered an extensively decomposed body hidden in brush beneath a tree on a local lover's lane. The body appeared to be that of a young woman, fully clothed, bound with rope at the ankles and wrists. There were no visible signs of trauma. Beneath the body, they found a small flying red horse pin, a souvenir of the Mobil Oil Company. Moritz brought the remains and a sample of the foliage that had been under the body back to Harvard. Three weeks later, after careful study of all the evidence, Moritz was able to tell the New Bedford police the name and address of the decedent, how, when, and why she was murdered, and who did it.

Her name was Irene Perry. She was twenty-two years old and had vanished in June when she left home to get ice cream for her two-year-old son. Among her remains were five small bones; Perry was four months pregnant at the time of her death.

Near Perry's body, investigators discovered a knotted loop of rope that appeared to have been used to strangle her. Harvard investigators did an experiment with fifty volunteer girls of the same age and size as Perry to measure the length of rope that would be needed to strangle them. After one hundred tries — none of the volunteers were actually harmed — the average was within a half inch of the noose found with the body. Chemical analysis of the rope revealed that it was a type sold in bulk and used in mills, farms, and industrial shops. A matching piece of rope was found in the basement of Perry's boyfriend, twenty-five-year-old mill worker Frank Pedro.

How long had Perry been dead? Four groups of carrion insects — those that deposit eggs on decomposing flesh — were found on Perry's body. Based on an analysis of the developmental ages of the larvae, investigators concluded that she had to have been dead for at least a month and could not have been killed after July 1. The foliage beneath her body included branches of sheep's laurel and low blueberry plants, which had grown during the current season until covered by the body. Based on the stage of development of the young leaves, the plants were killed on or after June 15. That left a two-week window, which was consistent with the date Perry was last known to be alive, June 29.

Pedro was charged with first-degree murder in Perry's death. Despite the scientific evidence linking him to the crime and likely to the great frustration of Moritz and Lee, Pedro was acquitted of the charge in court.

A compelling reason for locating a Department of Legal Medicine at Harvard was the potential for collaboration with the university's prestigious School of Law. A close relationship between the two departments could result in a true medicolegal program, with medical examiners providing lectures about medical evidence to law students and lectures for medical students about legal matters.

The Department of Legal Medicine planned to conduct a series of moot court sessions with medical and law students participating as a practice exercise. Medical doctors were generally ill-equipped for the adversarial arena of the courtroom. The average doctor was no match for an attorney skilled in the rhetorical arts. An unprepared doctor could be led beyond observable facts into speculation or doubt or be made to look like a liar, incompetent, or a quack. The moot court sessions were mock trials, a practice exercise. It was a useful way for medical students to learn how to answer questions, how to separate fact from opinion, and how to testify while under verbal attack.

Lee felt strongly that the Department of Legal Medicine should also begin conducting educational conferences. These meetings of professionals from across the country were important ways to learn the latest methods and procedures. Conferences and seminars were traditional ways groups of professionals kept up with current research and news, heard from leaders in the field, and maintained relationships with colleagues, and Lee pushed to schedule the first one.

May 17, 1940
Lee sent Moritz the outline of a two-day medicolegal conference that could be held once or twice a year. The intended audience was doctors and medical students from Harvard, Tufts, and Boston University, the Massachusetts State Police, Boston city police, undertakers, FBI special agents, and the press. Subjects to be covered during those two days included:

Causes of death:
Gunshot wounds
Incised and punctured wounds
Burns
— Electrical (lightning, power)
— Chemical (acid, alkali)
— Flames (inhaled, swallowed, external, moderate, or destructive)
— Scalds
— Insolation

Asphyxiation

— Drowning (fresh water, salt water)
— Hanging
— Strangulation
— Suffocation

Poison
— Inhaled
— Injected
— Absorbed
— Swallowed
— Alcohol
— Carbon monoxide

Diseases
— Coronary disease
— Other diseases

Abortion

Conditions of body after death:

Effects of:
— Immersion
— Heat and cold
— Incineration
— Insects or other animals
— Embalming
— Burial
— Agents to destroy body and evidence
— Natural decomposition

- Rigor mortis
- Areas of lividity to determine position of body at death
- Examination of alimentary tract to determine stage of digestion

Procedure in cases of different types:
Accident
Murder
Suicide
Dropping dead
Found dead
Hospital cases

Protection of evidence:
- What to look for
- How to gather up a body
- How and where to look for means of identification
- Care and disposal of effects
- Not too much haste to bury or dispose of body

Each topic would be presented from the viewpoint of those in medicine, law, the insurance industry, and police. Lee's plan also included a detailed list of potential speakers.

Lee proposed holding the conference in Boston in the fall of 1940. It would include a banquet at the Ritz-Carlton during which the attorneys general from Maine, New Hampshire Vermont, Rhode Island, Connecticut, and Massachusetts would speak. For the keynote address, Lee suggested either Governor Saltonstall or Alan Gregg of the Rockefeller Foundation. The exhibits Lee envisioned at the conference included books useful for police and medical examiners, samples of records and reports, displays of photographs, X-rays, shooting targets, powder marks, and body identification by dental records.

Despite Lee's enthusiasm and detailed plans, no such conference was held in the fall of 1940. Perhaps it was too soon for the department to undertake a major professional conference. Moritz did not support the idea at the time.

Lee did manage to persuade Leary, the medical examiner for the Southern District of Sussex County, to attend the annual meeting of the National Association of Coroners in Philadelphia, a city where the debate on changing to a medical examiner system was beginning to take shape. It was inconceivable to Lee that Philadelphia — the country's third-most populous city and the birthplace of medical education in America — was still using the coroner system, although it at least had a decent coroner physician, William "Waddie" Wadsworth. When Wadsworth took the position in 1899, he was one of the few doctors in America employed full-time as a coroner's physician. A colorful figure who kept a "crime museum" stocked with weapons and other occupational artifacts at the city morgue at Thirteenth and Wood Streets, Wadsworth was well regarded as a knowledgeable expert in the medical investigation of death — a refreshing change from the quacks and politically compromised doctors who often filled the role in nineteenth- and twentieth-century America.

At their 1940 annual meeting, members of the Medical Society of the State of Pennsylvania had passed a resolution recommending the abolition of the coroner system and its replacement with a hierarchy of medical examiners trained in pathology. Although only advisory in nature, the recommendations of medical societies were given serious consideration by lawmakers. Discussion at the next coroners' association meeting was expected to be lively.

Dr. J. W. Battershall, the medical examiner in Bristol County and past president of the Massachusetts Medico-Legal Society, received a provocative invitation from

P. J. Zisch, executive secretary of the coroners' group. "I cannot impress upon you too forcibly the advantages that you will secure by coming to Philadelphia to attend our Convention," Zisch wrote. "I say this in all sincerity."

Unable to go to the meeting in Philadelphia, Battershall sent the letter to Lee, who was expecting visitors to The Rocks, where she then lived full time, and could not attend the meeting herself. Neither Moritz nor Alan Gregg were available either. Still, Lee thought somebody from Boston should accept the invitation and attend the meeting.

"It seems to me that possibly the future of the Medical Examiner system may be at stake and that certainly the Medical Examiners should be well represented at this meeting," she wrote to Burwell. "I think it's important that the right people be urged to go and speak for the Medical Examiner system."

Lee pulled out all the stops to convince Leary to attend the meeting. She resorted to flattery and offered to pay his travel expenses. "Of all men connected with legal medicine, none stands higher than you in the respect and admiration of those who know, and no one could be a better representative not only of the profession, but also of the Massachusetts Medico-Legal Society," she wrote to the medical examiner.

Reluctantly, Leary acceded to Lee's entreaty. "In my opinion efforts to convert that particular group of persons to a belief in the Medical Examiner would be a waste of energy," he replied to Lee. "However, since I understand that they are going to discuss the Medical Examiner System, and since you feel that we should be represented at the meeting I shall be happy to attend . . . Though not on the program, and not a member, I hope that I shall be permitted to represent vocally the birthplace of the system."

The coroners' association meeting was uneventful. Leary was correct that no minds were changed. The coroner system was not abolished in Philadelphia at the time. The 1940 debate was one infinitesimally small incremental step in the city's progress toward the medical examiner system.

After the Philadelphia coroners' association meeting, Wadsworth wrote to Lee to follow up and make arrangements for visiting the Magrath Library of Legal Medicine, which had doubled in size to two thousand volumes. Wadsworth appears to have made the unfortunate error of misstating the name of the library, apparently referring to it as "Magrath's library." Lee was quick to disabuse him of that notion.

"I judge from your letter that you believe the Library of Legal Medicine was formed by Dr. Magrath or the choice of its books, perhaps, guided by him, and I must correct that impression," she replied by letter. "The Library was formed entirely apart from him and named in his honor." She did not say in her letter to Wadsworth that the library consisted of her books, selected and purchased by her. Why she stopped short is not clear.

In the first year of operation, the Department of Legal Medicine had assembled a teaching faculty that included Moritz, Leary, Brickley, and Dr. Joseph T. Walker, director of the Massachusetts State Police laboratory. Two doctors were in fellowship training, and five others taught on a part-time basis or were involved in research, including an attorney who was a fourth-year medical student. The department conducted a course on legal medicine for third-year medical students of Harvard, Tufts, and Boston University that had an average lecture attendance of 200 to 250 students.

During the year, staff members of the

department were involved in the investigation of seventy-two deaths in Massachusetts and performed fifty-six autopsies. In sixteen cases, Moritz and his colleagues examined autopsy material that had been sent in to the department from other jurisdictions.

Of the fifty-six autopsies conducted by members of the Department of Legal Medicine, new evidence disclosed during the examinations resulted in a complete change in the criminal status of thirteen cases. Nine cases that were suspected homicides were determined to be accidental, suicide, or natural causes. In four cases, homicides would have gone undetected were it not for the postmortem examination.

"It is interesting to speculate as to the number of cases of homicide that go unrecognized each year because of incomplete investigation of cases of obscure death," Moritz wrote in the department's first annual report.

Along with investigating deaths in Massachusetts, Moritz consulted in the investigation of murder cases in Maine, Rhode Island, and New York. He also maintained an active public speaking schedule, presenting talks on legal medicine to lay audiences, medical societies, and lawyers in Connecticut, Illinois, Missouri, Nebraska, New

Hampshire, New York, Ohio, Pennsylvania, and Rhode Island.

Drawing from the knowledge gained during his fellowship in Europe, Moritz also wrote a book, *The Pathology of Trauma.* He dedicated it to Frances Glessner Lee.

8
CAPTAIN LEE

Lee had a dream: one modern, centralized medical examiner's office located in Boston for the investigation of all unexpected or suspicious deaths in the Commonwealth of Massachusetts. A facility with a morgue and laboratories equipped for toxicology, microscopic pathology, X-rays, and photography.

There would be one chief medical examiner for the Commonwealth and several assistant medical examiners at the headquarters and a sufficient number of deputy medical examiners to attend scenes anywhere they occurred. The staff would be civil service employees, removed from influences of politics and corruption. Through its affiliation with Harvard's Department of Legal Medicine, the office would become the training ground to produce a stream of medical examiners, growing until there were enough qualified professionals for the entire country.

Legal medicine expertise in Boston would be available for investigations throughout New England and across the United States. The agency would serve as a veritable national institute of legal medicine, consulting with local police, coroners, and medical examiners from coast to coast, a forensic medicine counterpart of the Federal Bureau of Investigation.

Dr. Roger Lee asked Lee to sketch out her plan for reorganizing the Massachusetts medical examiner system. He knew people who could get the ear of Governor Saltonstall. Lee's scheme for Massachusetts ran to four typed pages, including a bibliography and a list of more than two dozen people from which an advisory board could be drawn.

As her personal physician, Dr. Lee advised Lee to start taking it easier. At sixty-two years of age, she had an enlarged heart, hyperglycemia, hypothyroidism, glaucoma, hearing loss, severe arthritis of both knees, and an untreated diaphragmatic hernia.

"I emphatically believe that you ought not to work as hard as you are working; that you should try to do all the work you have to do in two hours; that you ought to be out of doors sitting for two hours and take a drive every afternoon," Dr. Lee said. His prescription: "You should take a minimum of alcohol. A moderate amount of tobacco is permitted. You ought to have a massage several times a week."

Despite the doctor's warnings, Lee hardly cut back on work. By 1941, she had sold her Chicago residence and was living full-time at The Rocks, much preferring the fresh air and rural way of life. She still maintained an active schedule, traveling throughout New England and the East Coast and frequently visiting her hometown. A modern, centralized medical examiner's office at Harvard was never far from her mind.

November 28, 1942

The Cocoanut Grove was a popular nightclub in Boston's Bay Village neighborhood. The club had music and dancing, floor shows, food, and free-flowing post-Prohibition alcohol. Once a speakeasy and mob hangout, the Cocoanut Grove was the place where film stars, athletes, and assorted celebrity seekers went to be seen.

A former complex of warehouses and a garage, the Cocoanut Grove had been renovated and expanded numerous times. The interior was a confusing maze of corridors, dining rooms, and bars. The club's newest room, the intimate Melody Lounge, was approached by walking along a corridor and down a flight of stairs.

The Melody Lounge featured a revolving stage and was decorated with a proliferation of artificial palm trees with paper fronds. Like the rest of the Cocoanut Grove, the Melody Lounge decor evoked a tropical resort, with rattan and bamboo accents and silky fabric draped on the walls and ceiling.

On Saturday night, the Cocoanut Grove was packed. Fire erupted in the Melody Lounge. The flames spread rapidly along the decorative material and may have been fueled by a flammable gas used as a refrigerant during World War II. Escape from the inferno was hampered by an inadequate number of exits. The club had only one door at the main entrance, a revolving door that was soon blocked by a crush of bodies trying to escape.

Moritz was involved in the recovery, identification, and postmortem examination of victims from the Cocoanut Grove fire. Officials approached the postfire recovery in a systematic way. A command post was established at the scene for the coordination and control of resources. Bodies were tagged at the scene before they were moved to the morgue.

Four hundred and ninety-two people died in the Cocoanut Grove fire — thirty-two more than the building's legally authorized capacity. The Cocoanut Grove was the second-deadliest single-building fire in U.S. history after the 1903 Iroquois Theater fire in Chicago.

After the Cocoanut Grove fire, Moritz and Lee discussed methods of using teeth to identify decedents after mass fatality incidents. "Among the victims there were approximately two hundred that were so badly burned that it was impossible to establish identification by their external physical characteristics," he wrote to Lee. A large proportion of the decedents had dental repairs that were recognized by their dentists and were identified this way, but it was impossible to find dentists to identify every decedent. "It seems that there should be some simple way by which a dentist could leave a code number of some kind on or in a repair so that it could be readily traced."

Lee was generous to the Department of Legal Medicine in ways large and small. When they needed $1,000 for stenographic assistance or $500 for the salary of a researcher to complete his investigation of seminal stains, she could be relied upon for the funds. Although often happy to give her money away, she was also financially shrewd enough to take full advantage of her gifts when it came to taxes.

In 1942, Lee was reminded by her accountant that she had been paying for the storage of her mother's Steinway piano for several years. He asked whether she wanted to continue paying that bill. The piano was a Model D Parlor Concert Grand, the second-largest grand piano made by Steinway. The custom-made case, carved and inlaid mahogany, was designed especially for Lee's mother by furniture designer Frances H. Bacon. Theodore Thomas, the founding conductor of the Chicago Symphony Orchestra, visited the Steinway factory to inspect and approve the instrument before its delivery to the Glessners. The piano had particular significance to Lee. Her parents purchased the piano in New York in 1887 on the same trip as her miserable tonsil surgery.

Lee decided to give the piano to Harvard. "I do not play the piano and my small cottage home is too restricted in both size and quality to house an instrument as handsome or as large," she wrote her friend, Dr. Roger Lee. "It would make me a great pleasure if I could present it to Harvard University for the President's home." Harvard president James Bryant Conant and his wife, Grace, were pleased to accept the piano.

"You might be interested to know that the piano is safely in Mrs. Conant's hands but that I was unable to get 'Department of Legal Medicine' inlaid on it anywhere," Lee wrote Moritz afterward. "Perhaps I can do better with the next donation."

Lee deducted the value of the piano from her personal taxes as a charitable gift and eliminated the cost of storing the piano. During the war, the Conants were displaced from Harvard's president's house, which was given over to the navy. The Conants lived temporarily in a much smaller home next door. They had no room for the piano and paid to keep Lee's piano in storage for the duration of the war.

A teaching institution needs teaching materials. Books are a good start, and Lee had created a library that was second to none. Other sorts of media are also valuable for instruction — photographs, illustrations, films, models. There weren't a lot of instructional materials available in the area of legal medicine or, as it was increasingly being referred to, forensic medicine, so Lee took it upon herself to have it created.

Lee was determined that her Department of Legal Medicine would have the latest and best in instructional media. She helped the department acquire photographs and lantern slides that were useful for lectures. Letters between her and Moritz indicate plans to produce an autopsy film for educational purposes. An artist was hired to cast the head of a volunteer to create three models depicting various injury deaths, intended for study. One of the plaster heads illustrated a victim with a gunshot through the temples. The second showed the victim of a hanging, a distinct ligature mark around the neck and the whites of his eyes with pinpoint blood spots, known as petechiae, characteristic of asphyxial deaths. The neck of the third head was severed deeply enough to show underlying structures in sufficient detail for a trained eye to discern that the victim was cut from his left to the right.

For an additional contribution to the teaching materials, a young doctor on his fellowship, Russell Fisher, worked on a "fauna of decomposition" exhibit with preserved examples showing the life cycle of insects commonly found in proximity to dead bodies. Recognizing the stage of development of these insects can help estimate how long a body has been dead.

While on his fellowship at University of Edinburgh, Moritz had told Lee about a collection of photographs of bullet wounds there that were useful for study. This gave Lee an idea. She offered to shoot hogs with a variety of bullet calibers at The Rocks, then have the skin preserved for demonstration of the wounds they produced.

Ultimately, shooting pigs at The Rocks wasn't necessary. Lee hired an artist to craft rectangular plaster plates, hand-painted to simulate wounds from a variety of ammunition fired from a range of distances. The finely detailed models showed the abrasion and stippling of an entrance wound and the jagged shape common of an exit wound. Forty-four gunshot wound models were fabricated at a cost of $60 per plate. The collection would have cost Lee more than $2,600. This represents a present-day expenditure of about $27,000, a substantial amount for an instructional visual tool.

Although she had grown to respect Moritz's abilities and intelligence, Lee sometimes wondered whether they shared a vision about the purpose and goals of the Department of Legal Medicine. A pathologist at heart, Moritz was involved in research of burn injury and publishing his results — typical work for a medical academic that

Lee considered important but a comparatively lower priority. She was more concerned with training, educating, and pushing the field of forensic medicine forward.

During a visit with Moritz in Boston in November 1942, Lee asked Moritz a series of questions about the Department of Legal Medicine and wrote down his immediate answers. Her intent was apparently to assess the doctor's grasp of the field of legal medicine and the department he led in order to ensure that their vision and goals were congruent. Lee returned to The Rocks and wrote down her own answers, which she sent to Moritz to review and give a more studied response.

"I hope you can take time to give me somewhat expanded answers," she wrote to Moritz. "I don't mean to be a pest but I'm trying to gather together some material which may be of use later."

Question 1: What is the overall picture — the final attainment aimed at?

Moritz's answer: "A medicolegal Institute covering the County and serving the State as a whole in an authoritative relationship."

Lee's answer: "To make available scientific (medical, legal or other) skill and knowledge for the solution of otherwise unexplained deaths, accidents, or those crimes concerned with personal injury and death, in order to determine the cause of death where it is obscure, to recognize preventable hazards of public health and to life, and to clear the innocent and expose the guilty."

Question 2: By what steps is this to be reached?

Moritz's answer: "Educate as many of the public as possible that our services are useful, and Watching for political opportunities."

Lee's answer:

"By simplifying and improving the Medical Examiner System where it already exists

By providing a Medical Examiner System in place of the prevalent Coroner System.

By improving the quality of Medical and other scientific services available to the State by
- Increasing knowledge and training
- Promoting a higher conception of the ethics of the service
- Actively participating in an effort to

283

pass new laws and amend existing laws governing the service

- Disseminating information and knowledge concerning scientific services already or potentially available to the State
- Promoting and partaking in scientific research"

In all, Moritz's original responses to Lee's questions fit on one piece of paper. Lee's answers run more than three single-spaced typed pages. It was clear that Lee, a woman without a college degree, had a fuller and more comprehensive concept of the mission of the Department of Legal Medicine than the country's top forensic pathologist. The limited role she was allowed to take in the development and direction of the department she was nearly single-handedly responsible for founding must have been a source of unending frustration for Lee. No doubt Moritz was discomfited by the presumptuousness of a layperson, no matter how gracious and generous, demanding that he take a test.

As a regular presence at Harvard Medical School, Lee had her own office in the Department of Legal Medicine and a key to the elevator in Building E-1. In light of her ongoing involvement in departmental matters, Moritz thought it proper for the university to give Lee an official position. Burwell wrote a letter to Jerome D. Greene, secretary to the Harvard Corporation, recommending the appointment of Lee as consultant to the Department of Legal Medicine. "One of the things which Dr. Moritz and I desire to have Mrs. Lee possess is a type of authentication which will permit her to get into touch with certain organizations and individuals in the country as an individual with a visible attachment to the University and the Department of Legal Medicine," Burwell said.

The recommendation was highly unusual, since Lee had no academic credentials. "It will be recalled that Mrs. Lee is a generous supporter of the Department of Legal Medicine, both materially and through her own activities," Burwell said to Greene in another letter.

On March 18, 1943, Lee was appointed consultant to the Department of Legal Medicine. Harvard Medical School wouldn't admit female students for two more years.

Moritz told Lee that the position of consultant was as official as any faculty appointment at Harvard Medical School.

"This title would, of course, entitle its holder to use University stationery and to speak as a representative of the University," he told her.

Lee thanked Burwell for the appointment. "I shall do my best to have something worthy of being consulted about," she told him.

Under ordinary circumstances, an appointment such as Lee's would be announced in the *Harvard Gazette,* the university's newspaper. But word came directly from the office of the secretary of the Harvard Corporation: "Not to be printed."

Lee was not identified in the medical school catalog as consultant to the department but rather as honorary curator of the George Burgess Magrath Library of Legal Medicine. Whether she was slighted because she was a layperson with no academic credentials or a woman among the all-male medical school faculty or for some other reason was not explained.

One of Lee's many long-standing interests was forensic odontology — the science of using the teeth and dental records for body identification. The horrors of the Iroquois Theater and Cocoanut Grove fires were never far from her memory. The unknown haunted her. Every time she heard of an unidentified body, she felt a tug at her heart.

The teeth are the hardest, most durable material in the human body. Teeth can tolerate decomposition or submersion in water, withstand temperatures up to two thousand degrees Fahrenheit, and survive explosions and extremes of physical forces. To a skilled eye, a single tooth can provide identifying information — a decedent's age, dietary habits, sex, and other characteristics. Through patterns of wear, missing or broken teeth, and dental repairs, teeth are as unique as fingerprints.

Lee wanted to take dental identification to a different level with a national database of dental records, much like the FBI's fingerprint filing system. An unknown body, she reasoned, found anywhere in the country could be identified through this dental record clearinghouse. But for a centralized database to work, for dental records to be classified and filed systematically, there must first be a standardized record, which did not exist at the time. Lee took it upon herself to design one.

In February 1942, Lee sent Moritz a list she called a "plan for unification of dental records":

1. "Names and addresses [of] principal Dental Schools or Colleges. Names and addresses of Deans or heads of same.
2. Obtain from above several sample blank forms on which they keep Dental Records.
3. Obtain from Federal Bureau of Investigation several blank cards (on which records are kept) which may be sorted by machine. State for what purpose these cards are wanted and ask for suggestions.
4. Send all above cards, information and copies (or originals) of correspondence to F.G.L."

At the same time, Lee proposed a dental study for the purposes of researching ways to use teeth to estimate time of death, determine manner of death, and assist in body identification. The study would include research into the following:

1. "Natural decomposition in various stages
2. Immersion in various stages
3. Incineration
4. Injuries due to acids or alkalis
5. Trauma"

With a trained and knowledgeable dentist on staff, the Department of Legal Medicine could significantly advance the field of forensic odontology. Once again, Lee's proposal went unheeded, for reasons that are not documented.

By 1944, despite Lee's best efforts to educate the public, coroners had been replaced with medical examiners in only a few northeastern states: Maryland, Massachusetts, Maine, New Hampshire, Rhode Island, and parts of New York and New Jersey. Nearly 90 percent of the U.S. population was still under the jurisdiction of coroners. Of the three hundred thousand deaths every year that were the result of violent or unknown circumstances, only ten thousand were within a jurisdiction with access to an investigation by a competent medical examiner. The number of murders that went undetected every year was likely in the thousands, and how many people were charged with crimes they did not commit is anybody's guess. In Massachusetts, the value of Moritz's forensic investigations spoke for itself. During his first two years on the job, his work cleared at least six individuals from homicide convictions and identified perpetrators in nine other cases where the police would have made no further investigations.

A few states had improved their laws somewhat. In Ohio, for example, the law regarding the circumstances under which autopsies were required had been updated more in line with a medical examiner system, but the state still had elected coroners signing death certificates.

Even where medical examiners practiced, flawed statutes limited their effectiveness. Some states didn't allow medical examiners to perform autopsies without the approval of the attorney general. Many states restricted the involvement of medical examiners to cases known to be the result of a criminal or negligent act. The problem was that it wasn't always clearly obvious when criminal or negligent acts had occurred, and deaths that appeared ambiguous were investigated further.

To Lee's disappointment, in the sixteen years since the National Research Council report was published in 1928, only one state had rid itself of coroners and adopted a centralized, state-wide medical examiner system — Maryland. Coroners in Maryland had been notoriously corrupt and ineffective. In cities such as Baltimore, coroners were politically connected doctors who were appointed to office and granted a lucrative side business. Since coroners came and went as centers of political power shifted, there was no incentive for them to maintain or improve their competence. They would keep the job, done well or not, so long as they were loyal to the right people.

The coroners of Baltimore and Annapolis were notoriously unreliable and abusive. The cause and manner listed on death certificates was usually made up without an investigation or even examining the decedent. Coroners found various creative ways to get payoffs from undertakers and grieving families. One tactic was reportedly to slow-walk the death certificate or withhold it from Vital Records. Since the death certificate was required to file probate and for various other purposes, a family member or their funeral director had to chase down the coroner and pay $10 for a document that should have cost fifty cents from Vital Records.

The state medical society, MedChi (short for the Medical and Chirurgical Faculty of the State of Maryland), didn't mince words. In testimony before state lawmakers, the organization's leaders called the existing system racketeering. In 1938, MedChi took the opportunity to introduce legislation abolishing the county coroner system and replacing it with a novel state-wide medical examiner system. The law established a chief medical examiner for the state of Maryland, based in Baltimore, who had autonomy to investigate unnatural deaths without the need for permission from prosecutors or police.

To insulate the chief medical examiner from public pressure and political influence, the office was put under the authority of an independent Post Mortem Examiner's Commission. This was an innovative model of governance that had not been done anywhere else. The members of the commission included the chair of pathology at Baltimore's two medical schools, the Maryland health secretary, the attorney general, and the Baltimore city health commissioner.

Today in Maryland, the chief medical examiner can't be threatened or intimidated or have his agency's budget cut in retaliation for not playing ball with political officials. He can only be fired by a majority of the five members of the Post Mortem Examiner's Commission. Maryland's centralized Office of the Chief Medical Examiner, insulated from political and public influences, is perhaps the fullest embodiment of Lee's vision of legal medicine in the United States.

In hopes of replicating the success of Maryland's system, Lee had personally been in touch with public officials, medical associations, legal organizations, and civic groups actively engaged in the abolition or improvement of the coroner system in Oklahoma, Ohio, North Carolina, New York, California, Washington, Colorado, Louisiana, Michigan, Indiana, and Nebraska. Like Magrath, Lee was a tireless advocate for the medical examiner system. She had her driver take her to speak at clubs and ladies' societies throughout New England to spread the gospel of scientific death investigation. Lee's correspondence lists her giving talks to the Kiwanis Club of Concord, the Laconia Women's Club, the Women's Club of Meredith, the Dover Women's Club, the Sandwich Women's Club, and the Science Club at Plymouth Teacher's College in Plymouth, New Hampshire. She undoubtedly spoke dozens of times on the subject of medical examiners to a wide variety of audiences in hopes of getting others to see the importance of her cause.

In 1943, Virginia's governor appointed a panel to study the abolition of the coroner system and draft a law for a medical examiner system. Lee traveled to Richmond to meet with Dr. William T. Sanger, president of the Medical College of Virginia, and Colonel Charles W. Woodson, superintendent of the Virginia State Police. It isn't clear whether Lee was able to schedule a meeting with Governor Colgate Darden, but she made several attempts to speak with him directly.

Lee prepared five pages of comments about Virginia's proposed medical examiner system. She suggested that the medical examiner's office be authorized under an independent commission, as it was in Maryland. The commission, she said, should consist of the state's attorney general, the superintendent of the Virginia State Police, the deans from the Medical College of Virginia and the University of Virginia Medical School, and the president of the state's medical society and bar association in alternating years. Her recommendations included changing the term for appointment to the proposed commission from three to five years, clarifying specific language, and suggesting how the management of autopsy records should be addressed. Each of her suggested changes was accompanied by an explanatory note.

Another place where Lee believed she could make a difference was the District of

Columbia. In her view, it spoke poorly that the nation's capital, home to several very fine medical schools, did not have a modern medical examiner system.

World War II had transformed Washington, DC, into a bustling city. Ramping up for war required an influx of personnel. From 1940 to 1943, the population of Washington ballooned from 690,000 to more than 900,000 with no end of growth in sight. Housing was in such short supply that temporary dormitories were erected on the National Mall. Just across the Potomac, the War Department dedicated its new five-sided headquarters — the largest building in the world at the time. The District of Columbia would never be the same.

It wouldn't be easy for Lee to advance her cause in the populous city. Abolishing coroners in the District of Columbia would literally take an act of Congress. Prior to the introduction of "home rule" in 1973, the governance of the district was under congressional jurisdiction. Congress controlled the budget and had ultimate authority over Washington.

Lee began her effort by lobbying elected officials from New Hampshire: Senators Styles Bridges and Charles W. Tobey and Representatives Foster Stearns and Chester

Morrow. She enlisted the help of Fulton Lewis Jr., a prominent radio personality for the Mutual Broadcasting System, based at WOL in Washington, DC. Building public support was critical for passage of for a medical examiner law. "Believing yours to be the most influential voice heard over the radio, I appeal to you to take up this matter," Lee wrote to Lewis.

At long last, a bill to establish a medical examiner office in the District of Columbia was introduced in Congress in 1945. Lee went into action to press elected officials:

> I cannot too strongly urge your support of this bill — it would be of inestimable value to the District of Columbia. Certainly the most scientific skill should be made immediately accessible in Washington, of all places, in determining the cause of unexplained deaths without first going through the clumsy laborious and expensive routine of the coroner's office.

The bill never made it to a vote. Despite the setback, Lee was undaunted in her reform efforts. She never expressed discouragement or a sense of defeat. What Lee could not accept was inactivity and resignation when faced with institutional inertia.

The important thing was to push ahead, one incremental step at a time. As she searched for ways to advance her agenda in whatever state she was invested in at the time, she also kept her eye on what was happening across the country.

Illinois, for example, had not advanced toward a medical examiner system in the decade she had been following the issue. Lee realized that if the goal of establishing a medical examiner system was unrealistic, then the existing system must be reformed from within by improving the knowledge and expertise of coroners and coroner physicians. What better way to do that than become one of them?

Although no longer a full-time resident of Chicago, in December 1941, the sixty-four-year-old Lee was appointed a consulting deputy coroner for Cook County, which includes the city of Chicago. She was paid $1 as a symbolic gesture to give her professional legitimacy.

She singled out Oscar Schultz for criticism for seeming to give up trying to reform Illinois. Schultz "is of the type who is licked before he starts," Lee confided to Moritz. "I think, although this is not for publication, that he spends a good deal of time and energy in explaining why he didn't do a thing, when a small amount of that same time and energy might have accomplished that thing."

Others across the country were aware of Lee's views and activism. When the coroner issue arose in Oklahoma, Dr. W. Floyd Keller, a pathologist and prominent member of the Oklahoma City Clinical Society, contacted Lee for advice. Existing Oklahoma law required a justice of the peace, who lacked medical or scientific training, to attend deaths as a coroner. Abolishing the coroner system would require changing that law. Lee urged Keller to stay the course, no matter what.

I earnestly hope that your law passes in January, but if it doesn't, don't let that stop you . . .

Our knowledge of the experience in other states suggests that the effort to bring this change about must be steadily maintained to the last minute — even, if possible, increased. It is my belief that in a matter of this kind it is necessary to have every potentially affected group actively enlisted on your side . . .

In some other states where this change from coroner to medical examiner has been attempted the medical men who worked so hard for it became discouraged when their efforts failed on the first try. They felt, and not without justice, that they could not continue to devote any more of their busy days to the cause. Disappointed, therefore, they quit, thinking to resume their activities later at a more suitable or convenient time. But what actually happens is that they fail by this lapse of time to capitalize on what has already been built up. The enthusiasm of the supporters is lost by even a temporary pause in the presentation of the need, the benefit and the advantage of the proposed change. The foundation disintegrates, and by the time the right moment seems to come around again, it means starting from scratch, doing all the work all over again.

The reform effort in Oklahoma failed. However, in Oklahoma City, an agreement was reached between city and county officials and the Oklahoma University Hospital. They created a county-wide homicide squad or what the *Daily Oklahoman* called a "murder-clue team" to attend all questionable and violent deaths. The practice of coroner inquests was discontinued. A justice of the peace still served as coroner, but he would be accompanied on every case with an OU Hospital doctor to examine the decedent and the scene before anything was disturbed.

Reforming laws was a work in progress. The medical aspects were being addressed by Harvard and subsequently by other medical schools as well. The other part of legal medicine's three-legged stool was the police.

Lee began to develop an affinity for police officers in the late 1930s. She was particularly interested in working with state police organizations. State police covered an entire jurisdiction rather than the limited territories of city or county police. State troopers tended to have more formal education, were better disciplined, and regularly underwent training, and Lee felt that the quality, ability, and organization of state police were superior to local law enforcement.

A police radio receiver was installed in Lee's cottage at The Rocks. She spent countless evening hours listening to police dispatch chatter. Through an atmospheric fluke, she was able to pick up broadcasts from the Virginia State Police, which she listened to so regularly that she became able to discern personalities and goings-on at different police barracks. The disembodied voices of the police radio were almost like family.

"I've fallen completely under the spell of the Virginia State Police, beginning with the Superintendent, his lovely wife and his two sweet little girls," Lee wrote to Woodson in Virginia, "and going down through H.Q. and Divisions 1 to 5 inclusive, and must confess that although Division 5 still qualifies as 'pet,' H.Q. and Division 1 are close runners up!"

Her relationship with police helped her formulate plans to improve their crime scene skills. She began with Colonel Ralph Caswell of the New Hampshire State Police. Caswell was a no-nonsense cop. A native of Stafford, New Hampshire, Caswell was appointed the head of law enforcement for the state's Department to Enforce Prohibition in 1922. When Prohibition ended, Caswell was appointed an investigator in the attorney general's office. As an investigator, he created the state's fingerprint database, and he was among the first detectives of the New Hampshire State Police when the agency was formed in 1937.

Caswell also served as a member of the State Liquor Commission, which oversaw the retail sale of alcohol in New Hampshire. Once, having found several cases of liquor on his porch, a gift from liquor dealers intended to win him over, Caswell called a press conference. He announced that he had broken every bottle of liquor and warned that any dealer who attempted to bribe him in the future would be banned from state liquor stores.

Lee knew Caswell through her brother, George, who was active in New Hampshire politics. When Caswell was appointed superintendent of the state police in 1937, he placed an unusually high priority on training for his troopers.

Lee began holding conferences to bring together police supervisory personnel with members of Harvard's Department of Legal Medicine. These one- or two-day conferences were held in the Magrath Library at Harvard, the New Hampshire State Police headquarters in Concord, and on many occasions at Lee's home at The Rocks. The conferences included sessions on weapons and ammunition, death by violence and poisoning, preserving evidence at crime scenes, and related topics. Moritz often presented a session describing the autopsy process.

The training received in Lee's conferences made police officers better prepared and more effective at crime scenes. In recognition of her contribution to the New Hampshire State Police, Caswell named Lee the organization's director of education. Caswell commissioned Lee as a captain in the New Hampshire State Police in 1943, the first woman in the United States to hold such a rank. She was sixty-six years old. Lee's commission granted her "general police power to enforce all criminal laws of the state, and to serve criminal processes and make arrests under proper warrants in all counties."

Some have characterized Lee's role with the New Hampshire State Police as merely honorary, but nothing could be further from the truth. "This was not an honorary post," Caswell later said. "She was actually a full-fledged captain with all the authority and responsibility of the post."

She never made an arrest during her career as a police officer. But from then on, Lee always carried a gold badge in her purse and identified herself as Captain Lee.

As her interest in the field of law enforcement grew, Lee envisioned the development of a new specialty within police work. Just as there were specialists in medicine — cardiology, neurology, and so on — there were areas of specialized expertise in law enforcement as well, such as fingerprinting and examination of questioned documents. She believed that homicide should be a specialty area with dedicated personnel trained with specific expertise.

She called the position she was thinking of a "medicolegal investigator," what would be known today as a homicide detective. While homicide squads existed in some police departments and there were officers called homicide detectives, none had the advanced legal medicine training Lee proposed. As her vision of the scope of the department solidified, Lee considered the purpose of the Department of Legal Medicine in regard to training specialized law enforcement officers to include:

1. "To create the profession of Medico-legal Investigator and to standardize its requirements.

2. To give the Medicolegal Investigator a proper attitude toward his calling as well as toward the public and to develop his sense of responsibility toward both.

3. To give him a background of the history of his profession as well as its relation to other branches of the government.

4. To train him in the basic skills and

304

abilities peculiar to his work.

5. To acquaint him with the general types of forms and reports he will be required to fill out.
6. To develop in him a sense of the need for full and generous cooperation with other government departments with which he works.
7. To stimulate in him a desire for further knowledge.
8. To teach him that Legal Medicine should be taken out of politics.
9. To teach him that he is a seeker for truth — that his duty is to present that truth and fearlessly adhere to it.
10. To instill in him the desire and ability to improve his profession, not alone in its workings, but in its repute in the minds of the lay as well as the professional public.
11. To develop in him a sense of loyalty to and pride in his profession and an appreciation of its scientific value and of its essential dignity."

But the momentum that had been building within the Department of Legal Medicine was brought to a halt by a disconcerting letter to Lee from Burwell, the medical school dean, in April 1944.

"An alarming possibility occurs," Burwell wrote. "Dr. Moritz has been offered an extremely attractive opportunity to take a position in another medical school. It is so attractive that he is bound to consider it seriously and I am sure that he is now doing it."

Suddenly, everything that Lee had worked so hard to build at Harvard seemed at risk of crumbling.

9
IN A NUTSHELL

May 15, 1944

"Five years ago the department consisted of a newly appointed professor and some empty rooms on the third floor of building E-1," Moritz wrote in a report to the medical school dean, Dr. Sidney Burwell. "No one, including the professor, had any definite idea of what was to be done or how to do it." Now, after five years of operation, Moritz said, it was time to step back to assess the experiment and discuss whether the Department of Legal Medicine had promise of ultimate success.

In many respects, the department appeared productive. Moritz was performing autopsies and consulting on deaths throughout Massachusetts. Members of the department were involved in research and publishing papers. Lectures were being delivered to medical students from Harvard, Tufts, and Boston University. But the collaboration that had been expected with Harvard's School of Law never materialized. Four doctors had been trained in the fellowship program, two of whom took positions at other universities to develop legal medicine programs of their own. Since the United States had been drawn into the war, qualified candidates for the fellowship training became unavailable. One of the fellows was called up by the army, leaving only one remaining at Harvard doing research.

"It is expected that at the conclusion of the war there will be more applications for fellowships in Legal Medicine than can be accepted," Moritz wrote in his report. The department desperately needed more faculty to handle the increase of activity expected when men were released from military service after the war.

The heavy workload was taking a toll on Moritz. As the department's only full-time faculty member, he found himself pulled in multiple directions. Attending medical meetings to represent legal medicine and Harvard was a professional obligation. Moritz was asked to give testimony about legal medicine before state lawmakers in Oklahoma, Illinois, Virginia, and other states. He consulted with universities developing legal medicine programs, including the University of Washington and the University of California, Los Angeles. At the same time, Moritz needed to be in the autopsy room, instructing students and fellows in postmortem examination. Many of his cases, of course, were criminal matters that ended up in court, meaning additional hours of preparation and testimony. Finally, he was also involved with Lee and the legal medicine conferences she was conducting for medical examiners, coroners and coroner physicians, prosecutors, police officers, and insurance company executives.

The bottom line: Harvard Medical School needed to increase the full-time faculty to at least three, with another pathologist aside from himself and a toxicologist. The salaries that were required seemed like a huge expenditure, but the return to the community in the form of autopsy services throughout the Commonwealth of Massachusetts could be substantial. Tufts and Boston University would also benefit as Harvard, by agreement, provided legal medicine lectures for all the medical schools in Boston.

"It is possible that the University did not fully realize the extent to which it was committing itself in undertaking the development of a department of Legal Medicine,"

Moritz wrote in his report. "It would be better to abandon the project entirely than to persist in an attempt so handicapped as to be fore doomed to failure."

If Moritz's report was a gambit to get increased funding and attention for the Department of Legal Medicine, it worked. The Rockefeller Foundation granted an additional $75,000 to the department over a ten-year period. Lee, who had been donating $1,000 a year to the department for three years to pay for expenses, increased her annual gift to $3,000 for five years. Moritz decided to stay.

Lee was pleased with his decision. But she couldn't help but notice the cracks in the veneer of their relationship as Moritz continued to lead the department as he saw fit, sometimes in direct contradiction of her wishes and proposals.

Despite the lukewarm response the rest of the university, particularly the law school, had to the Department of Legal Medicine, Lee was convinced that Harvard could do for law enforcement what its prestigious School of Business had done for the corporate world. Harvard MBAs practically ran the country, and the distinction of that degree was far beyond the value of a piece of paper.

Degree programs for police had been developed at several colleges, including the University of California and the University of Chicago. But no curriculum offered to police officers at the time included material on legal medicine. There was nowhere in the United States to be trained as a homicide detective. Lee and Moritz spent a great deal of time discussing how to address this lack of police training. Neither of them were certain what police wanted or needed to know or whether police departments would be interested in enrolling in educational programs at Harvard.

Colonel Caswell, the New Hampshire State Police superintendent, sent Lee on a mission to survey police departments in New England. Driven by a state trooper in a police cruiser, Lee visited with state police and medical examiners in New Hampshire, Massachusetts, and Maine. Captain Lee was shown professional courtesy along the way.

Lee questioned police leadership about legal medicine training, assessing their familiarity with the subject area and soliciting ideas for topics that should be covered in a course. She produced a detailed, nine-page report of her survey. One insight Lee gained was that within police departments, different people needed to understand different things. Officers who investigated unexplained deaths should know the practical aspects of legal medicine. But before you could reach these officers, the "top men" in each department needed to be educated about what legal medicine was and how it could help their investigations. "In a word, to sell Legal Medicine to the State Police heads in order that they may be enlightened enough to detail their Troopers to take the next course" was what Lee recommended in her report.

It was clear that legal medicine education had to be taught from the top down. Lee suggested a nontechnical one- or two-day course for police chiefs and top investigative officers that explained what could be found out with legal medicine, what material and information were needed, what would be taught to the troopers, and how it would help police departments.

For police officers, Moritz and Lee considered developing a one-year course at Harvard to provide in-depth training in forensic investigation. Moritz circulated a letter to police departments in New England to gauge interest in the proposal and to recruit the first class of twelve students. The proposal withered on the vine when too few candidates were found with the basic prerequisite of two years of college, including physics and chemistry coursework.

As an alternative, Lee suggested an intensive course — a one-week seminar held in the Magrath Library. The course shouldn't be overly technical, just what state troopers absolutely needed to know. "The men dealt with are those of average education without technical medical knowledge," Lee said. "They are to be taught the practical how-to-do aspects of crime detection from the medical point of view, in words of one syllable, to make them efficient in bringing in the material for examination . . . While it would be a feather in a Trooper's cap to take a course at Harvard, he shouldn't be frightened off by fear of it being over his head."

As Lee well knew, no aspect of any investigation was more important than the crime scene. There was only one opportunity to process a crime scene the right way. An error or oversight at the scene could alter the trajectory of an investigation. Police had to be taught to use their powers of observation before stumbling through a crime scene and disturbing the facts. They needed to know how to recognize evidence that may be significant in order for it to be preserved and documented. *How does one teach how to observe?* Lee pondered.

"The matter of providing students with first-hand experience in at-the-scene observation became of paramount importance and was under frequent discussion" between Moritz and herself, Lee said. Using an actual crime scene would be ideal but not practical.

"The problem of teaching a group of students was insurmountable as they could not, in a body, be taken to the scene of an unexplained death to study at their leisure," Lee said. "Why not? Because time was important, conditions changed, crowds of 'interested bystanders' get in the way, but chiefly because until a case has cleared the courts it should not be a matter for free public discussion. And once it has cleared the courts, the clinical material has undergone such changes as to be valueless for teaching purposes, and the scene and its surroundings have been practically wrecked."

Students could be shown photographs or movies from crime scenes, but that process would be leading them by the nose, pointing out evidence to them. That was very different from the process of finding evidence at an actual crime scene, with no photographic framing to direct the attention.

314

"It has been found that visual teaching is the most valuable, but lantern slides and motion pictures, although important, do not give the third dimension, nor the opportunity for prolonged study that is requisite," Lee said.

Out of the blue, Lee thought of the Chicago Symphony Orchestra diorama she had created for her mother and the boxes of dollhouse furnishings and bisque pieces in the attic of The Rocks. "Why not let me make a model that will contain the settings for a scene and the body in its place," she said to Moritz. "Could you not teach from that?"

Lee contacted her carpenter, Ralph Mosher, who lived in Malden, Massachusetts. Mosher did carpentry work and other various odd jobs at The Rocks, most recently building a wine cellar. "I have some special work to be done which I can only describe as the making of a particular type of wooden box, to be approximately 18 × 18 inches square," she wrote to Mosher. "There will be detail work which I can explain later."

Mosher wrote back asking for clarification. "If you will send me the details I will be glad to do it for you," he said. "If you give me a little idea of what tools I would need, it would help. I may have to come by train and would not want to bring unnecessary tools."

The Rocks had a workshop with nearly all the heavy carpentry and metalworking equipment Mosher would need. "The work I want done is building some model miniature rooms, so what you will need in the way of tools will be your smallest and finest ones," Lee told Mosher.

Lee envisioned creating a series of dioramas presenting crime scenarios that were purposefully ambiguous, forcing the student to observe and ponder. She believed it was important that the dioramas look as realistic as possible, lest police officers think they were being asked to play with dollhouses. She decided early on to work in a familiar scale — one inch to one foot, the same proportions she had used for the Chicago Symphony Orchestra and Flonzaley Quartet models. Lee's dioramas would be designed for an investigator about six inches tall.

The first diorama Lee made was based on a case investigated by Magrath of a man who hanged himself under curious circumstances. The dead man had been an unpleasant, manipulative fellow who repeatedly coerced his wife by threatening suicide until he got his way.

"In the original the old man went to the cellar carrying a rope in his hand — he placed the rope over some overhead piping and attached one end of it thereto, the other end containing a noose," she said to Moritz. "After that he stood on a convenient box, bucket or crate with the noose around his neck and waited to be coaxed down." One day, his stand broke, unexpectedly resulting in his strangulation.

In order to conceal the real decedent's identity in the diorama, Lee decided to have the death take place in a typical New England barn rather than a cellar. To build the barn, Lee had Mosher salvage aged wood from an old barn building that had been on The Rocks property when it was acquired. Mosher used a saw to carefully remove the naturally bleached and worn surface of the lumber, creating sheets of wood one-twelfth of an inch thick. The sheets were cut into half-inch strips, then glued together to make scale-model two-by-six-inch planks with aged wood on both sides.

Mosher's barn is twenty-seven inches tall from the base to the weather vane and about two feet on each side. Lee filled the interior with straw and an assortment of farm implements, including a scythe made from an oyster knife. Through the back window is a view of the Franconia Mountains from Bethlehem Junction, Lee's local railroad station. Over the barn door hangs a horseshoe with the open side down — the unlucky way. An inch-tall hornet's nest, camouflaged so well it is easily overlooked, is tucked beneath the eaves.

Inside the barn, the lifeless body of Eben Wallace (the name Lee invented for the tiny decedent) dangles from the hoist, a flimsy wooden crate crushed beneath his feet.

Work began on the dioramas amid World War II. Many materials were rationed or scarce, such as steel and other metals, some kinds of wood, and even the equipment necessary to make the dioramas. Before Mosher could make miniature pieces for the dioramas, he needed to make miniature tools — small-scale chisels and planes to work the wood. Lee tried to purchase a $13.95 jeweler's lathe from Sears Roebuck and Co. in St. Johnsbury, Vermont, but was informed that electrical motors were rationed for the war and she needed to apply for permission from the War Production Board. Lee filled out a form PD-1A, the Application for Preference Rating, in order to acquire the jeweler's lathe. In the spot for the purpose for which a priority was requested, Lee wrote, "Dioramas (miniature models) for scientific study and instruction." It took two months, but Lee got her jeweler's lathe. She was not so fortunate in securing a priority number for a saw and motor that Mosher also needed.

The war caused hardships for everybody. Obtaining materials and spare parts could be difficult. Even when it came to asking International Harvester for materials, being the daughter of a beloved cofounder proved no benefit at all. When Lee needed a replacement exhaust pipe for the International Harvester A-6 truck at The Rocks, the company told her that they could not send a replacement until the old one was returned. This did not sit well with Lee, as that would require the truck to be out of commission for several days while waiting for the replacement part. "We are in the midst of haying and it would greatly inconvenience us to be without the use of this truck for three or four days," she wrote to the company in which she still held a substantial portion of stock. It was no use. Nothing would trump government war rationing.

Sheet metal, nails and screws, hinges, wire — all varieties of metal items were scarce. If a screw was available, it may not be the right size or color. Since nails at the small scale Lee needed for her dioramas were not commercially available, Mosher had to make his own. Even a half-used spool of wire was precious for Lee's project. In the winter of 1944, a friend in Cambridge sent Lee a length of wire. "The package containing the wire which you sent me has been received, and I am extremely grateful to you for your thoughtful and generous gift," she wrote. "It will be far more value in my work on the NUTSHELL models for the Department of Legal Medicine at the Harvard Medical School than you can have any conception of, for it is much needed, and as you know, is pricelessly rare."

Quarter-inch brass hinges, necessary to hang miniature doors with hardware in the correct proportions, were unavailable anywhere. Lee searched hardware stores and suppliers far and wide to no avail. The closest fine brass hinges she could find were half-inch, which were each individually ground down to the proper size to represent a three-inch hinge.

One of the scenarios Lee wanted to model was a car wreck, with a female driver dead behind the wheel. Unbeknownst to the viewer, the woman had been beaten to death by her husband and the crash staged to cover up his crime. The student's challenge would be to discern whether the driver had been killed by the collision or if she was already dead when it occurred.

Because of rationing of steel and rubber, Lee could not find a realistic vehicle of the correct scale for her models. Production of toy cars and trucks was suspended during World War II, and some companies went out of business. With some determination, Lee was able to find one vehicle — a 1:12 scale red roadster — but thought better of trying to simulate a realistic crash with her precious toy.

At another point, Lee needed clear plastic Lucite for windows, one-eighth of an inch thick, thirteen pieces of various small size. She told her supplier in Boston that she would buy a piece of one-eighth-inch Lucite of any size that she could cut the pieces from. "Lucite is on priority and cannot be purchased," the supplier told her. All the company had was a fourteen-inch panel of quarter-inch Lucite that had been rejected by the navy because it scratched too easily.

"I shall be very glad to have the panel of Lucite as I can use it to very good advantage," Lee wrote along with an order for brad nails. "Thank you for obtaining the precious articles for me."

For some of the models, Lee was forced to use glass taken from a picture frame for windows. Once the war had concluded, she was able to acquire thin sheets of acrylic for window panes.

Lee spared no effort or expense to give her dioramas authenticity. For whiskey bottles to ornament the models, she acquired labels of Town Tavern and Crab Orchard brand liquor from the National Distillers Products Corporation from which she made miniatures. She hired an artist to paint backdrops and another to create a miniature oil painting of her cottage at The Rocks, an inch tall and twice as wide, to hang over a living room fireplace.

For a kitchen scene, Lee purchased a working hand mixer made of gold, a small bauble meant to hang from a charm bracelet, which she painted gray to look like steel. This one piece of jewelry, just a prop, likely cost more than a day's wages for the typical worker at the time.

Unlike the beautiful dioramas of fancy rooms produced as a hobby by Lee's friend and Prairie Avenue neighbor, Narcissa Niblack Thorne, Lee wanted her models to look realistic — lived-in and shabbily cluttered. The deaths Lee chose to depict were those of people of modest means, far removed from the social circles of her upbringing. Her dioramas included prostitutes, a prisoner, the poor, and the marginalized. Finding furniture and other furnishings for such humble settings proved difficult. Lee wrote a miniature furniture maker in Dunstable, Massachusetts, that while "I have never seen more exquisite work not more faithful replicas than yours, not even Mrs. Thorne's," his work was too good for her purposes.

"I am not representing the finest pieces nor period pieces, but am trying to show the typical furnishings in lower middle-class homes, or in poverty-stricken shacks or tenements," she wrote the craftsman, "mostly the furniture of that nondescript type which one cannot imagine as even having been procurable at any place but a secondhand store."

Many of the furniture pieces were handmade by Mosher: scale-sized wardrobes, bedside tables, chairs. To make sure that the results were as realistic as possible, Lee asked a forestry professor at Yale for a list of varieties of wood with a grain fine enough to be plausible at 1:12 scale.

Realistic human figures for Lee's death scenes did not exist commercially either. All the figures available in the dollhouse supply catalogs were posed in a fixed position with the feet on a base to stand upright. This was not at all suitable for Lee's purposes, so she made her own. The heads, left over from the miniatures she had made decades previously, were finished with wigs or painted plaster to simulate hair. Torsos and limbs were filled with sawdust, cotton, sand, or lead shot as necessary to give the body the proper heft and appearance. Stiff wire was employed to hold a body in position and represent rigor mortis. Lee carefully painted the porcelain skin of the figures to show lividity, carbon monoxide poisoning, decomposition, and signs of violence.

Dressing the dolls was an exacting affair. "The most difficult matter is the texture of the material used — that of men's suits being perhaps the hardest to simulate," Lee said. "The material must meet many requirements: they must be thin and pliable, but not transparent, they must be capable of taking a crease, they must not ravel easily and for draping purposes, they must be such that they can be wet without damage, and of course the color and pattern must be correct, but while all these can sometimes be found in one piece of goods, it may still be unusable as the texture is out of proportion."

Lee reveled in the most minute details. "Most of the furniture and small objects work — doors and dressers open, stove lids lift, corks come out of bottles, grind-stone is a real one and turns, halter and belt buckles work, some books open and have printed pages inside, the knitting is real," she wrote. The figures, although fully clothed, had underwear on beneath. Anything less would be indecent.

Lee carefully applied red nail polish to simulate blood spatter on walls, puddles of blood, and bloody footprints on the floor. The walls around light switches were smudged with fingerprints. With cloth wrapped around her fingertip, Lee spent hours rubbing a worn spot on a piece of linoleum to make it look authentically aged. She included things that would never be seen by observers — a stamp-size poster for a boxing match inside a saloon that is only visible to a six-inch-tall patron walking inside and graffiti scrawled on a jail cell wall.

"I found myself constantly tempted to add more clues and details and am afraid I may get too 'gadgety' in the process," Lee said to Moritz. "I hope you will watch me and stop me when I go too far."

Within months, Lee and Mosher had made a barn, a bedroom, a kitchen, a living room, and at least three other dioramas. In honor of Isaac Scott, Mosher built a log cabin based on Lee's childhood playhouse built by the designer. Another model was inspired by the garage at her parent's Prairie Avenue home. Many more dioramas were planned. "I have in prospect, or completed, two hangings; two shootings; two assaults with blunt weapon; one natural cause; one drowning; one found dead; one arson (I do not know yet how that gentleman was killed — am open to suggestions); and one poison," she told Moritz. "I need more traffic accidents — hit and run, collision and non-collision with some good evidence (shreds of clothing et cetera, but not too commonplace or obvious), also another shooting or two, a stabbing, more poisonings, carbon monoxide, and a couple of puzzling Found Deads."

The most elaborate diorama Lee built consists of two nearly identical side-by-side rooms. On the left, the scene shows the moment after a man was shot to death. He is sprawled on the living room floor. The room to the right, finished exactly the same as the other, shows conditions after a trooper helpfully moved the victim to the couch. The trooper is standing, taking notes, while the wife sweeps up the debris of china broken when her husband collapsed. In the officer's hand is a pencil made from a toothpick, with a real lead. The notebook has tiny indecipherable notes. Around his neck, on a very fine platinum chain, is a whistle that actually works. Although at first glance they appear nearly identical, there are more than thirty differences between the two scenes that the student observing them is expected to detect.

It is difficult to assign an accurate monetary value to the dioramas. Lee did not keep itemized accounting on each model, and some materials were used in more than one. By some estimates, the cost of material and labor in producing each diorama ranged from $3,000 to $6,000, representing an expenditure of $40,000–$80,000 today.

One of Lee's early models was a rural two-room cabin. Its resident was clearly not a wealthy man — the tar-paper roof had been patched — but had the basic necessities: a comfortable chair in a warm spot near the wood stove, a wide, iron-framed bed, and a simple kitchen with a kerosene stove and well-stocked with food. After spending countless painstaking hours and thousands of dollars to make an exquisitely detailed diorama, Lee took a blowtorch to her work. Inspired by the Frederick Small murder and arson, Lee carefully burned most of one corner of the cabin until the bed began to fall through the floorboards. In the foreground, on top of a chest of drawers, is a soot-smudged alarm clock.

The first week-long seminar in homicide investigation for police officers took place in 1945. Two sessions were to be held each year, in April and October, around the conference table in the Magrath Library. Lee hailed the seminar as a new chapter in scientific police work.

"Believing firmly that the efficient policeman is an informed policeman [I have] made every effort to provide the police students with the most modern and progressive scientific training possible to procure for them," she said. "The old days are gone — the days when 'brogue and brawn' were the requisites to make a city foot patrolman, and today the policeman is an educated, well-trained gentleman," she said.

Lee orchestrated the homicide seminar like a social engagement. Attendance at the seminar was by invitation only. During her travels visiting various police departments, Lee kept notes on potential students. She looked for police officers who were bright, had attended college, and were early enough

in their career to take full use of the specialized training. If an officer was within a few
years of retirement, Lee ruled him ineligible
for the seminar, believing that he wouldn't
make full use of the training in his remaining time on the force. Lee also personally
interviewed the student candidate's supervi-
sors and chief to make sure they were committed to taking full advantage of the training. She did not want to waste a slot in the
classroom if the graduate would later be assigned to a desk or the evidence room.

She insisted that all law enforcement
agencies pay the full price for the seminar
and that it be paid for by the department
and not by the officer. This was to get agencies invested in the program, literally and
figuratively.

During the week of the seminar, officers
heard lectures about blunt and penetrating
injuries, asphyxiation, poisoning, fires,
drowning, and a variety of causes of death.
They observed an autopsy performed by
Moritz, and of course, they interacted with
Lee's dioramas, which she called the Nutshell Studies of Unexplained Death.

At the end of the first day of the seminar,
officers were assigned two Nutshell dioramas to study. They were given about ninety
minutes to observe each one. Later in the

week, each officer stood before the class and gave a verbal report. After some discussion, the point intended to be illustrated by each model was disclosed to the students.

The models were installed behind black cabinets in a darkened gallery. Most of the illumination was from the miniature light bulbs within the dioramas. Lee sat in the room while the students worked, making herself available to answer general questions but never giving away hints.

Students were told that the dioramas weren't meant to be solved like a real criminal case. The models don't contain complete information — there are no autopsy findings, witnesses can't be asked questions, and in most cases, the full faces of the dead are never shown.

"It must be understood, these models are not 'whodunits' — they cannot be solved merely by looking at them," Lee said. "They are intended to be an exercise in observing, interpreting, evaluating and reporting."

Most importantly, the Nutshells were intended to teach the viewer to resist jumping to conclusions, making a snap judgment, and only noticing evidence fitting a favored hypothesis. "One of the essentials in the study of these Nutshells is that the student should approach them with an

OPEN MIND," Lee said. "Far too often the investigator 'has a hunch,' and looks for — *and finds* — only the evidence to support it, disregarding any other evidence that may be present. This attitude would be calamitous in investigating an actual case."

Lee encouraged students to think of the Nutshells as a moment frozen in time — "as if a motion picture were stopped at such a point." Some sequence of unknown events had occurred, and the diorama represented the moment when the officer arrived on the scene.

"The students should be warned that they must whittle their perceptions down to as fine a point as possible in order not to overlook pertinent details," Lee said. "It should be explained to them that much of the detail in the models has nothing to do with the actual problem, but is present as scenery — stage setting — in order to show the kind of people who occupied the premises or their state of mind."

Lee recommended that students observe the diorama slowly and methodically, beginning at one spot to their left and looking around the room in a clockwise direction, from the periphery to the middle of the room. She urged them to look at everything with an open mind and without judgment and allow the truth suggested by the evidence to let itself be known.

The seeds of legal medicine planted in the police officer's homicide seminar would need tending if the field was to grow and flourish. Knowledge and skills introduced during the seminar had to be kept updated. Lee wanted the officers trained in her seminars to keep the momentum going, to maintain the professional relationships they formed during the week, to network and exchange information and work together on major cases as necessary. To that end, at the same time as she began the homicide seminar, she formed a nonprofit organization called Harvard Associates in Police Science. Graduates of the seminar were given membership in HAPS, which held advanced homicide seminars and promoted professional development. According to its articles of incorporation, the purposes of HAPS were:

"To organize and unite persons who have completed a Seminar on Legal Medicine for Police Officers at Harvard Medical School
To encourage the enlargement and improvement of medical science in crime

detection

To encourage research work in scientific crime detection

To promote the highest standards among law enforcement officials having charge of criminal investigations

To meet in Convention and disseminate precise data to members in respect to crime prevention and detection, and to put forth full power in any movement that has as its aim crime reduction

To provide the police with the latest developments in laboratory and other scientific aids in crime detection

To bring about closer cooperation between police and medical science."

Lee treated the officers attending the homicide seminars very well, making sure that they were as comfortable as possible. She purchased cigarettes for the men — about eight cartons of cigarettes supplied the group for a week — and in a shrewd piece of marketing had packs of matches with "Legal Medicine" printed on them. It was her hope that the officers would take the matches to prompt conversations about legal medicine back home.

On the second night of each seminar, Lee hosted a fine dinner at Boston's Ritz-

Carlton. She spent lavishly on these dinners, fussing over the smallest details. Lee personally drew up the seating chart for the dinners, placing officers from the most distant cities next to each other to facilitate friendships and conversation. Insisting on the finest in food, drink, and service, Lee spent an amount comparable to $25,000 for a dinner with forty guests. The floral centerpieces alone cost more than $6,000 in present-day money. Lee insisted that her police officers dine on gold-leaf place settings, so the hotel spent the equivalent of $66,000 to purchase a set of china that was reserved exclusively for the homicide seminar.

"These were wonderful affairs," recalled Charles L. Banino, general manager of the Ritz. "She treated her guests as if they were royalty. They could have anything they wanted and as much as they wanted — as long as they behaved like gentlemen."

A typical menu included boola-boola soup, paillettes, celery hearts, radishes, olives, broiled filet mignon with sauce bordelaise, petits pois a l'étu, Anna potatoes, endive and watercress salad, omelette suédoise flambée, coffee, mints, and cigars. For many of the officers attending the seminar, it was the finest meal they had in their lives.

Lee was "probably the fussiest patron we ever had," Banino said, "and we loved her."

The opulent meal was part of Lee's overall desire to impress upon the students that they had been privileged to receive specialized training from some of the best minds in the country. The officers now belonged to an elite corps and were expected to conduct themselves accordingly. They had been given a gift in the education they were receiving and had a duty to apply their newly gained knowledge in their work.

Upon completing the seminar, each student was given a diploma from Harvard Associates in Police Science. It was important to Lee that they have a diploma that said Harvard on it, to let them know they had accomplished something significant. Each student was also given a HAPS lapel pin and a group photo of the entire class as a keepsake.

At the conclusion of the seminar, Lee rose to address the group of police officers.

There is no place for guesswork in any sort of police work whatever, especially not in homicide investigation. The investigator seeks out the truth, the whole naked incontrovertible truth, let it finish where it may. He is not protecting or avenging

335

anyone, but is seeking, through patient pains-taking accurate hard work, what happened, never making a guess and then searching for evidence to support it. Patience, an infinite capacity for taking pains, absolute accuracy, thoroughness, there is no substitute for these. If you cannot approach a case with these convictions, you should resign at once. There is no place for you either in police work. Say to yourself over and over "There is absolutely no place for guessing in police work" and perhaps you will learn it.

Lee planned on donating the Nutshells to the Department of Legal Medicine at Harvard. "I am making arrangements to determine, through my tax advisor, how the models may take their place in the Department of Legal Medicine most advantageously for all concerned," she wrote Burwell. "When this has been decided I will write you a formal offer along the lines that you and I have discussed."

Months later, Lee made a formal offer to Harvard. "I dislike to attach conditions to a gift but for the sake of clarity I will say that I understand these models will be adequately installed and protected," she wrote. "I prefer that they shall not be on public exhibition but that they will be kept for the use and, I hope, benefit of those who are taking our seminars."

Harvard thanked Lee for the promised donation with a tea party on January 23, 1946. The guest list included Harvard president Conant and his wife, Dr. and Mrs. Roger Lee, Dean Burwell and his wife, Alan and Velma Moritz, Alan Gregg of the Rocke-feller Foundation, Lee's son, John Glessner Lee, and Lee's daughter Martha Batchelder.

Despite the outward show of generosity, Lee was growing unhappy with Harvard and the Department of Legal Medicine. Moritz had accepted a position as chief pathologist at Peter Bent Brigham Hospital alongside his regular duties, taking more time and at-tention away from departmental matters. Lee had the sense that she was tolerated at Harvard only because of the promise of her estate. In all fairness, she was exploiting Harvard to her advantage as well, using the university's prestige to advance the field of legal medicine. But she didn't feel that she was being taken seriously for her contribu-tions.

Lee "expressed the opinion that she was not as hospitably received in the Depart-ment of Legal Medicine as she would like to be and was eager to be," Burwell wrote in a memorandum, "and that she was too much of an honored guest and not enough of a participant."

10
MURDER AT HARVARD

In the spring of 1946, state lawmakers in Virginia passed Senate Bill 64, which abolished the coroner system and established the office of chief medical examiner to investigate unexplained deaths. To shield the medical examiner from public pressure and political influence, he was under the authority of a five-member independent commission, much like the arrangement Lee widely recommended. Lee wasted no time ensuring that Virginia's system got off on the right foot by advocating they hire a former Harvard legal medicine fellow as the first chief medical examiner. Two candidates were at the top of her list — Dr. Herbert Lund and Dr. Herbert Breyfogle. They were both young, brilliant, and well qualified for the job.

A third candidate, Dr. Russell Fisher, had received his medical education at the Medical College of Virginia. MCV president Dr.

William Sanger asked Moritz to take Fisher in Harvard's fellowship program with the thought that he may return to Virginia as medical examiner one day. Lee felt that while Fisher was intelligent and capable, he would not be ready for such a pivotal role for a few more years because he had not yet finished his pathology training. Lee shared her views with Sanger and Colonel Woodson, superintendent of the Virginia State Police, both members of the commission overseeing the medical examiner's office. In a unanimous decision, the commission appointed Breyfogle as Virginia's first chief medical examiner.

The law that established the office of chief medical examiner also authorized the creation of a Department of Legal Medicine at the Medical College of Virginia. Breyfogle was appointed an assistant professor, and operation of the new department commenced in 1948.

It didn't take long for newspaper reporters to hear about the scientific homicide seminars for police officers at Harvard and the unusual crime scene models used for instruction. The odd combination of murder and dollhouses was ready-made for feature stories. The *Boston Globe, Providence Sun-*

day Journal, and many other newspapers did stories about the Harvard Department of Legal Medicine and the heroic exploits of a new generation of scientific medical examiners.

These stories tended to cast Lee as a peripheral figure if she was mentioned at all — a wealthy matron who made morbid dollhouses — and understated her role as a leader in the field and a driving force behind the Department of Legal Medicine. Lee was willing to accept this self-effacement if it made a useful hook for a story and helped spread the word about legal medicine. Moritz apologized to Lee that she was kept anonymous and not given credit for her pioneering work.

"As for my 'complete anonymity' is concerned, it doesn't exist," she told Moritz. "I have had all kinds of write-ups from the beginning. Let's put all our efforts into bringing the subject of legal medicine before the public and making it both understood and valued as well as popular. It really doesn't matter to any but a few who is backing it, and those few know, so let's call it a day."

The biggest score to date happened in the spring of 1946 when Lee was approached for a story in *Life* magazine. *Life* was the country's preeminent pictorial news weekly with a circulation of about 13 million readers. The large-format magazine was known for its superior photography and was anxious to feature the Nutshell Studies of Unexplained Death.

A *Life* photographer spent several days at Harvard shooting the dioramas. The magazine wanted to present the Nutshells to its readers as they were to students in the seminar, with the brief preliminary report assigned to each diorama. There was one problem: the magazine wanted the answers behind each scene.

"LIFE is still very much interested in getting a story, but feels the 'solutions' are indispensable," magazine staffer Jeff Wylie told Lee. "I explained that you had said we would be free to draw our own conclusions and I told the editors that I thought you would confirm correct deductions that we might make. The editors now, in the cantankerous way that editors have, want to know why — if you will confirm our guesses — you can't agree to give us the full solutions. In other words, LIFE doesn't want to play a guessing game."

Participating in the story was an opportunity to bring legal medicine to a huge national public audience. But if everybody knew the solutions, the value of the Nutshells for teaching would drop to zero. Lee compromised. She allowed *Life* to use witness statements but not the complete report used during the homicide seminar. She let the magazine reveal some clues but withheld the solutions.

The Nutshells made their national debut in the June 3, 1946, issue of *Life*. An unbylined feature ran on three pages in the front of the magazine, in a prime spot as the first photo feature after the letters to the editor. Lee was mentioned as the founder of the Department of Legal Medicine but not shown in a photo. There were photos of four of the Nutshells: Living Room, Dark Bathroom, Two Rooms, and Striped Bedroom. The only photograph of people was four men looking at the Barn.

Troopers who had attended the Harvard seminar were pleased to report back to Lee how they applied the training to investigations. After one seminar, Lieutenant R. F. Borkenstein of the Indiana State Police Laboratory told Lee about a recent case involving a man who had been found immersed in water for about three months, his body so badly decomposed that the local police and coroner had abandoned the possibility of identifying the man through fingerprints.

Having learned about skin slippage and degloving — in which the epidermis separates from the underlying layer of the skin — at the homicide seminar, Borkenstein thought to look inside the gloves the decedent was wearing when he was found. The gloves had been discarded along with the dead man's clothing but had not yet been destroyed. Inside the gloves was skin with legible fingerprints, leading to the identification of the decedent.

"The Coroner, an undertaker, was not familiar with the fact that the skin from the hands separates under these conditions," Borkenstein told Lee. "The cause of death will probably never be known as no autopsy was done. I am lighting a torch to carry against this condition, and hope that something will come of it in the future."

Knowledge imparted at the homicide seminars was propagated when students returned home. A Delaware trooper presented a training session based on his experiences at Harvard, including the observation of an autopsy. One of his trainees, based on this secondhand information, interrupted a coroner's physician who was about to begin a postmortem examination by opening the decedent's skull. "That's wrong," the trooper told the doctor. "The abdomen should be opened before the skull. That's how they do it at Harvard." Sawing the skull can damage veins in the membrane surrounding the brain, obscuring the signs of intracranial bleeding. Opening the abdomen first allows the blood vessels of the head and neck to drain into the torso, so any blood on the surface of the brain wasn't caused by the saw.

The coroner's physician did not take kindly to the unsolicited advice and walked away. A supervisor called the trooper into his office to explain himself. "I thought you had us take a course because you wanted us to learn something and then put that to use?" the trooper said. "There is a right way and a wrong way, and that was the wrong way."

April 16, 1947

In the homicide seminar during the first week of April 1947, Moritz presented a session on how he and the Boston medical examiner's staff recovered and identified the 493 victims of the Cocoanut Grove fire and the chemical analysis for fumes that may have been responsible for many of the deaths. J. H. Arnette, a chemist with the

Texas State Police laboratory, was in attendance to hear Moritz's presentation. One week after his return to Texas City, a cargo ship in the city's port loaded with two thousand tons of fertilizer exploded. Arnette, having just attended the seminar, knew exactly how to begin the process of recovering and identifying the casualties. He set up a command center at the scene to centralize the recovery of remains and obtained tags to identify victims before they were removed from the scene.

At least 581 people were killed, including all but one of the twenty-eight-member Texas City Volunteer Fire Department. More than sixty victims were never identified, and scores of victims were never found. It was the worst industrial accident in American history, and without the influence of Lee's seminar, the aftermath would have been overwhelming for the local law enforcement.

Eighteen men went through fellowship study at Harvard's Department of Legal Medicine during its first decade of existence. Of those eighteen, half were still working in the field as medical examiners by 1947 — in Massachusetts, Virginia, and Vermont. The remainder had returned to general pathology or were working in other fields.

By this time, medical examiners had replaced coroners in ten states. Some progress had been made toward Lee's goal, but three out of four Americans still lived under the jurisdiction of coroners.

The Department of Legal Medicine, through the efforts of Moritz and Lee, had been actively involved in efforts to reform laws in Massachusetts, Rhode Island, Vermont, Maine, Connecticut, New York, Ohio, Louisiana, Oklahoma, Michigan, North Carolina, California, Colorado, and Iowa. With the assistance of Moritz and his Harvard group, legal medicine programs had begun at the University of Washington, University of Cincinnati, University of Colorado, Medical College of Virginia, and University of California, Los Angeles.

Still, the Department of Legal Medicine was far from its goal of serving as a resource for investigations throughout Massachusetts, much less as an institute of forensic medicine with a national scope. Statistically, considering the fifty thousand deaths every year in Massachusetts at the time, there should have been about ten thousand cases meriting an investigation by a competent medical examiner. About half of those cases, or around five thousand a year, would require a forensic autopsy. But members of the Department of Legal Medicine were involved in only fourteen hundred investigations in 1947. They performed 385 autopsies, including 121 for Suffolk County medical examiners and 204 for investigations conducted by the state Department of Public Safety. This volume of autopsies was barely enough for medical examiners to maintain proficiency in the procedure.

Lee told Alan Gregg of the Rockefeller Foundation that she had doubts about Moritz's commitment to legal medicine and hinted at dialing back her financial support for the department. "She thinks [Moritz's] heart is still in pathology and always will be," Gregg noted in his diary. "Mrs. Lee intimates rather directly that the next major financial contribution from her is more likely to be in her will than anywhere else. It is her hope that Harvard will 'do as much for the police as it has for the businessman,' and, quite understandably, she feels that the recent state of affairs is somewhat remote from that objective."

While the Department of Legal Medicine was performing short of expectations, Lee's homicide seminars had been consistently successful. Two groups of around thirty students were trained every year. By 1949, the seminars had been attended by officers from nineteen states and two Canadian provinces, special agents of the FBI, and the U.S. Army Military Police.

Lee ran the homicide seminar entirely by herself, with no financial or administrative help from Harvard. Cara Conklin, her personal secretary, handled all the correspondence. Lee arranged for the speakers, most of them affiliated with the Department of Legal Medicine, and paid the travel expenses of those from out of town. She spent a week in Boston before each seminar to personally oversee arrangements for the classroom and the banquet. Lee treated everybody to the elegant dinner at the Ritz-Carlton, provided cigarettes and matches, paid for the diplomas and lapel pins, and personally covered all the expenses related to the homicide seminars. Meanwhile, the proceeds from the seminar in the form of registration fees went to the Department of Legal Medicine, which Lee was also still supporting financially.

Despite its success, not everybody at Harvard was supportive of the police homicide seminar. There were some who thought cops were out of place on an Ivy League campus. Dr. George Minot, corecipient of the 1934 Nobel Prize for his pioneering work on pernicious anemia, dashed off his thoughts in a letter to Burwell. "Why should Harvard Medical School have anything to do with courses for training policemen or their associates?" Minot said to Burwell. "It seems that the Medical School is to become involved in giving courses or instruction to individuals who haven't the slightest idea of ever getting any degree. There is, of course, no question that well trained individuals in so-called police laboratories are well worthwhile but I am simply asking myself why should Harvard have anything to do with this anyhow."

Lee believed that police work was not beneath the Ivy League and used her influence to ensure that the homicide seminar remained at Harvard. She also began inviting female police officers to the homicide seminar in 1949. The first women to attend, in April 1949, were also among the first female troopers of the Connecticut State Police: Evelyn J. Briggs and Kathryn B. Haggerty. After that point, every seminar included at least two female students.

Lee went out of her way to make sure that the women felt welcome at the homicide seminar. While female police officers weren't unheard of at the time, they were sufficiently rare for male students to think the women were secretaries or had blundered into the wrong room. "We were informed by some of the male members of the group that our entrance on the first day had been somewhat disconcerting to them," said state trooper Lucy E. Boland, who was among the second group of women to attend the homicide seminar in October 1949. "They were startled when Captain Lee introduced us as State Policewomen."

Boland described an incident during a laboratory exercise in which students observed the effect of poisons on mice. After assuring Lee that she had no fear of mice, Boland was startled by a sudden movement out of her peripheral vision and jumped back, bumping into Lee. "I was embarrassed because of the fact that I had bumped into her, but ashamed of my retreat after having boasted that I was not afraid," Boland said. "Captain Lee immediately put me at my ease, however, when she told me that she has no fear of mice, but that frogs petrify her, since she never knows where they are going."

Interacting with female police officers was good for the male students at the seminar. During breaks, men flocked around the female officers to talk about how they were faring in police work. "Few of the States represented at Harvard had ever had any contact with policewomen and were amazed to find that Connecticut is so healthily supplied," Boland said. "Many of them said that they have been fighting for years to have women added to their departments, without success, but felt that, after talking to us, they could go back to their superintendents, commissioners, etc with added ammunition for the fight."

February 9, 1948

A larger goal, introducing legal medicine to the general public, remained elusive. Lee had another ambitious idea: a dramatic theatrical film about the Department of Legal Medicine. Through a friend in the New York City publishing world, Lee got the ear of Samuel Marx, a story editor in charge of the screenwriting department of Metro-Goldwyn-Mayer Pictures. "We feel that an interesting motion picture of a semi-documentary nature can be made dealing with your work in the field of crime," Marx told Lee. He dispatched a young writer, Alvin Josephy, to Boston.

Back at The Rocks, the police radio kept Lee in touch with her extended law enforcement family during the long, lonely days. "I have listened with increasing interest and appreciation to the Virginia State Police broadcasts until I feel as if each one of you is my personal friend," she wrote to Major James Nunn, who was the acting state police superintendent while Colonel Woodson was on active duty during the war.

Lee sent personalized Christmas letters and spoiled her boys in Virginia and New Hampshire with gifts of smoked turkeys, boxes of fresh citrus, and copies of Dr. LeMoyne Snyder's book, *Homicide Investigation: Practical Information for Coroners, Police Officers, and Other Investigators.* Snyder, who received his medical education at Harvard, was medicolegal director for the Michigan State Police. He was involved in the formation of the Department of Police Administration at Michigan State University — now the School of Criminal Justice — and the Michigan Crime Laboratory.

Published in 1944, *Homicide Investigation* was the standard textbook for police academies and university criminal justice programs for more than three decades. When the first edition was published, Lee wrote to Snyder to praise his text. Snyder replied with flattery. "Your remarks made me feel very good indeed, particularly as you are recognized throughout the country as a real authority on the subject," he said.

In 1948, Snyder passed along to Lee an inquiry from a friend, Erle Stanley Gardner, author of the Perry Mason novels. The bestselling author in America at the time, Gardner regularly contributed to major magazines throughout the country. A practicing attorney as well as a writer, Gardner had recently begun a project to reinvestigate cases of people who claimed to have been railroaded by authorities and convicted of murders they did not commit. Gardner enlisted the help of police, investigators, forensic scientists, and other experts in what he called the Court of Last Resort. Gardner ended up writing a feature article on the project for *Argosy,* a pulp magazine trying to clean up its image by shifting from fiction to true-crime articles.

Sometime later, Gardner read an article in the *Los Angeles Times* about the homicide seminar for police officers at Harvard and became interested in wrangling a seat for himself in the classroom. The seminar was something new and different and might result in some ideas for his writing. Snyder, a member of Gardner's expert panel for the Court of Last Resort, introduced the author to Captain Lee.

Lee was uncertain at first. "I thought it over for a long time, for I have strenuously avoided inviting outsiders," she told members of the HAPS board. "But, I thought he might do some good."

Gardner was invited to attend the homicide seminar in October 1948. Learning the modern methods of scientific death investigation was an eye-opener for him. "He was the most interested, and the most deeply affected person by the group of men he met," Lee said.

Lee challenged the author about his Perry Mason books. "Your stories are formulaic," she complained to Gardner. "The police are portrayed as uneducated fools who are bettered by a defense lawyer who acquits his client based on mistakes that never should have happened. Why don't you write stories that depict the police accurately?"

"If I told the truth," Gardner said, "the book would end after a page and a half."

"I just can't believe this is the kind of people that make up the State Police," he told Lee.

"They are," she said, "and the sooner you get through writing about Perry Mason and the police going around in circles about him, the better."

During the week of the homicide seminar,

Gardner happened to be finishing a Perry Mason novel — *The Case of the Dubious Bridegroom*. During breaks in the sessions, Gardner dictated the novel by telephone to his secretary in Temecula, California.

Gardner's impression of Lee was memorable. She was "a perfectionist in every sense of the word," he said. "When she gave her banquets . . . she gave hours of careful consideration to the seating arrangements, the floral decorations and to the program. I don't think there was any detail too small or insignificant to be given careful consideration.

"Because she had an orderly mind and a logical mind," Gardner said, "she was able to comprehend police work in a way that enabled her to make a shrewd and accurate appraisal of individual cases as well as overall planning of what was being done and an accurate estimate of what should be done."

Sold on the importance of legal medicine, Gardner telephoned Harry Steeger, publisher of *Argosy* and another member of the Court of Last Resort expert panel. Steeger traveled to Harvard from New York City for the last day of the homicide seminar. Afterward, Gardner and Steeger discussed a book, perhaps a series featuring a state trooper or medical examiner who used the latest scientific tools to solve murders.

The Case of the Dubious Bridegroom was dedicated to Captain Lee. In the foreword, Gardner wrote:

This book was written under rather unusual circumstances. The last part of it was dictated while I was in Boston attending a seminar on Homicide Investigation at the Department of Legal Medicine of the Harvard Medical School.

I had for some time heard about these seminars, which are sponsored by Frances G. Lee of New Hampshire (a Captain of the New Hampshire State Police). Invitations to attend are as sought after in police circles as bids to Hollywood by girls who aspire to be actresses . . .

Back of all this, and as the guiding spirit, is Captain Frances G. Lee. I don't believe she has ever overlooked a detail in her life. Captain Lee has reconstructed in small scale (one foot to the inch) some of the most puzzling crimes which have been encountered by police . . .

This is a marvelous work that Captain Lee is doing . . . I have dedicated this book to her as an expression, in some measure, of my appreciation; and in admiration of the manner in which her mind, working with the accurate precision of a railroad watch, has brought into existence the over-all plan of a course in training that is helping to make the competent state police official as much a professional man as the doctor or lawyer.

Gardner autographed the first copy of *The Case of the Dubious Bridegroom* off the printing press and sent it to Lee. He also sent autographed copies to each officer attending the homicide seminar. Lee wrote to Gardner's editor at William Morrow & Company with an unusual request for one uncut sheet from the printer, called a signature, with the first thirty-two pages of *The Case of the Dubious Bridegroom.* "I want to have it photographically reduced to my scale and use it in a tiny book for one of my Nutshell models," she explained. "I hope this is not asking too much. And I also hope for permission to reproduce that much of the book — of course not for sale! And please don't tell Mr. Gardner."

An enthusiastic convert to legal medicine, Gardner promised Lee a "book in which a state police organization is shown to an advantage." This proposed book could appear under his own name or one of the numerous pseudonyms he used, including Charles J. Kenny, Carleton Kendrake, and A. A. Fair. But he had one favor to ask of Lee — her assistance in getting authentic background experience with state police. He wanted to spend time with police to glean realistic details for his stories, to follow the progress of actual murder cases. Names and other details would be changed to avoid violating privacy or risking a lawsuit, fictionalized for the purposes of Gardner's story. "One of the things that I do want is to see some organization of state police working on a difficult murder case — watch the way the whole thing is handled, and pick up on my background from seeing the machinery in operation," he told her.

Lee believed that Gardner could be useful for the advancement of legal medicine and cultivated her relationship with him. With Gardner's name, a book that was authentic and favorable to police would be tremendously valuable to bringing legal medicine to the general public. "A lively correspondence with Erle Stanley Gardner has developed," she told Moritz. "I fancy we can swing him to write just about anything we want."

Contacting her state police friends in Massachusetts, New Hampshire, Connecticut, Pennsylvania, Maryland, and Virginia, Lee arranged a road trip for Gardner. She told Woodson, head of the Virginia State Police, that Gardner admitted that he had been "taking the wrong attitude towards the police, tending to belittle them in favor of some amateur detective hero, and he intends writing a book using a trooper as the star performer. I believe he can do the police much good if he will write from their angle, provided he gets the background complete and accurate, and this is most important."

Gardner attended a second homicide seminar, held during the last week of April 1949. This time, he was accompanied by *Argosy* publisher Harry Steeger and other members of the Court of Last Resort panel — LeMoyne Snyder, private detective Raymond Schindler, and lie detector expert Leonard Keeler. Immediately after the homicide seminar, Lee and Gardner spent two weeks traveling from state to state, from Boston to Richmond, driven by Lee's chauffeur. Gardner brought along cameras and dictation equipment, working while on the road.

In Baltimore, Lee and Gardner met with members of the Maryland Post Mortem Examiners Commission at the Elkridge

Country Club. Dr. Howard Maldeis, who had been chief medical examiner since the system was created a decade earlier, unexpectedly fell ill and died in January. Maryland was in need of a new chief medical examiner.

Maryland's medical examiner was under the authority of an independent commission, with laws that ensured their independence and autonomy. There were two well-regarded medical schools in Baltimore — Johns Hopkins and the University of Maryland — and the city was positioned to take a lead role as a nucleus of legal medicine.

Lee told the commission members that Russell Fisher was Moritz's brightest prospect. Fisher had completed his pathology training and a three-year research fellowship. Young and ambitious, Fisher had missed his opportunity to return to Richmond as chief medical examiner for Virginia. Lee recommended Fisher highly for the position in Maryland. Gardner vouched for Fisher as well, assuring the commission members that the pathologist was smart and had the strength of character to resist attempts at political influences.

In September 1949, Fisher was appointed chief medical examiner for the State of Maryland. Within a year, he began a fellowship training program. The ultimate vision for the Maryland Office of the Chief Medical Examiner was an Institute of Legal Medicine like at Harvard.

Back at Harvard, the Magrath Library of Legal Medicine, which was the largest of its kind in the world when founded with one thousand books, grew through Lee's diligent acquisitions to a collection of three thousand books and periodicals. Included in the library's holdings were numerous rare and valuable texts, Magrath's case files, one-of-a-kind documents, and what is the most comprehensive collection of documents related to the Sacco and Vanzetti case in the United States.

In early 1949, the head of the medical library once again approached Moritz with the idea of consolidating the department's books with the central library. "I am reluctant to give you a verbatim copy of that part of Mrs. Lee's personal letter to me of November 15, 1938 that pertains to the Magrath Library," Moritz responded. "I can assure you, however, that she was firmly opposed at that time of a transfer of any of the library from this department and I have no reason to believe that she has changed her mind."

■ ■ ■ ■

The Metro-Goldwyn-Mayer studio was interested in doing a different kind of motion picture, a film done in a documentary style, telling a fictionalized true story. The appetites of American film audiences had changed since World War II. They wanted motion pictures that were more realistic, less idealized reflections of everyday life. Crime stories and mysteries were perennially popular genres, but legal medicine presented an untapped approach.

"Our belief is that a very effective story can be developed from this material," read an MGM report. "The most interesting thing about it is that the detective in the case is not the usual Dick Tracy type, but a doctor — a Medical Examiner — for a refreshing change. As a matter of fact, the Medical Examiner is involved in real police cases, yet for some reason or other he has never, or rarely at least, been used in pictures."

MGM forged an agreement with Moritz to develop a motion picture tentatively titled *Murder at Harvard.* The story writing assignment was given to Leonard Spigelgass, who most recently had cowritten the screenplay for *I Was a Male War Bride.* The studio agreed to pay $10,000 to Harvard University in return for the cooperation and assistance of the Department of Legal Medicine. Moritz would be given final word on the script to ensure technical accuracy.

University officials were unsure about the propriety of lending the Harvard name to an endeavor in popular entertainment. Burwell, the medical school dean, pressed the case to the Harvard Corporation. Legal medicine had been hampered by archaic laws and a lack of financial support, he argued. This wouldn't change until the general public was aware of the need for improvement. "I am of the opinion that a good motion picture might do more good on behalf of public enlightenment as to the need for improvement in the practice of legal medicine than thousands of pages written for medical journals and thousands of speeches made before medical societies and bar associations," Burwell wrote in a letter to the Harvard Corporation secretary. In the end, the Harvard Corporation allowed MGM to use the university's name.

Spigelgass drafted a ten-page synopsis for *Murder at Harvard* that opened with the various experts involved in the investigation of suspicious and violent deaths sitting around a conference table in the Magrath Libra "Mrs. Lee has in the meantime joined th group," Spigelgass wrote. "The conference is adjourned and we cut to Mrs. Lee's most recent contribution to the teaching collection of Nutshell Studies of Unexplained Deaths. Until now Mrs. Lee's presence at the conference has been unexplained. She is obviously an anomalous figure in the cast. Until now the story has not had a principal character nor has it had cohesive action. It has been a documentary account of a joint enterprise between university and state law enforcement agency depicting the nature and magnitude of the problem presented by obscure deaths and the surprises that come when expertness is applied to its solution."

As Spigelgass envisioned it, the camera would close in on the Burned Cabin diorama and fade into a flashback of George Burgess Magrath's investigation of the Florence Small murder and arson. From there, the film would tell the story from the founding of the Department of Legal Medicine to the present day. Lee told Spigelgass that she did not desire personal publicity but wanted popular attention focused on the field of legal medicine. She recommended that he base his story on the Irene Perry murder.

Spigelgass wrote Lee out of the story. Due

desire to focus public attention on
d of legal medicine rather than
Lee's role in the development of
ısic science was marginalized. Her
contributions as a reformer, educator, and
activist were largely lost to history.

Shortly after Lee reviewed the film script,
Scientific Monthly, a publication of the
American Association for the Advancement
of Science, contacted Moritz about writing
an article about scientific crime detection
techniques. Moritz suggested that the magazine ask Lee to write the article, which they
did. For an organization like the American
Association for the Advancement of Science
to consider seeking a contribution from a
person who essentially didn't even have a
high school diploma, much less a professional credential, was astonishing.

Lee thought so too. "I would like to accept your offer," she replied to their inquiry,
"but . . . I am totally unqualified to write
such an article as you suggest."

She also didn't have the time to do it.
Aside from a full schedule of meetings and
giving talks to community groups, Lee was
busy editing a collection of papers based on
presentations to the homicide seminar for
Charles C. Thomas, publisher of Snyder's
Homicide Investigation.

When Howard Karsner retired as director of the Pathology Institute at Western Reserve University, Moritz jumped at the chance to take the position he had long coveted. Lee was not surprised that he chose to leave Harvard. Moritz had had to be coaxed and prodded along the way into legal medicine, making no secret of his preference for clinical pathology and research. Legal medicine was still in adolescence, not yet accepted as a legitimate field of medical practice. It was a sordid and tawdry business, doctors playing cops and robbers, and never warmly welcomed in the refined environment of the Harvard campus.

"Members of the faculty of the Harvard Medical School looked down upon Legal Medicine," Lee said. "They felt that when Dr. Moritz, a pathologist of note, had been willing to take a position as head of the Department of Legal Medicine, that it was a step down or several steps down."

Moritz felt that he had done what he had been asked to do — develop an academic medical department — and it was time to turn his attention to his own interests. He explained his motivation in a letter to Lee:

I am not unmindful of my obligations to

you, to Harvard University and to the Rockefeller Foundation. I am not unmindful of the many persons in this department who may be disturbed to a greater or lesser degree by my leaving. However, I have devoted twelve years, which is approximately one-third of the productive period of my life, to legal medicine and I am now faced with the crucial decision of what I want to do during my last fifteen years. I have decided to turn to something that will probably be less important from the standpoint of social welfare but will undoubtedly give me more pleasure in the doing.

By then, the relationship between Moritz and Lee had cooled but was still cordial. Moritz bristled at Lee's meddling in department affairs and continual demands for her seminars. For her part, Lee felt that Moritz was always more interested in his own career than the field of legal medicine. In time, Lee had come to learn that he could be duplicitous, taking credit for her work while saying things behind her back to undercut support for her ideas.

On the heels of Moritz's departure, medical school dean Sidney Burwell announced his retirement. Like sand shifting beneath

Lee's feet, everything was uncertain — the book Lee was working on, *Murder at Harvard,* the homicide seminars, even the Department of Legal Medicine itself.

11
THE DECLINE AND FALLS

February 28, 1949

Moritz's departure threw the Department of Legal Medicine into turmoil. After a decade of his leadership, with Lee in the background, everything that had been built to date was threatened unless a strong successor could be found to carry its mission forward. Without a department head with the stature of Moritz, there was concern that other personnel might leave for more secure and rewarding situations.

"We will be sunk if any or all of them should leave us at this time for self-protective reasons," Lee told her friend, the internist Dr. Roger Lee. "If you will think with me of the seriousness of our predicament: if we lose the only people who are trained for the special work they are doing, it would set us back tremendously as there is no outside field from which to recruit other workers."

Moritz nominated Dr. Richard Ford to replace him as head of the Department of Legal Medicine. Ford had graduated from Harvard Medical School and did a surgical internship at Boston City Hospital before spending three and a half years in the Pacific during World War II. He had served in combat with a portable surgical hospital, and for the last eighteen months of the war, he had commanded an airborne hospital. He was commissioned as a major before returning home in 1945. After his fellowship training in the Department of Legal Medicine, Ford was appointed Leary's successor as medical examiner for the Southern District of Suffolk County. Ford was a first-rate forensic pathologist, dedicated to his work as medical examiner. Within pathology, his main interest was trauma — the types of injuries he had treated during the war.

The war seemed to have affected Ford deeply. He had a dark side with a tendency for outbursts of a fiery temper. Visitors to his office were often disturbed by grisly crime scene and autopsy photos on display. Despite his personality issues, Ford's abilities as a forensic pathologist and medical examiner were unquestioned. Lee was willing to give Ford the benefit of the doubt and work with him in the Department of Legal Medicine. "The more I see of Doctor Ford the more highly I think of him," she told Dr. Lee.

In the spring of 1949, MGM producer Frank Taylor sent Moritz a script for *Murder at Harvard* that the pathologist considered acceptable. Since he was no longer with Harvard, whether the film could still go forward depended on several factors, including the consent of Ford as the acting head of the Department of Legal Medicine. Ford agreed to cooperate with MGM.

Moritz wrote Burwell encouraging Harvard to allow MGM to make the motion picture for the sake of legal medicine. "During the past ten years I have traveled from one end of the country to the other in an attempt to arouse public interest in the need for improvement in the practice of legal medicine," Moritz said. "It seems to me that a proper kind of motion picture prepared and distributed by an organization such as Metro-Goldwyn-Mayer Corporation might well accomplish more in a few months than could be accomplished in many years by any other means."

Harvard had one objection to the motion picture: the title. The university did not want a picture distributed under a title that was "lurid or otherwise offensive." *Murder at Harvard* became *Mystery Street*.

As Lee suggested, the story of *Mystery Street* is based loosely on the case of Irene Perry. Details were changed to fictionalize the incident. In the film, Barnstable County police officer Pete Morales, played by Ricardo Montalban, is investigating the discovery of a skeletonized body found on the Cape Cod seashore. With little more than a box of bones for evidence, Morales seeks assistance from the Department of Legal Medicine at Harvard. Dr. Arthur McAdoo, the Moritz/Ford department head portrayed by actor Bruce Bennett, employs the latest ripped-from-the-headlines scientific methods to help solve the case, including identification, ballistics, and forensic photography that had been pivotal evidence in the Ruxton murder case. Using forensic anthropology, McAdoo determines the decedent's age, sex, occupation, and cause of death — a bullet wound. Morales thinks he has the guilty man, but McAdoo's dispassionate adherence to following the scientific facts wherever they lead shames the cop into investigating further, leading to the apprehension of the real murderer. In a nutshell, science clears the innocent and convicts the guilty.

Mystery Street was the first major theatrical motion picture filmed on location in Boston. Filming took place during October and November 1949, with Harvard Square, Beacon Hill, and the Harvard Medical School campus featured in the film. Scenes depicting the Department of Legal Medicine include shots of the bullet wound models and manikin heads acquired by Lee, but the Nutshell Studies of Unexplained Death do not appear in the film.

According to the agreement with MGM, $10,000 was to be paid to Harvard for the Department of Legal Medicine as soon as shooting of the movie began in October. By December, Harvard had not yet received the money.

Ever shrewd in the ways of business, Lee demanded that MGM hold up their end of the agreement. She insisted that Ford step up and take responsibility as head of the department and collect the money from the studio. Ford, in turn, sought direction from Dr. George P. Berry, successor to Burwell as dean of the medical school, since the deal had been made before he arrived at Harvard, and he was not part of the agreement between the studio and the university.

"Mrs. Lee has asked me repeatedly

whether the money was yet forthcoming," Ford said to Berry. "She has stated emphatically that the original arrangements for this motion picture concerned her alone . . . I gather from several conversations with Mrs. Lee that she has a very proprietary interest in this whole matter."

Failure to collect the money owed to Harvard could jeopardize gifts from Lee in the future. "I am . . . absolutely certain that if [payment] does not come to the Department not only will it jeopardize the quarter of a million dollars eventually promised but it will also cut off the generous gifts which have been received continually into our special fund for the last ten years," Ford said.

Harvard got the money.

Mystery Street opened to positive reviews. The *New York Times* critic said, "There is more science than mystery in this cops-versus-killer number, but it is an adventure which, despite a low budget, is not low in taste or its attention to technical detail, backgrounds and plausibility. It is strong on authenticity." Spigelgass was nominated for the Academy Award for his story.

Today, *Mystery Street* is an obscure film noir murder mystery. To fans of forensic science, *Mystery Street* is known as the first modern procedural crime drama. The forerunner of *Quincy M.E., CSI: Crime Scene Investigation,* and programs of that ilk, *Mystery Street* established a formula that has become one of the most popular genres in film, books, network and cable shows, podcasts, and reality-based programming. Interest in forensic science is so pervasive among the general public that it has produced a so-called *CSI* effect — people now have unreasonably high expectations about scientific evidence.

It soon became apparent that Ford did not have the temperament to head the Department of Legal Medicine. He had little appetite for research, teaching, or the administrative duties that came with the department chairmanship. Lee confronted Ford bluntly with what she saw as a serious problem. "I must confess that it is a mystery to me why the Department of Legal Medicine should be dying on its feet," she wrote to him, "but it certainly is moribund at present, and I shudder to think of the enormous task of reestablishing its former, none too perfect, activities . . . . Have you any suggestions as to how the Department can be restored to life?" Ford had no suggestions to offer.

Lee shared her dismay at the state of her

beloved department with Alan Gregg of the Rockefeller Foundation. "I must confess that I am greatly disappointed in Dr. Ford, as it seemed to be that he was a well-trained and skillful man who was really enthusiastic about Legal Medicine (and I am still of that opinion) but for some reason that I cannot fathom he seems unable to recognize a big opportunity when it lies right in his hand," she told Gregg. "I am loath to discuss this situation with him, as I have already tasted his quick and fiery temper and feel that I have already had all the unpleasantness that I should accept from the personnel of the Department."

Lee hadn't always agreed with Moritz, but at least he got things done. Ford seemed content to sit and wait for something to happen. Under his leadership, the Department of Legal Medicine was doing little research or anything else of note.

Lee had received pushback about the homicide seminars in particular. Allowing state police on the medical school campus was pushing things, but Harvard drew the line at city cops. The university would not allow Boston police officers to attend the homicide seminars, even though the conferences were entirely organized and underwritten by Lee.

"In my opinion, the Department is rapidly dying on its feet," Lee told Gregg, "and that after another year of such a continued slump, I should have no further interest in giving it either my financial or moral support." Gregg advised Lee to cut back her involvement with Harvard — both personally and financially.

Lee made some decisions. She would continue to use Harvard for her homicide seminars but withdraw any other support for the department. There would be no more gifts during her lifetime. And the Nutshell Studies of Unexplained Death would not be given outright to Harvard Medical School. A letter to her banker regarding her taxes for the year 1950 made her intentions clear. Lee asked her banker about the legitimacy of deducting the $3,720 in wages paid to her cabinetmaker, Alton Mosher. "Although no models were presented to Harvard in 1950, two models were loaned for each seminar," Lee wrote. "I call your attention to this item only because Mr. Hovey has raised the question of it being a proper deduction since the models are no longer becoming the property of Harvard."

True to his word, Gardner returned to

forensic science in his 1950 book *The Case of the Musical Cow.* The novel, dedicated to Moritz, is based on a case the pathologist was involved in during his fellowship training in Scotland. Rather than featuring Perry Mason — to the chagrin of many readers who bought the book — the protagonist is a state trooper who uses the police crime lab to clear an innocent suspect and convict the guilty. Gardner paid tribute to Magrath as well, dedicating his 1955 Perry Mason book *The Case of the Glamorous Ghost* to George Burgess Magrath.

Lee and the Department of Legal Medicine were singled out for praise in Gardner's 1952 book *The Court of Last Resort,* which devotes a chapter to the Harvard homicide seminar. "Captain Frances G. Lee is a fabulous character, a woman of around seventy who has donated a fortune to establish a school of legal medicine at Harvard University," he wrote.

After the photo feature in *Life* magazine, Lee and her Nutshell Studies of Unexplained Death were featured in numerous newspaper stories and in national magazines: *Saturday Evening Post, Coronet, Yankee, Popular Mechanics* and many others. The angle of a wealthy elderly woman who made dollhouses of death was irresistible.

Lee felt that writers like Gardner and *Argosy* publisher Harry Steeger were using her to draw in readers. She wanted the focus on legal medicine rather than her — at least during her lifetime.

"I have had to restrain their eagerness at times as they seemed to want to use me as the dramatic figure in their publicity and I feel that the subject itself is dramatic enough and that it is in better taste to omit the personal slant," Lee told her advisory board. "But once I am safely dead, there is nothing I can do about this — if it will further the development of the work, let them use me if it will be right in your eyes, but otherwise leave me out of it," she said. "During my lifetime I shall make every effort to stay in the background."

Despite her aversion to publicity, fame accrued from newspaper and magazine stories brought Lee unwanted attention. She was bombarded with letters from people who had heard about the millionairess and her interest in police science. People wrote her with pleas for help, requests for money, and offers for commercial endorsements. Some told sad stories of injustice and baffling mysteries. She begged off pleas for help from convicted murderers, the desperate loved ones of missing persons, the institutionalized, and the mentally ill who sent Lee pages of scrawled handwriting. "In desperation, I am writing you this letter that you will be able to help, or advise me, as to what I can possibly do to be released from this place, as I am not insane," wrote a resident of the Mayview State Hospital who claimed to have been deliberately inoculated with syphilis.

"Dear Lady" began a letter simply addressed to "Mrs. Frances Glessner Lee, Harvard University, Cambridge, Mass." that Lee apparently ignored. "I am interested in what I read in article 'Murder at Harvard' of you in Sunday Star believe that you could solve some things that Puzzle me since I first got really wise to them 1897–1898."

Lee was offered investigative and forensic artist services and approached with an assortment of endeavors. The Automotive Safety Association tried to pique her interest in traffic safety. An entrepreneur from Long Beach wanted Lee's help in launching a national database of shoplifters and petty thieves for use by retail businesses.

John Crocker Jr., a young clergyman at Trinity Church in Boston's Copley Square, wrote Lee on behalf of Charles E. Warren, a lifer at Charlestown Prison. "He has read of your interests and work in penology in Earl

[sic] Stanley Gardner's book 'Court of Last Resort,' " Crocker wrote. "He himself is in the process of writing a book about himself and the Charlestown Prison. I have not read any part of the book, but he has been in the prison longer than anyone now there. He wants very much to interest people of real stature in his case."

Lee's reply was civil but direct. "While I am entirely sympathetic with your activity on behalf of Mr. Charles E. Warren I am sorry that I am not in a position to give him any assistance," she replied. "I am interested solely in medicolegal subjects and know nothing concerning the subject of criminology, and I cannot add the smallest iota of additional burden to that which I already carry. I admire and like Mr. Erle Stanley Gardner but his over-enthusiastic friendship has given his readers a false impression of what I do."

An exception was made for a distraught mother whose teenage son died by autoerotic asphyxiation. This dangerous practice involves the use of strangulation or suffocation to heighten sexual arousal during masturbation. Partially suspended or strangled by a rope or belt, a person takes himself to the threshold of unconsciousness. Death can be an unintended consequence.

The mother, a woman by the name of Mrs. Wright of Anaheim, California, asked Lee about the shocking and disturbing circumstances under which her son was found, unclothed and with a cord wrapped around his body. The death was ruled a suicide. Mrs. Wright wondered whether it could have been murder. Did such things happen?

Lee took the questions to her experts at Harvard and reported back to Mrs. Wright, explaining the death, mother to mother, compassionately and yet with an unflinching clinical frankness that laid out the facts for the grieving mother to dispel her lingering doubts.

"This appears to be an accidental death, in no way out of keeping with adolescent sexual experimenting," Lee told Mrs. Wright. "Cases of this type are not common, but occur with sufficient frequency to be well recognized."

Mrs. Wright's questions were answered in the format used in law enforcement:

Q.1. Will the rings in the trachea fracture by hanging, especially when all of the weight is not on the noose around the neck?

A.1. Not ordinarily, but it could happen.

Removal of the neck organs could produce these fractures under certain circumstances.

Q.2. Should the eyes have been completely closed if the subject were conscious when hanged?
A.2. This is inconclusive. It might be either way.

Q.3. Isn't it possible that the subject was unconsciousness when hanged?
A.3. Possible, but unlikely. There is no proof and appears to be no evidence that would suggest this possibility.

Q.4. Have you ever known of a male tying himself around the scrotum?
A.4. No, but I have known of other acts as unaccountable or even more so. Great ingenuity is often exercised in sexual experimentation.

In 1950, at seventy-three years of age, Lee faced her greatest challenge to date: a diagnosis of cancer. She was admitted to Phillips House in Boston where she had spent so much time with Magrath years earlier. With the specter of her own mortality looming, Lee took steps to ensure that the flame of legal medicine would not be extinguished by her death. She established a trust and formed the Frances Glessner Lee Foundation to continue sponsorship of the homicide seminars for police officers and Harvard Associates in Police Science.

In order to make sure that her directions were followed to the exact degree, Lee formed an advisory board consisting of five people she considered most trustworthy and fully informed of her vision of legal medicine: her daughter, Martha Batchelder; former U.S. Army Judge Advocate Ralph G. Boyd of Boston; Charles Woodson, superintendent of the Virginia State Police; Francis I McGarraghy, former Air Force criminal investigator and FBI special agent; and her banker, Allan B. Hussander.

"Each member of the Advisory Board has been chosen by me, primarily because I had some implicit confidence in his ability and good judgement," Lee told members of the board, "but also because I believed in his understanding of and sympathy with my aims."

In 1951, Lee wrote a letter to her advisory board that she labeled "Top Secret."

It seems to me well that you should know something of my problems in starting the

Department of Legal Medicine at the Harvard Medical School. First, I am, and always have been, a lone worker and have never found it satisfactory to work at something that has been gone over and over by others until the original meaning and spirit have all been worn out of it. Therefore, when an opportunity came to me to start something completely new in the medical line, I was delighted to take it on. As a girl, I was deeply interested in medicine and nursing, and would have enjoyed taking a training in either one. This was not possible, so Legal Medicine, including medicine and just ordinary common sense, together with some smattering of detective work, made an immediate appeal to me. However, I found that no one including alas! my own self, knew exactly what Legal Medicine was supposed to mean, and at the time — around 1930 — that I first took an active part in its development, there was very little printed material available to help me. So it was necessary to proceed by mainly strength and awkwardness, but fortunately with the skill, knowledge and training of Doctor Magrath to guide me (he, in turn, had really started from scratch), I have been able to accomplish a good deal. Considering that in 1930 the world in general, the medical world in particular, and specifically I myself, had very little idea of "what it was all about." I feel that great strides have been taken in the twenty years since the beginning of the Department at Harvard.

First, I think it was timed right; next, I think that Dr. Sidney Burwell, who became dean at about that time realized that Legal Medicine was the first entirely new department in a medical school in many years, and so decided to ride to personal success on it; and third, I think that Dr. Moritz, the first active head of the Department, was eager for personal publicity and thought he might get it through Legal Medicine.

For me, it has been a long, discouraging struggle against petty jealousies, crass stupidities, and an obstinate unwillingness to learn that has required all the enthusiasm, patience, courage, and tact that I could muster. Being by nature and training a somewhat shy and timid person, this has been a lonely and rather terrifying life that I have lived. Chief amongst the difficulties I have had to meet have been the facts that I never went to school, that I had no letters after my name, and that I was placed in the category of "rich woman who

387

didn't have enough to do." Also, being a woman has made it difficult at times to make the men believe in the project I was furthering, although sometimes, I must own, being a woman had its advantages . . . But the discouragements have been plentiful and severe, but still I feel that I have surmounted most of them and have succeeded in my purposes, perhaps more than I deserved but not more than the magnitude my subject merited.

In the first place, everyone had to be taught what Legal Medicine is, and its potential value, both those who could sponsor it and those who could practice it, as well as the general public who could benefit by it. The President and Fellows of Harvard had to be taught, the Dean of Harvard Medical School had to be taught, and the doctors and lawyers had to be taught. The police had to be taught, most of all of these holding away from it with reluctance to learn. The police superintendents had to be taught, but they were almost without exception willing to learn and send their men to take the course I was finally able to persuade an unwilling Department Head to permit me to offer, and there was the bright spot, the police students themselves, who have been enthusiastic participants and supporters from the outset . . .

Having, during my long life, had a good deal of experience in amalgamating some rather heterogeneous groups of people, I wished to make our classes not "just another school," and so chose to keep the classes small and to inject a definite social quality into them. For this reason I have persisted in giving the class dinners, much against the wishes of the head of the Department, who insistently said, "those dinners are expensive; all that money could be used in the Department to better purpose." But even in the few years of their existence I can plainly see the value of the social contacts these dinners have forwarded. The establishment of the little organization called Harvard Associates in Police Science is another stepping stone along the path toward friendships. It is my firm belief that this society can become powerful for good, for the betterment of the police training, and for improvement in medical investigations . . .

While I know it is said that there is no one in the world whose place cannot be filled, still I believe that Legal Medicine will take something of a slump when I die, for, though I say it myself, I have had enthusiasm, willingness, courage, patience, and persistence, and believe my personality has been effective in what I have been trying to accomplish. I have dearly loved our graduates; have been proud and happy in their successes, and understanding and sympathetic when luck went against them. They have been wonderfully dear and sweet to me and have brought a beautiful happiness to my last years. I have been meticulous in never asking for or seeking a favor, and I conjure you to be the same . . .

My whole object has been to improve the administration of justice, to standardize the methods, to sharpen the existing tools, and to make it easier for the law enforcement officers to do "a good job" and to give the public "a square deal."

Harvard has not been very broad-minded or very generous in its attitude toward the Department of Legal Medicine, but the Rockefeller Foundation has been much more sympathetic. Dr. Moritz was willing to "play ball" as long as there was something in it for him, but never without a fight; and Dr. Ford is much the same, although Dr. Moritz was active and Dr. Ford is inert. Had there been true collaboration from the beginning, Legal Medicine could have been much farther advanced than it is today, but perhaps that would have been growing too fast.

But at any rate, here we are. Please don't let things slump down and disappear. You five will have to learn to go ahead, no matter how many times you are knocked down. But you men already know this far better than I have ever learned it, and then there are five of you to compare the bruises.

What follows in the letter to her advisory board are more than five single-spaced pages with detailed instructions about conducting the week-long homicide seminar, the selection and vetting of students, a timetable for organizing the seminars, how to line up speakers for lectures, and the seating arrangements and menus for the group dinner. No aspect of the seminar was overlooked. According to Lee's directions, the dinners "must be carried out with conspicuous elegance, generosity, and friendliness."

Then she returned to continuing her work:

I suspect that since you are mostly men, you may not run into some of the difficulties that I have from the very outset, but I will hereby warn you that you will find the

Department personnel in no way under-standing of the value or meaning of the Seminars. They see no reason for putting the subjects in a certain order — in their minds, if a subject is to be discussed dur-ing the Seminar week, it makes no differ-ence at what place it is brought forward. Actually, it makes much difference — first things first, and the Class as a whole is not ready for certain subjects until they have been prepared for them. It must be remembered that these men are not scien-tists and there is no intention of making them into scientists. They are not trained in laboratory technique, but it is well for the development of Legal Medicine that they should know how easily certain tests can be made, so they may have a person in their organization who can make these tests for them when needed. Also the chemical demonstrations serve to break up what could easily be too long a day overfilled with too much concentration. These men are adults, some years re-moved from school, and to sit in inactivity from nine to five for nearly a week is dif-ficult for them. This is one reason for cigarettes and is the main reason for plac-ing certain features on the program at the points where they are found . . .

It has been my intention in whatever I have done, to bring about an up-grading of the police in the United States and to thereby place them in a position where they are deserving of the respect and honor which is rightfully theirs, and I charge you with continuing my efforts along these lines to the end that there may be an improvement in the administration of justice in this country. If, singlehanded, I have been able to accomplish as much as I have, you — five of you — with your wider experience and stable masculine judgment, should be able to accomplish wonders . . . I am herewith handing you a lighted torch to bear, with complete confidence that you will not let the flame go out, and so accept my heartfelt thanks and appreciation for the help you have already given me by showing your interest and belief in my work and for the comfort I have in knowing that it will be carried on — farther and more widely than I have been able to do — when I have to leave it.

As for Harvard, Lee was unsparing with her views:

For the past 20 years I have given all of my time and energy and thought, indeed all of my waking hours, to the effort to establish securely Legal Medicine in the United States, not merely to establish a department of Legal Medicine at the Harvard Medical School, although that has been a basic part of the overall picture. Harvard has the reputation of being old fogeyish and ungrateful and stupid and I have indeed found this reputation to be deserved. I therefore have no special wish to further Harvard, but I do feel that there is already there a department together with its library and other equipment, much of which is unique and cannot be duplicated. Moreover, Harvard has a clear cut and well recognized reputation as the first department of Legal Medicine in this country. Therefore I recommend to the Board and to the Foundation that they favor Harvard whenever possible, but I have placed certain restrictions upon Harvard . . . I warn you each and every one that Harvard is clever and sly and will need to be watched constantly or she will take advantage of you and apply any funds you may grant her to her own purposes. This has been so marked a tendency in my lifetime that I have preferred to spend the money myself to procure what I wanted and then to give the result to Harvard. I suggest that whenever possible, you do the same.

Lee concluded her top-secret letter with final words of advice for her advisory board:

Don't forget, it is Legal Medicine to be built up, not Harvard Medical School. Also keep an eye upon tax problems.

Despite the increasing disabilities of advancing age, including heart disease and repeated fractures, Lee maintained a busy schedule for the remaining eleven years of her life. Active in professional associations, Lee attended the second meeting of the American Society for Forensic Science. She was the first female member of the International Association of Chiefs of Police, frequently attending their meetings as well as those of the Massachusetts and New Hampshire Medico-Legal Societies, the New England Policewomen's Association, and many others.

Along with Ralph Mosher's son, Alton, Lee resumed work on several more Nutshell Studies of Unexplained Death dioramas. Alton created a scale model of the Swedish porch of Lee's residence — an enclosed stone patio with a fireplace. Every miniature stone used in the model matched the shape of the actual Swedish porch, reproducing the authenticity to the most minute detail. Lee also worked on a multiple-room diorama and a large model of an apartment building.

The Rocks also continued to be a gathering place for law enforcement officials to visit. Lee's son, John, described the activity at his mother's house during a weekend visit:

We had not been visiting more than a few hours when who should arrive but Captain Schwarz of the Connecticut State Police, and wife. Needless to say, the conversation fell heavily on police work and legal medicine affairs for the remainder of the weekend. Interesting, but I couldn't contribute much, as my own crimes are not for public discussion. The latest of these was covering the 220 miles to Littleton in five and a half hours, flat, including breakfast. This averages 40 mph including breakfast, which mean I spent a lot of time at 65 or more, which is too fast for Vermont's twisty roads. So when the Captain, who had traveled the same route, started to compare notes on elapsed time, I was understandably vague.

December 21, 1951

Lee visited the FBI again and attempted to schedule a meeting with J. Edgar Hoover to discuss the need for a national dental record database that could be invaluable for identifying unknown bodies throughout the country. Hoover told Lee that his official duties, regretfully, made it impossible for him to meet during her visit to Washington, DC, and referred her to one of his staff. According to a Director's Office memo circulated to FBI associate director Clyde Tolson, "When informed of Mr. Hoover's absence, Mrs. Lee declined to talk with anyone else and stated that she wanted to arrange an appointment with Mr. Hoover to discuss a matter that she had written about."

This time, Lee did not get her audience with Hoover.

In the mid-1950s, Harvard officials began considering gently guiding Lee to the door. Lee turned seventy-six years old — the age of mandatory retirement at Harvard — in 1954. The Harvard Corporation noted this fact within weeks of her birthday. In April, the corporation secretary contacted Berry, the medical school dean, about whether Lee's honorary curatorship of the Magrath Library should be terminated.

By then, Lee's involvement with Harvard was limited. She was mostly at the medical school only for the twice-yearly homicide seminars for police officers, and her titles with the university were largely ceremonial. Aside from occasional requests for lecturers at the homicide seminar, the burden she posed on the university was minimal. Berry questioned whether it was prudent to bite, however gently, a hand that fed the university.

"No salary from Harvard is involved," Berry said to the corporation secretary. "Mrs. Lee has made generous contributions to our work. Unless changes in the times have posed financial problems for her since she told us about the plans she had for the disposition of her estate, I believe that the Department of Legal Medicine will find that she has left substantial sums in her will. In the light of these circumstances, I hope that the Corporation will agree that an exception is justified."

David W. Bailey, secretary of the corporation, told Berry that Lee would be allowed to keep her honorary title. "I have talked again with President Pusey about the matter, and he agrees that under the circumstances it will be a happy thought to leave Mrs. Lee's present appointment undisturbed despite the fact that she has almost totted up the psalmist's four score years."

Berry shared the good news with Ford. "You will agree with me, I am sure, that persuading them to continue to let her hold this honorary post was in our best interests!" Berry said.

The following year, the issue of Lee's "retirement" was put to rest for good. "So you may have a written record in your files, I write to tell you that we do wish to continue Mrs. Lee on the University's roster as Honorary Curator of the George Burgess Magrath Library of Legal Medicine even though she has passed the compulsory retirement age. It is reasonable to assume, furthermore, that we shall continue Mrs. Lee in the honorary post indefinitely."

Colonel Woodson, superintendent of the Virginia State Police, received an enticing invitation from Lee through her foundation — the opportunity to spend two weeks in England and one week in Germany for the purpose of studying the police systems in those countries.

Being a prominent member of the law enforcement community and an officer in the International Association of Chiefs of Police, Woodson thought it prudent — even though he had known Lee for years and was a member of her advisory board — to check with the FBI to see whether the agency knew of any affiliation with subversive organizations of individuals. It was the height of the Cold War in 1955, and a link to communism could ruin a career.

The FBI special agent in charge of the Boston field office filed a report to Hoover about meeting Lee at a reception she held at The Rocks for the annual conference of the National Association of Attorneys Generals. "This reception reportedly cost CAPTAIN LEE approximately $3500 and she imported caterers from New York City to handle all arrangements," the report said. "The Bureau has previously been advised with regard to the background of Captain LEE. She is approximately 75 years of age, practically an invalid, and has been deeply interested in Criminology and Legal Medicine for many years."

The all-clear was given by teletype from the Boston field office to the FBI headquarters, then relayed back to Woodson: "NO DEROGATORY INFO CONTAINED IN BOSFILES PERTAINING TO HER."

In the late 1950s, the tranquility of The Rocks was disturbed by a work crew from the New Hampshire Highway Department. A new expressway was being surveyed that would transect the Glessner estate, separating about a third of the land from the rest of the property.

Approaching eighty years old, practically deaf and blind, Lee was as willing as ever to muster up a battle. "I've been fighting the Highway Dept. to take their darned road elsewhere, but to no use," she wrote in a letter to her son, John.

According to Lee, the highway crew said to her, "As soon as it is determined exactly how much of your land we will take you will be offered a fair price for it."

"Oh no, it won't be a fair price," she responded. "You will offer me the lowest figure you think you can get away with. If you don't do that you will show that you are not a good businessman."

The work crew and Lee parted as friends. "If I must lose my farm, you will find me a good loser," she told them. "I will not make unnecessary difficulties but will cooperate with you to the best of my ability." They agreed to do the same.

Lee invited the work crew to lunch and served them cocktails before the meal. "I had them come up to lunch two weeks ago and gave them a swell meal," she wrote to her son. "We had some drinks all around before lunch and I drank to them individually and by name and added 'down with the Highway Department!' "

Work crews drilled core samples to assess the underlying geology of the area. "I was praying for quicksand but they got solid granite," Lee said. They gave Lee two pieces of granite core taken from her property, heavy cylinders of gray rock about two feet long. She had the granite polished and made into table lamps.

The road surveyed by the work crew became I-93, which now runs from Boston through Concord and the White Mountains to Waterford, Vermont. Lee remained living in her cottage at The Rocks until, as time went on, difficulty walking limited her mobility. In 1957, Lee purchased a prefabricated house trailer and had it placed behind the cottage. Gleaming aluminum finished in white and lavender enamel, the mobile home looked like a space-age module in the rustic setting of The Rocks. Lee was delighted with her new scaled-down home. Inside the trailer, she could move about without a wheelchair or walker. Everything was new and worked. It was well-illuminated, had plenty of hot water for one person, and had more electrical outlets than

Lee knew what to do with. Alton Mosher set a table and comfortable chair in front of a large window with a view of Mount Washington, and Lee planned to begin writing her own books there.

Lee's spirit and energy never flagged, despite ongoing health problems and repeated bone fractures. In the summer of 1958, she broke a rib while leaning over an armchair to pick up a letter that had dropped to the floor. Whatever the obstacle, Lee put it behind her at day's end with a shaker of cold, delicious martinis. "The cocktail hour has come to be important time with me — not for the liquor, but for the pause, the relaxation, the daintiness and prettiness of the service," she said in a letter to her family. "In the day to day living, it is unwise to let it become entirely utilitarian — some of the graces and formal gracious living must be included or one would go completely to seed."

In another letter to her family, Lee reflected on her life. "As I sit quietly here, an old woman, I think back over my life and realize what a wonderfully rich life it has been," she said. "Recently I read somewhere that when we are young, we cannot understand the problems of the old for we haven't experienced them yet ourselves, and when we are old we have largely forgotten the problems of the young. But I haven't forgotten, and I believe I am nearer a sympathetic understanding of the problems of those younger than they think possible. Anyway, it's a good world and I am grateful I have been given a chance to play a part in it."

In February 1961, Parker Glass, assistant to Ford in the Department of Legal Medicine, wrote to Lee with heartbreaking news. An accumulation of snow and ice on the roof of Building E-1 had allowed water to leak onto the Nutshell Studies of Unexplained Death. Several dioramas had suffered water damage.

"The most serious damage is to the large model in the center of the room, the water from the roof coming directly into that model," Glass wrote. "When discovered, the model (I suppose because of the excessive dampness) had been growing mold on many of the leather and cloth components. It is truly a sorry sight to see."

Lee inspected the Nutshells, made the necessary repairs as possible, and had them back in their cabinets in time for the police homicide seminar in the fall of 1961, the last one she attended even as her cancer had returned and spread.

12
POSTMORTEM

January 27, 1962

Frances Glessner Lee died at her home at The Rocks a month short of her eighty-fourth birthday. The immediate cause of Lee's death was intestinal obstruction, which was related to liver cancer that had metastasized from breast cancer. She had ascites — an accumulation of fluid in the abdominal cavity — due to the liver failure as well as decompensating heart failure that produced a generalized swelling of her body.

The mass for Lee at the Littleton church was attended by most of the employees of The Rocks, most of the staff from the Department of Legal Medicine, six New Hampshire state police officers in uniform, and eight or ten police officers from other states. She was buried in the Maple Street Cemetery in Bethlehem, New Hampshire.

News of Lee's death brought accolades from throughout the United States and overseas. "Mrs. Lee was unquestionably one of the world's most astute criminologists," said Parker Glass, who had been secretary for the Department of Legal Medicine since the days of Magrath. "She was acquainted with and respected by top criminologists all over the world."

Cyril Cuthbert, founder of the forensic science laboratory at Scotland Yard, said Lee was "the only person in the world going out of her way to teach legal medicine to police."

Erle Stanley Gardner's obituary of Lee appeared on the front page of the *Boston Sunday Globe*. He gave the newspaper his obit at no charge as a labor of love.

She was . . . my personal friend because I appreciated her grim, relentless pursuit of an objective, her uncompromising insistence on the best and her loyalty to the causes she espoused and to her friends generally.

Capt. Lee had a strong individuality, a unique, unforgettable character, was a fiercely competent fighter, and a practical idealist.

The cause of legal medicine and law enforcement suffered a great blow with her passing and yet for years the country will benefit because of her dogged determination, her down-to-earth grasp of the problems with which she was confronted, and her unswerving determination to find a solution by persistence, diplomacy, charm, and, if all else failed, by downright battering ram in-fighting.

She was a wonderful woman.

During her lifetime, Lee was bestowed numerous honors and awards. She was given an honorary doctorate of laws from New England College in 1956, and two years later an honorary law degree from Drexel University. Lee was an honorary captain in the Maine State Police, the Vermont State Police, the Massachusetts State Police, the Virginia State Police, the Connecticut State Police, and the Chicago Police Department, an honorary major in the Kentucky State Police, and an honorary captain in the U.S. Navy. In recognition of her extraordinary contributions to the advancement of legal medicine and forensic pathology, the Institute of Medicine of Chicago created a category for Lee: Citizen Fellow of the Institute of Medicine.

One recognition that was never granted to Lee — the one that would have held the most profound meaning for her — was an honorary degree from Harvard.

Without the support of Lee, the Department of Legal Medicine at Harvard Medical School went into a death spiral.

By 1963, Harvard estimated that consulting on nearly four hundred postmortem cases a year cost the university about $50,000 annually — an amount considered an unacceptable burden on the medical school. A committee reporting to Harvard president Nathan M. Pusey and medical school dean George P. Berry recommended that the Department of Legal Medicine be made into a division in the Department of Pathology.

After repeated clashes with his colleagues, Ford was relieved of his academic duties, and his appointment to the Department of Legal Medicine ended in June 1965. He continued to serve as Suffolk County medical examiner. Harvard ceased operations of the Department of Legal Medicine on June 30, 1967. All the books and other material in the Magrath Library of Legal Medicine were subsumed in the collection of the medical school library, now called the Countway Library of Medicine.

Lee's legacy at Harvard is commemorated

with the appointment of the Frances Glessner Lee Professor of Legal Medicine. As of this writing, this position is held by a pediatric anesthesiologist who is the director of the Center for Bioethics. Harvard does not have a forensic pathologist on the medical school faculty.

As head of pathology at Case Western Reserve University, Moritz was involved in the founding of the Law and Medicine Center, which aimed at becoming one of the country's premier institutes of forensic medicine education. In a 1958 *True* magazine article, Moritz estimated at the time that as many as five thousand homicides went undetected every year in the United States. "It is an amazing truth that in most localities of the United States the official medical examination of unexplained deaths is so casual and inexpert that clever murderers often go free," he said.

Moritz was involved as an expert witness in the July 4, 1954, murder of Marilyn Reese Sheppard in Bay Village, Ohio. An investigation by Cuyahoga County coroner Dr. Samuel Gerber, a well-regarded medical doctor, pointed to the victim's husband, neurosurgeon Dr. Samuel Sheppard. Sam Sheppard was found with nonlethal injuries and claimed that a "bushy-haired man" was responsible for killing Marilyn and attacking him.

The investigation was conducted poorly from the onset, beginning with the failure to secure the crime scene. The Sheppard house was open to bystanders, including Cleveland Browns quarterback Otto Graham, a friend of the family. Local newspapers turned on Sheppard. Coverage of the case was so intense that the U.S. Supreme Court ruled that the excessive publicity denied Sheppard a fair trial.

Sheppard was acquitted of murder in a 1966 retrial. By then an alcoholic unable to practice medicine anymore, he later performed as a professional wrestler as "Killer" Sam Sheppard. The Sheppard murder was the basis for the television series *The Fugitive* and the subsequent theatrical film.

Moritz lived until 1986 when he died of natural causes at age eighty-eight.

On August 3, 1970, Dr. Richard Ford died of a self-inflicted gunshot to the head.

Lee left an estate worth almost $1 million at the time of her death. In her will, the bulk of the estate was divided between her two surviving children — John G. Lee and Martha Batchelder. A portion of Lee's estate was set aside for the Frances Glessner Lee Fund for the Study of Legal Medicine. Harvard was never mentioned in Lee's will. The university was left nothing.

In 1978, John G. Lee and Martha Batchelder donated The Rocks to the Society for the Protection of New Hampshire Forests to continue the conservation and restoration efforts began by their grandfather, John Jacob Glessner, a century earlier. As a provision of their gift, The Rocks must always have a crop in their fields. For more than three decades, that crop has been Christmas trees. The Rocks is open to the public and hosts activities throughout the year, ranging from a network of well-maintained trails to school trips for children to learn about making maple syrup.

In August 2018, the New Hampshire Division of Historical Resources unveiled a highway historical marker on Route 302 at The Rocks, honoring Lee as the mother of forensic science and creator of the Nutshell Studies of Unexplained Death.

Ownership of the Glessners' Prairie Avenue residence went through several hands over the years. The heirs of the Glessner property deeded the residence to the Armour Institute, now the Illinois Institute of

Technology, which leased it to the Lithographic Technical Foundation. The house was used by the vocational school until 1965 when it was put on the market for $70,000. With no takers, H. H. Richardson's landmark residence was slated for demolition.

The Prairie Avenue residence was saved from the wrecking ball when a handful of local architects and preservationists joined to form the Chicago School of Architecture Foundation. The foundation bought the house for $35,000 in December 1966. Programming and exhibitions began within a year, and a regular tour program started in 1971.

In 1994, the foundation spun off the Glessner House museum as a separate nonprofit corporation. The Glessner House museum is open to the public for tours and special events in the Historic Prairie Avenue District on Chicago's South Side. With the original floor plan intact, the residence has undergone extensive work to restore original appearances and furnishings. Members of the Glessner family have returned many pieces of furniture and decorative objects to bring the residence back to its heyday. Three generations of Glessners are responsible for the Prairie Avenue house surviving to this day.

In March 2019, the Glessner House museum unveiled the restoration of Lee's childhood bedroom, including her bed designed by Isaac Scott.

Lee presided over every homicide seminar without fail until shortly before her death. In her later years, speaking to her involved yelling into a hearing aid the size of a pack of cigarettes that she held aloft. The seminars continued to be held at Harvard under the supervision of her daughter, Martha Batchelder, until 1967 when Harvard ended the training seminars for police officers.

Russell Fisher, chief medical examiner for the State of Maryland, who had trained with Moritz and was one of Lee's favorites, approached Harvard about continuing the homicide seminar in Baltimore. With the consent of Lee's heirs, the President and Fellows of Harvard College voted to permanently loan the Nutshell Studies of Unexplained Death to the Maryland Medical-Legal Foundation for the purposes of training police officers in the renamed Frances Glessner Lee Seminar in Homicide Investigation.

When the first Frances Glessner Lee

Seminar in Homicide Investigation was held in Baltimore during the week of May 6–10, 1968, the Nutshell cases were assigned to participants by Fisher. The reviewer of the cases, the keeper of Lee's confidential solutions to the dioramas, was Parker Glass, the Department of Legal Medicine secretary who, aside from Lee, had spent more time with the dioramas than anybody else. Having looked at the Nutshell Studies for more than twenty years, Glass couldn't help but notice a few things out of place, possibly the result of jostling during the trip from Boston.

"There are two minor items that might be changed," he wrote in a letter to Fisher's secretary, Dorothy Hartel. "In the scene showing the gal dead in a closet with her throat cut, the little knife is missing. Should be beside her hand on the floor. In the living room scene showing the wife dead on the stairway, there is a vase on the floor beside the divan. It should not be there. One of the boys [attending the seminar] insisted that this was indication of some kind of struggle in the room. If I am invited for next seminar, I perhaps could look over the models in their new home for any misleading changes."

Today, the Frances Glessner Lee Seminar in Homicide Investigation is held at the Forensic Medical Center for the State of Maryland in Baltimore. The seminars are conducted in accordance with the traditions set by Lee, although admission is more open than her strict invitation-only rules. Students still receive a diploma that says "Harvard Associates in Police Science" and a HAPS lapel pin. Every seminar has a group photo.

On the second night, seminar participants go out for a fine dinner at one of the best steakhouses in Baltimore. Food is not served on gold-leaf place settings, but it's still a pretty good meal.

In 2017, after the seminars had been conducted in Baltimore for half a century, a law firm representing the President and Fellows of Harvard College sent a letter to Harvard Associates in Police Science. The attorneys said that their clients were "troubled by the implication that Harvard Medical School and your organization are affiliated." At the request of the President and Fellows of Harvard College, lest students mistakenly believe they received a degree from Harvard, the HAPS website and the diplomas given at the conclusion of the homicide seminar now include the disclaimer "Not affiliated with Harvard University."

The Nutshell Studies of Unexplained Death are still used as Lee intended, for training police officers to observe and report their findings. One of the dioramas — Two Rooms — was irreparably damaged or destroyed in the 1960s, leaving eighteen in existence used for teaching. The disposition of Two Rooms is unknown.

Although more than seventy years old, the Nutshell Studies of Unexplained Death serve a purpose that cannot be duplicated by any other medium. Not even state-of-the-art virtual reality approaches the experience of viewing a three-dimensional setting.

Despite their continued usefulness, after more than seven decades, the materials Lee used to make the Nutshell Studies were suffering the ravages of time. Some materials were cracking and warping. Exposure to years of heat and ultraviolet light had caused damage to some surfaces. Several of the dioramas contained sheets of asbestos that in some cases was crumbling and could be dangerous to those who maintained the models. An aging electrical system posed an unknown risk of fire.

During 2017, for the first time since they had been assembled by Lee, the Nutshell Studies underwent an extensive conservation by experts from the Smithsonian Institution's American Art Museum. Under the direction of object conservator Ariel O'Connor, the dioramas were painstakingly cleaned, repaired, and strengthened to slow or stop the effects of aging.

Smithsonian lighting director Scott Rosenfeld replaced the incandescent bulbs in the Nutshell Studies with custom-made computer-controlled light-emitting diodes encased in small glass bulbs to mimic vintage lighting. The electrical system now uses less energy, produces less heat and damaging wavelengths, and poses less risk of fire.

By the time the team of conservators, artists, model makers, and lighting experts had finished working on the dioramas, the Nutshell Studies were preserved for generations.

For three months, the Nutshell Studies of Unexplained Death had their first — and likely only — public exhibition at the Smithsonian's Renwick Gallery, across the street from the White House in Washington, DC. More than one hundred thousand people attended the exhibition, *Murder Is Her Hobby.* It was, at the time, the second-most attended exhibition in the history of the museum.

Upon the conclusion of the Renwick exhibition, the dioramas were carefully packed in custom-made boxes and returned to their cabinets in the Forensic Medical Center in Baltimore where they continue to be used in the homicide seminar. The Nutshell Studies are not open to the general public.

Today, the United States is served by a patchwork of 2,342 separate death investigation systems — some state-wide, some by county, some regional. There are no federal laws or national standards about how unexplained deaths are to be investigated. There is little consistency from place to place in terms of who conducts a death investigation, that person's qualifications, the conditions under which a forensic investigation is indicated, and how it is conducted. How a death is investigated depends on where a person dies. Since Boston introduced medical examiners in 1877, the growth of medical examiner systems throughout the United States has been painfully slow. Of the 3,137 counties in the United States, more than

418

two-thirds are still served by coroners. About half of the total U.S. population is still under the jurisdiction of coroners.

Every year, approximately 1 million sudden and violent deaths in the United States are referred for forensic investigation. At least half a million of these unexplained deaths are never subject to a thorough inquiry by a qualified forensic pathologist. There is no way to estimate how many murders slip below the radar every year in the United States.

As of this writing, medical examiner systems are present in the District of Columbia and twenty-two states: Alaska, Arizona, Connecticut, Delaware, Florida, Iowa, Maine, Maryland, Massachusetts, Michigan, New Hampshire, New Jersey, New Mexico, North Carolina, Oklahoma, Oregon, Rhode Island, Tennessee, Utah, Vermont, Virginia, and West Virginia. The most recent state to convert from coroners to medical examiners was Alaska in 1996.

Less than a third of the twenty-eight states with coroners require them to have training in forensic science.

Eleven states are exclusively on the coroner system (Colorado, Idaho, Kansas, Louisiana, Nebraska, Nevada, North Dakota, Ohio, Pennsylvania, South Dakota, and

Wyoming), while seventeen states have both coroners and medical examiners. For example, Los Angeles, Ventura, San Francisco, and San Diego have medical examiners, while the remainder of California is served by coroners.

Despite the efforts of Lee, Oscar Schultz, and many others going back to the 1940s and earlier, Cook County — which includes the City of Chicago — didn't have a medical examiner until 1976. As the only medical examiner office in Illinois, the agency covers half of the state's population. The rest of Illinois is under the jurisdiction of 101 coroners — some elected, some appointed — of various backgrounds. By law, they are required to take a one-week course of basic coroner training upon assuming office.

Only one jurisdiction — Charleston, South Carolina — has ever reverted from medical examiners to a coroner system. In 1972, the city implemented a dual system in which a medical examiner shared responsibility with a coroner. As one might expect, the approach was plagued with conflict. Public confidence in death investigation was such that political efforts were undertaken to pull all funding from the medical examiner's office. Since 2001, Charleston has been served by elected coroners.

The reasons for inertia against adoption of medical examiner systems are the same as they were in Lee's time: political opposition, resistance to giving up a local authority, the fairly high initial investment cost to set up a well-equipped medical examiner office. One of the most serious obstacles to the wider acceptance of the medical examiner system is a severe shortage of manpower. There simply aren't enough forensic pathologists to serve the entire United States.

According to the National Association of Medical Examiners, there are four to five hundred forensic pathologists working as medical examiners in the United States. The country needs two to three times as many to sufficiently cover the population, but medical schools are not producing forensic pathologists in great numbers.

Of the eighteen thousand young doctors who graduate from medical school every year, only 3 percent, or about 550 individuals, choose to train in pathology. After a three-year residency, most of these pathologists work in hospitals or clinical laboratories, with less than 10 percent electing to undergo an additional year of fellowship training to specialize in forensic pathology.

Since Lee established the first training program at Harvard's Department of Legal Medicine, the number of forensic pathology fellowship training programs in the United States has grown to thirty-nine. At present, there are seventy-eight forensic pathology fellowship positions approved by the Accreditation Council for Graduate Medical Education. Only fifty-four of these positions are actually funded, and about 20 percent are vacant in any given year for lack of a suitable fellowship candidate.

In recent years, an average of thirty-eight board-certified forensic pathologists enter the workforce annually. This number is not enough to replace pathologists who are reaching retirement age and leaving the workforce, much less to expand medical examiner systems throughout the country. There remains a persistent shortage of qualified forensic pathologists in the United States.

Attracting doctors to careers in forensic pathology is difficult. Since medical examiners are typically government employees, the pay is generally less than what can be earned as a pathologist in a hospital or the private sector. The work is frequently unpleasant and often done in facilities that are aging and underfunded. Whether these trends can be changed remains to be seen.

Despite Lee's abiding belief in the superiority of the medical examiner system as opposed to coroners, it would be inaccurate to claim that medical examiner systems don't have problems. A search of news stories from recent years will reveal scandals and crises in Boston, Connecticut, Los Angeles, Chicago, Delaware, and many other medical examiner offices.

A study by the U.S. Department of Justice found that investigators examine the crime scene in only about 62 percent of cases referred for medicolegal investigation. The prudent approach to questionable deaths is to have a trained investigator at every scene, every time. Fewer than half of the forensic investigations involve an autopsy, and despite what viewers of procedural crime dramas are led to believe, death scenes are processed for criminal evidence in only about 5 percent of investigations.

According to Dr. Randy Hanzlick, past president of the National Association of Medical Examiners, about a third of medical examiner offices in the United States lack a toxicology laboratory. The same proportion lack a histology laboratory, and an equal number lack in-house X-ray services. The absence of these essential tools can lead to cutting corners, needless delays, and other tragic unforeseen circumstances.

In 2013, an eleven-year old boy died while staying at a Best Western motel in Boone, North Carolina. He was found to have died from carbon monoxide intoxication. Exhaust from a swimming pool pump was drawn into the victim's room by the ventilation system. Two other people had died in the same motel room two months earlier. However, blood tests that revealed carbon monoxide intoxication were sent to a state laboratory by the medical examiner. Results took more than six weeks and were received a week before the child died. A forensic medical center with an in-house toxicology laboratory should have carbon monoxide results in a week or less. Had a warning about a potential carbon monoxide leak into a motel room been raised in a timely manner, a death may have been avoided.

In many instances, the problems affecting forensic medical centers are a lack of resources, a lack of funding, a lack of training and adherence to standards of practice, and a lack of support.

The science of forensic science is always evolving. DNA "fingerprinting" is a good example. Since DNA evidence emerged into the public consciousness in the 1990s, more than 360 people convicted of crimes have been exonerated by DNA evidence according to the Innocence Project. The number of innocent people who were executed or died in prison will never be known.

The problem with DNA evidence is that the results can be misinterpreted. Several prominent news stories highlight the problem of DNA evidence misused to implicate an innocent person. A recent study by the National Institute of Standards and Technology revealed that 74 out of 108 crime laboratories the agency tested falsely implicated an innocent person in a hypothetical crime. DNA fingerprinting is among the areas being given a second look for scientific reliability, along with bite marks, arson evidence, and conditions such as shaken baby syndrome.

The pursuit of truth must be relentless, Captain Lee reminds us. Scientific facts must be followed wherever they lead to clear the innocent and convict the guilty.

A NOTE FROM THE AUTHOR

On a winter morning in 2012, I was among a dozen or so editors touring the State of Maryland's state-of-the-art forensic medical center in Baltimore. We all worked for Patch, an organization of hyperlocal news sites owned at the time by AOL-Huffington Post. Through covering the news at my site, I became acquainted with an individual active in my community, Mike Eagle, who worked as the director of IT for the Office of the Chief Medical Examiner. I asked Mike to give us a tour of the state's new facility, which he was kind enough to do.

We met with the chief medical examiner, Dr. David Fowler, for an informal, off-the-record chat in a fourth-floor conference room. In the next room, behind a door labeled "Room 417 Pathology Exhibit," was the famous collection of eighteen incredibly detailed dioramas known as the Nutshell Studies of Unexplained Death.

I knew all about the Nutshell Studies and their creator, Frances Glessner Lee. At least I thought I did. I first wrote about the Nutshell Studies in 1992 for *American Medical News,* the weekly newspaper of the American Medical Association. At the time, *American Medical News* paid very well for feature stories with a medical interest angle, such as doctors with unusual hobbies. I wrote articles about a medical motorcycling club, a rather genial biker gang of doctors and allied health professionals, and a surgeon who studied ancient Egyptian medical texts.

Of the thousands of stories I wrote over the years, the Nutshell Studies is the one that stuck with me. I had come to know the previous chief medical examiner, Dr. John Smialek, and a handful of others at the OCME by return visits to see the Nutshell Studies. Friends and family, knowing about my connection, periodically asked me to arrange a visit to see the dioramas. Every time I looked at the models, I noticed new things. The Nutshell Studies never ceased to amaze me.

After meeting with Dr. Fowler on that winter morning, Mike led our group around the dazzling 120,000-square-foot forensic medical center. We saw the brightly lit two-story autopsy rooms — each a huge, gleaming, voluminous space — the biosafety suite with smaller autopsy rooms under negative pressure, the radiology room with a CT and a low-dose full-body X-ray machine, and the histology and toxicology laboratories. It was all very impressive. The OCME of Maryland, regarded as one of the best in the United States, had a stellar facility to match its reputation.

While showing us Scarpetta House, the studio apartment–like forensic investigator training facility on the OCME's fourth floor gifted by novelist Patricia Cornwell, Mike mentioned to our group that the agency had an opening for a new position — an executive assistant to the chief medical examiner who would serve as public information officer for the OCME. They were looking for somebody with media experience, ideally with a medical background, who had a basic grasp of the law and was comfortable dealing with police, lawyers, and the public. The OCME never had a public information officer before, so this was something new.

My background seemed to fit the criteria. I had been an EMT-paramedic and even completed most of nursing school before sidling into journalism. I worked in and around hospitals for years. Police and lawyers don't rattle me. Would I like to work in the same building as the Nutshell Studies? Yes, please.

I got the job. The leap from journalism to forensic medicine isn't as far as it might seem. Both fields are dedicated to establishing facts: who, what, when, where, why, and how. Both require critical thinking and a skeptical attitude. Medical examiners, in a sense, write the last chapter of a person's life.

It didn't take long for a variety of diorama-related tasks to be added to the miscellany of my duties. Jerry D, the keeper of the secret Nutshell Studies solutions, asked me to change the light bulbs in the dioramas as they burned out and showed me where the keys to the cabinets are kept. There is no manual or instructions for the dioramas, so I learned a lot about them. When filmmakers and photographers requested access to the Nutshell Studies, they were directed to me because I was the only person willing to take the time to accommodate them. I met members of Frances Glessner Lee's family when they came to visit and was honored to share a fancy dinner with two of her grandchildren — John Maxim Lee and Percy Lee Langstaff — during the Francis Glessner Lee Seminar in Homicide Investigation. My understanding of Frances Glessner Lee deepened by engaging with people like William Tyre, executive director and curator of the Glessner House museum in Chicago.

Although there was no formal title, I became the de facto curator of the Nutshell Studies. I collected images, artwork, and documents related to the models. When the dioramas, fragile seventy-year-old artifacts at risk of irreparable damage, underwent conservation by experts from the Smithsonian American Art Museum in preparation for their first and only public exhibition, I was present to observe at every step. The examination of the dioramas by conservator Ariel O'Connor and her team revealed an abundance of previously unknown information about the composition of the materials Lee used and how she constructed the models.

When people see the Nutshell Studies, they often ask the same questions. How did Lee get involved in forensic science? How did she choose the cases to depict in the dioramas? Why didn't she go to college? What was she like as a person? Although I'd known about Lee for twenty-five years, maybe knew more about her than anybody else on earth, I didn't know the answers to those questions.

Lee has been the inspiration for a documentary, a coffee-table picture book, at least two collections of poetry, and even a plot arc on a popular forensic science television drama. Her life story had never been told. Articles about Lee and the Nutshell Studies that I read in print and online were riddled with errors and misinformation. Lee is depicted as a rich old woman who made morbid dollhouses. I knew she was so much more than that. She was an agent of change: a reformer, educator, and advocate.

The need for Lee's story to be told became increasingly obvious. Who could be trusted to tell the story fairly, honestly, diligently, and thoroughly? Who could be relied upon to present the facts without trying to make Lee serve an agenda? The only person I'd trust is me. So I undertook this assignment out of respect and obligation to Lee's legacy.

Lee demanded that investigators relentlessly pursue the facts to determine the truth and follow the evidence wherever it leads. The telling of her own story deserves no less. I approached this subject as a journalist, reporting on historical events. I have endeavored to present the facts without speculation or embellishment. I don't know if I could ever have met Lee's exacting standards of perfection, but I hope that I have done her justice.

READING GROUP GUIDE

1. Before Lee and others began reforming the field of forensic science, coroners regularly committed malpractice either through ineptitude or corruption. Do you think cases like these still occur today? How can this be avoided?
2. Lee came from an elite Chicago family that was famous for its patronage of the arts. Discuss Lee's (and her brother George's) childhood. How did it influence her as an adult?
3. When nine-year-old Lee needed to have her tonsils removed, one doctor recommended coating her tonsils in cocaine before removing them, while another recommended using ether as an anesthetic. What was your reaction to these dangerous medical practices?
4. Lee navigated a world run by wealthy men with ease, even gaining the respect and friendship of a few. Discuss the ways

she formed relationships with them. How did she go about earning their trust?

5. A large part of Lee's success was aided by her wealth. In what areas was she successful without the influence of money?

6. Characterize the relationship between Lee and Dr. Magrath. In what ways were they similar? How were they different? Was their relationship mutually beneficial?

7. Many of Lee's projects, especially the *Anatomography in Picture, Verse and Music,* blended scientific studies with artistic creations. Do you think this sets Lee apart from many of her contemporaries? What are the benefits of combining these two seemingly incongruous styles?

8. Moritz dedicated a book to Lee and even asked her to be the editor of a medical journal. Given the gendered prejudice of the time — women weren't even allowed to attend Harvard — discuss the significance of Lee's efforts being recognized by a prominent man in the field.

9. Lee was zealous in her protection of the medical library she cultivated for Harvard. Why do you think that is?

10. Despite her huge role in the development of the Harvard Medical School, Lee's promotion to Consultant to the Department of Legal Medicine was not

acknowledged in the school catalog. Why do you think, after all her work, she could not be publicly recognized? Can you think of other instances in history when women's achievements went unrecognized? Can you think of a modern occurrence?

11. Lee wanted all attention to remain focused on legal medicine and chose to stay out of the limelight. Do you think this forwarded her cause? In what ways would public recognition have been beneficial?

12. Some have noted that Lee did not have many close associations with other women and seemed to prefer to collaborate with men. Many of her greatest accomplishments were achieved in partnership with men — Lee and Magrath, Lee and Moritz, Lee and Gardner. Why do you think she may have sought the company of men over that of other women?

13. Women like Evelyn J. Briggs and Kathryn B. Haggerty were eventually incorporated into the forensic training program. What challenges do you think they faced as women in a primarily male environment? Discuss the ways Lee made them feel comfortable.

14. The venture to instill a medical examiner system in each state has been slow-going: as of 2019, out of fifty states, only twenty-

two have medical examiner systems in place. Do you think Lee would see this slow transformation as a victory?

NOTES

ABBREVIATIONS
ARM Alan R. Moritz
CHM Center for the History of Medicine at Countway Library, Harvard University
CSB C. Sidney Burwell
FGL Frances Glessner Lee
GHM Glessner House museum
RAC Rockefeller Archive Center

NOTES
1: Legal Medicine

Lee unable to attend seminar due to heart attack: Letter from FGL to ARM, August 10, 1944, CHM.

"Men are dubious of": Pete Martin, "How Murderers Beat the Law," *Saturday Evening Post,* December 10, 1949.

"The models are none": Letter from FGL to ARM, August 10, 1944, CHM.

"Resolved that Mrs. Frances G. Lee": Resolu-

tion enclosed in letter from ARM to FGL, October 6, 1944, CHM.

One in five deaths are sudden: About 10 percent of deaths are due to violence or unnatural causes, and about 10 percent of deaths are due to unknown or obscure causes that require inquiry. Committee on Medicolegal Problems, "Medical Science in Crime Detection," *Journal of the American Medical Association* 200, no. 2 (April 10, 1967): 155–160.

The earliest methodical inquiries: Sources for historical descriptions of coroners include Jeffrey Jentzen, *Death Investigation in America: Coroners, Medical Examiners and the Pursuit of Medical Certainty* (Cambridge, MA: Harvard University Press, 2009), and Russell S. Fisher, "History of Forensic Pathology and Related Laboratory Sciences," in *Medicolegal Investigation of Death,* 2nd ed., ed. Werner U. Spitz and Russell S. Fisher (Springfield, IL: Charles C. Thomas, 1980).

Coroners are responsible for answering two questions: Theodore Tyndale, "The Law of Coroners," *Boston Medical and Surgical Journal* 96 (1877): 243–258.

One of the earliest American inquests: Portions of this section are drawn from Bruce

Goldfarb, "Death Investigation in Maryland," in *The History of the National Association of Medical Examiners*, 2016 ed., 235–264, https://www.thename.org/assets/docs/NAME%20e-book%202016%20final%2006-14-16.pdf. Other sources include Julie Johnson-McGrath, "Speaking for the Dead: Forensic Pathologists and Criminal Justice in the United States," *Science, Technology, and Human Values* 20, no. 4 (October 1, 1995): 438–459; Michael Clark and Catherine Crawford, eds., *Legal Medicine in History* (Cambridge, UK: Cambridge University Press, 1994); Jentzen, *Death Investigation in America;* Fisher, "History of Forensic Pathology."

Thomas Baldridge's instructions: William G. Eckert, ed., *Introduction to Forensic Sciences*, 2nd ed. (New York: Elsevier, 1992), 12.

"Upon notice or suspicion": Aric W. Dutelle and Ronald F. Becker, *Criminal Investigation*, 5th ed. (Burlington, MA: Jones & Bartlett Learning, 2013), 8.

Baldridge inquest: J. Hall Pleasants, ed., *Proceedings of the County Court of Charles County, 1658–1666*, Archives of Maryland 1936, xl–xli; "An inquest taken before the Coroner, at mattapient in the county of St maries, on Wednesday the 31. Of January

1637," USGenWeb Archive, http://files
.usgwarchives.net/md/stmarys/wills/briant
-j.txt.

Earliest known forensic autopsy in America:
"Early medicine in Maryland, 1636–
1671," *Journal of the American Medical Association* 38, no. 25 (June 21, 1902): 1639;
"Judicial and Testamentary Business of
the Provincial Court, 1637–1650," Maryland State Archives, vol. 4: 254.

The deficiencies of the coroner system: Julie Johnson, "Coroners, Corruption and
the Politics of Death: Forensic Pathology
in the United States," in Clark and Crawford, *Legal Medicine in History,* 268–289.

Nonsensical causes of death: Raymond
Moley, *An Outline of the Cleveland Crime
Survey* (Cleveland: Cleveland Foundation, 1922).

Leonard Wallstein's report: Leonard Michael Wallstein, *Report on Special Examination of the Accounts and Methods of the Office of Coroner in New York City* (New York:
Office of the Commissioner of Accounts,
1915).

"Outrageous crooks who dispensed": Jentzen,
Death Investigation in America, 25.

Cleveland Police Department's eight-week
course: Raymond Fosdick, "Part I: Police
Administration," *Criminal Justice in Cleve-*

land (Cleveland: Cleveland Foundation, 1922), 34–35.

"These detectives are supposed": Moley, *Cleveland Crime Survey,* 8.

"Suffolk County had more coroners": James C. Mohr, *Doctors and the Law: Medical Jurisprudence in Ninteenth-Century America* (Baltimore: Johns Hopkins University Press, 1996), 214.

"You have in the coroner": Tyndale, "Law of Coroners," 246.

The scandal that precipitated the end of the coroner system: Martin, "How Murderers Beat the Law."

Chicago Police Department: "History," Chicago Police Department, accessed April 20, 2018, https://home.chicagopolice.org/inside-the-cpd/history/; on Orsemus Morrison, see *A History of the City of Chicago: Its Men and Institutions* (Chicago: Inter Ocean, 1900), 440–441.

The first death Morrison investigated: Richard L. Lindberg, *Gangland Chicago: Criminality and Lawlessness in the Windy City* (Lanham, MD: Rowman & Littlefield, 2015), 3–5.

John Jacob Glessner in Springfield: Timothy B. Spears, *Chicago Dreaming: Midwesterners and the City, 1871–1919* (Chicago: University of Chicago Press, 2005), 24–50.

Isaac Scott: Percy Maxim Lee and John Glessner Lee, *Family Reunion: An Incomplete Account of the Maxim-Lee Family History* (privately printed, 1971), 354; David A. Hanks, *Isaac Scott: Reform Furniture in Chicago* (Chicago: Chicago School of Architecture Foundation, 1974).

2: The Sunny Street of the Sifted Few

After a two-day train ride: Lee and Lee, *Family Reunion,* 348.

"Aunt Helen made the move": Frances Macbeth Glessner Journal, Glessner Family Papers, GHM (hereinafter cited as Journal), July 22, 1878.

Twin Mountain House: Lee and Lee, *Family Reunion,* 348.

Henry Ward Beecher: Robert Shaplen, "The Beecher-Tilton Affair," *New Yorker,* June 4, 1954, https://www.newyorker.com/magazine/1954/06/12/the-beecher-tilton-case-ii.

"He took a fancy": Lee and Lee, *Family Reunion,* 350.

"My dear, a summer": Lee and Lee, *Family Reunion,* 350.

"One of the finest": Journal, July 29, 1883.

Buildings at The Rocks: For information about The Rocks, see *A Historical Walk Through John and Frances Glessner's Rocks Estate* (undated booklet); "Heritage and History," The Rocks Estate, accessed September 14, 2018, http://www.therocks .mobi/about.html.

Frances Glessner invited local residents to visit: Lee and Lee, *Family Reunion,* 357–358.

"One day, a mountain wagon" and following quotes: Journal, 356–357.

Prairie Avenue, Chicago: William H. Tyre, *Chicago's Historic Prairie Avenue* (Chicago, IL: Arcadia Books, 2008).

Glessner wanted an architect of note: Lee and Lee, *Family Reunion,* 327–330.

Henry Hobson Richardson: Finn MacLeod, "Spotlight: Henry Hobson Richardson," *ArchDaily,* September 29, 2017, https:// www.archdaily.com/552221/spotlight -henry-hobson-richardson.

"I'll plan anything a man wants" and following quotes: Journal, 327.

Frances's description of Richardson: Journal, May 15, 1885.

Description of the Glessner home: Lee and Lee, *Family Reunion,* 322.

Reactions to the Glessners' new home: Lee

and Lee, *Family Reunion,* "House Remarks," May 1887, 340.

"Prairie Ave. is a": Lee and Lee, *Family Reunion,* 338.

H. H. Richardson's death: Lee and Lee, *Family Reunion,* 329.

"The house responds": *Family Reunion,* 326.

The orchestra and special occasions: Lee and Lee, *Family Reunion,* 326.

"Cannabis indicie (Indian hemp)": Journal, May 11, 1884.

The Monday Morning Reading Class: Genevieve Leach, "The Monday Morning Reading Class," *Story of a House* (blog), August 4, 2016, https://www.glessnerhouse.org/story-of-a-house/ 2016/8/4/the-monday-morning-reading-class; Genevieve Leach, "The Monday Morning Reading Class, Part 2," *Story of a House* (blog), August 14, 2016, https://www.glessnerhouse.org/story-of-a-house/2016/8/14/the-monday-morning-reading-class-part-2.

"The ladies' fingers were": John Jacob Glessner, *The Story of a House* (privately printed, 1923).

Invitation to the Monday Morning Reading Class: Judith Cass, "Monday Class in Reading to Hold Reunion," *Chicago Tribune,* April 2, 1936.

"The nervous strain of school": Lee and Lee, *Family Reunion,* 325.

"Over the thresholds": Lee and Lee, *Family Reunion,* 325.

"Rendezvous for George's friends": Lee and Lee, *Family Reunion,* 326.

"Never shall I forget": Lee and Lee, *Family Reunion,* 349, 351.

"Does not make up easily with strangers": Journal, July 26, 1885.

Evening entertainments: William Tyre, "Tableaux Vivants," *Story of a House* (blog), September 1, 2014, https://www.glesserhouse.org/story-of-a-house/2014/09/tableaux-vivants.html.

"We have been most": Journal, July 27, 1884.

"He said there was": Journal, May 15, 1887.

"D is for Doctor Lincoln": Journal, July 3, 1887.

Fanny began to accompany local doctors: FGL, manuscript written for *Yankee Yarns* radio show, 1946, GHM.

"But cooking and surgery": FGL, *Yankee Yarns* manuscript.

"I am unmarried and": Harvard College Class of 1894 Secretary's Report, 1909, 172–173.

"Yes, he's a bachelor": C. A. G. Jackson, "Here He Is! The Busiest Man in the City," *Sunday Herald,* March 4, 1917.

Fanny rode the Ferris wheel: Journal, June 25, 1893.

Material about the Glessners at the 1893 World's Fair is based on various passages from the Journal during 1893.

Anthropometry: Oliver Cyriax, Colin Wilson, and Damon Wilson, *Encyclopedia of Crime* (New York: Overlook Press, 2006), 14–15.

For a thorough and compelling account of H. H. Holmes, see Erik Larson, *The Devil in the White City: Murder, Magic, and Madness at the Fair that Changed America* (New York: Vintage Books, 2003).

"Before summer was out": Harvard College Class of 1894 Secretary's Report, 1897.

"On Wednesday, Frances was": Journal, March 29, 1896.

Stephen Dill Lee: "About Stephen D. Lee," Stephen D. Lee Institute, http://www.stephendleeinstitute.com/about-sd-lee.html.

Asa Candler: Lee and Lee, *Family Reunion,* 255.

Women in medicine in the late 1800s: "A Timeline of Women at Hopkins," *Johns Hopkins Magazine,* accessed April 6, 2019, https://pages.jh.edu/jhumag/1107web/women2.html.

Sarah Hackett Stevenson: William Tyre,

"Mrs. Ashton Dilke visits the Glessner house," *Story of a House* (blog), February 18, 2013, https://www.glessnerhouse.org/story-of-a-house/2013/02/mrs-ashton-dilke-visits-glessner-house-html.

Wedding section is from Lee and Lee, *Family Reunion,* 391–394.

"Then they — the two": Family Reunion, 394.

3: Marriage and the Aftermath

The newlywed couple: Much of this section is drawn from Lee and Lee, *Family Reunion,* 258.

The Metropole Hotel: "The Metropole Hotel," My Al Capone Museum, accessed September 27, 2018, http://www.myalcaponemuseum.com/id224.htm.

Friction in the marriage: Lee and Lee, *Family Reunion,* 259–263.

"The Doctor said several": Journal, December 11, 1898.

"She has been quite": Journal, December 11, 1898.

"Extremely outspoken and partisan": Lee and Lee, *Family Reunion,* 260.

Gifts of stock: Journal, December 27, 1903.

Iroquois Theater Fire: Bob Specter, "The Iroquois Theater Fire," *Chicago Tribune,* December 19, 2007, https://www

.chicagotribune.com/news/nation-world/
politics/chi-chicagodays-iroquoisfire-story
-story.html.

"It has all been": Journal, January 4, 1904.

George Glessner went to the theater: Journal, January 4, 1904.

John's lymph glands: Lee and Lee, *Family Reunion,* 403–404.

"I can remember eating": Lee and Lee, *Family Reunion,* 404.

"Once she undertook to": Lee and Lee, *Family Reunion,* 404.

Miniature orchestra: Lee and Lee, *Family Reunion,* 398.

"New Years was Frances' birthday": Journal, January 5, 1913.

"Every member of the organization": Journal, January 19, 1913.

The Flonzaley Quartet: Lee and Lee, *Family Reunion,* 398–401.

"An unhappy time for all": Lee and Lee, *Family Reunion,* 404.

Candy making: Lee and Lee, *Family Reunion,* 403.

"Particularly notable for being": Chicago Daily Tribune, July 21, 1915, 15.

Detailed notes on visitors: Based on review of correspondence and records at GHM.

"Dear Mother Lee": Letter from George Wise

to FGL, July 17, 1918, GHM.

Finger Tip Theater: William Tyre, "Chicago's Tiniest Theater," *Story of a House* (blog), June 22, 2015, GHM, http://glessnerhouse.blogspot.com/2015/06/chicagos-tiniest-theater.html.

"The auditorium will seat": "Hop o' My Thumb Actors Delight at Finger Tip Theater," *Chicago Daily Tribune*, March 20, 1918, 15.

"If one has an imagination": Tyre, "Chicago's Tiniest Theater."

"There seemed to be": "Hop o' My Thumb."

"I am glad to": FGL, letter to the editor, *Chicago Tribune*, March 30, 1918.

"I didn't do a lick": Martin, "How Murderers Beat the Law."

"All this time": FGL, *Yankee Yarns* manuscript.

"Said au revoirs to": *Chicago Tribune*, November 15, 1918.

"Writing to the Monday Morning": Siobhan Heraty, "Frances Glessner Lee and World War I," *Story of a House* (blog), December 15, 2014, GHM, https://www.glessnerhouse.org/story-of-a-house/2014/12/frances-glessner-lee-and-world-war-i.html.

4: The Crime Doctor

"Dead bodies of such persons": George Burgess Magrath, "The Technique of a Medico-Legal Investigation," Meeting of the Massachusetts Medico-Legal Society, February 1, 1922.

"We should do our": Magrath, "The Technique of a Medico-Legal Investigation."

"The duties of this office": Myrtelle M. Canavan, "George Burgess Magrath," *Archives of Pathology* 27, no. 3 (March 1939): 620–623.

"If the law has": Erle Stanley Gardner, *The Case of the Glamorous Ghost* (New York: Morrow, 1955), dedication.

"He was always cheerful": Letter from FGL to Erle Stanley Gardner, August 1954, GHM.

"You ought to set": William Boos, *The Poison Trail* (Boston: Hale, Cushman, & Flint, 1939), 40.

"More than most men": Letter from Frank Leon Smith to Erle Stanley Gardner, February 19, 1955, GHM.

"His statements were the": Boos, *The Poison Trail,* 41.

Magrath in the courtroom: "Like a Lion Resting," *Boston Globe,* December 18, 1938, D5.

"He went into something": "Like a Lion Resting."

"Get three drinks into": "Like a Lion Resting."

"As a Medical Examiner": Letter from FGL to Erle Stanley Gardner, August 1954, GHM.

Avis Linnell case: "Quick March in Poison Tragedy of Dead Singer," *Boston Sunday Globe,* October 22, 1911, 1; "Murder Ends a Love Dream," *Boston Sunday Globe,* January 7, 1912, 8; Timothy Leary, "The Medical Examiner System," *Journal of the American Medical Association* 89, no. 8 (August 20, 1927): 579–583.

"It is as quick": "Murder Ends a Love Dream."

"There was no primary suspicion": New York *Post,* November 24, 1914, CHM.

Marjorie Powers case: "Authorities Probe Death of Girl in Bathtub," *Pittsburgh Press,* November 15, 1912, 1; "Another Boston Girl Thought Victim of Man," *Daily Gate City,* November 15, 1912, 1; "Cummings Arrested on Woman's Death," *Boston Globe,* November 15, 1912, 1; "Boston Girl Not Victim of Foul Play," *Lincoln Daily News,* November 15, 1912, 7; "Girl's Death Natural, Employer Re-

453

leased," *Philadelphia Inquirer,* November 16, 1912, 2.

Brimfield lawsuit: "Sues for $10,000," *Boston Globe,* February 6, 1913, 1; "Widow Sues Medical Examiner Magrath," *Boston Globe,* January 12, 1915, 1.

Magrath framed for larceny: "Three Accused of Conspiracy," *Boston Globe,* January 26, 1915, 1; "Men in Morgue Under Arrest," *Boston Globe,* August 9, 1914, 1.

The governor's decision: "Not to Reappoint Dr. Geo. B. Magrath," *Boston Globe,* July 16, 1914, 1.

Brimfield lawsuit resolution: "Medical Examiner Magrath Exonerated," *Boston Globe,* January 13, 1915, 1; "Reads Three Depositions," *Boston Globe,* January 15, 1915, 1.

Larceny plot falls apart: "Green Witness in Own Behalf," *Boston Globe,* January 28, 1915, 1; "Green Admits He Did Wrong," *Boston Globe,* January 28, 1915, 1; "Search Left to Subordinate," *Boston Globe,* January 27, 1915, 1; "Jury Returns Sealed Verdict," *Boston Globe,* February 2, 1915, 1.

Green, Miller, and Kingston arrested: "Like a Lion Resting."

"The coroner is not": Editorial, *New York*

Daily Globe, March 2, 1914.

Reform of New York's coroner system: Milton Helpern and Bernard Knight, *Autopsy: The Memoirs of Milton Helpern, the World's Greatest Medical Detective* (New York: St. Martin's Press, 1977), 11.

Death of Eugene Hochette: "Point to a Murder Hid by Coroner's Aid," *New York Times,* November 25, 1914, 1.

"I should say that": "Murder Hid by Coroner's Aid."

"A practically perfect instrument": New York Tribune, February 25, 1915, 7.

Early days of the New York City medical examiner's office and laboratory: S. K. Niyogi, "Historic Development of Forensic Toxicology in America up to 1978," *American Journal of Forensic Medicine and Pathology* 1, no. 3 (September 1980): 249–264; Deborah Blum, *The Poisoner's Handbook* (New York: Penguin Press, 2010); Helpern and Knight, *Autopsy: The Memoirs of Milton Helpern.*

"The rear end": Boston Post, November 8, 1916, 7.

Boston molasses disaster: Stephen Puleo, *Dark Tide: The Great Boston Molasses Flood of 1919* (Boston: Beacon Press, 2003).

"As though covered in": Puleo, *Dark Tide*. 109.

Sacco and Vanzetti case: "Sacco and Vanzetti: The Evidence," Massachusetts Supreme Judicial Court, accessed March 2, 2019, https://www.mass.gov/info-details/sacco-vanzetti-the-evidence; Felix Frankfurter, *The Case of Sacco and Vanzetti* (New York: Little Brown, 1927); Dorothy G. Wayman, "Sacco-Vanzetti: The Unfinished Debate," *American Heritage* 11, no. 1 (December 1959).

5: Kindred Spirits

Prairie Avenue in the early 1900s: This section drawn from public signage produced by the Prairie Avenue Historic District and Tyre, *Chicago's Historic Prairie Avenue,* 97–114.

The White Schoolhouse: "List of Dealers," undated notes, correspondence, GHM.

Phillips House: Frederic A. Washburn, *The Massachusetts General Hospital: Its Development, 1900–1935* (Boston: Houghton Mifflin, 1939).

"He used to tell": Letter from FGL to Erle Stanley Gardner, August 1952, GHM.

Magrath's stories: Ruth Henderson, "Remember G.B.M.?" *Kennebec Journal,*

February 22, 1950.

Florence Small murder: Lowell Ames Norris, "Inanimate Objects Often Expose Cruel Murder Secrets," *Sunday Herald,* May 21, 1933; "Dr. Magrath Tells of Unusual Cases," *Boston Globe,* February 26, 1932, 16; "Florence Small Lost Her Head," *Criminal Conduct* (blog), accessed April 5, 2017, http://criminalconduct .blogspot.com/2011/11/small-remember ance.html.

"I consider this one": Norris, "Inanimate Objects."

"Showed the stove had": Norris, "Inanimate Objects."

"An innocent man would": Norris, "Inanimate Objects."

Consulting with Charles Norris: "Dr. Magrath Tells of Unusual Cases."

"I'm still trying to": FGL, *Yankee Yarns* manuscript.

"He was a brilliant raconteur": Letter from FGL to Erle Stanley Gardner, August 1954, GHM.

The Hall-Mills murders: Julie Johnson-McGrath, "Speaking for the Dead: Forensic Pathologists and Criminal Justice in the United States," *Science, Technology & Human Values* 20, no. 4 (Autumn 1995): 438–459; Mara Bovsun, "A 90-Year Mystery: Who Killed the Pastor and the Choir Singer?" *New York Daily News,* September 16, 2012, http://www.nydailynews.com/news/justice-story/90-year-mystery-killed-pastor-choir-singer-article-1.1160659; Sadie Stein, "She is a Liar! Liar!" *New York Magazine,* April 1, 2012, http://nymag.com/news/features/scandals/hall-mills-2012-4/.

Study on coroners and medical examiners: Oscar Schultz and E. M. Morgan, "The Coroner and the Medical Examiner," *Bulletin of the National Research Council* 64 (July 1928).

"You know, I won't": FGL, *Yankee Yarns* manuscript.

6: The Medical School

Description of the autopsy conducted by Magrath: Letter from Frank Leon Smith to Erle Stanley Gardner, February 19, 1955, GHM; "The Routine Autopsy," Ed Uthman (website), June 2, 2001, http://web2.iadfw.net/uthman/Autop.html; "Autopsy Tools," Ed Uthman (website), February 24, 1999, http://web2.iadfw.net/uthman/autopsy_tools.html; Nicholas Gerbis, "What Exactly Do They Do During an Autopsy?" *Live Science,* August 26,

2010, https://www.livescience.com/32789 -forensic-pathologist-perform-autopsy-csi -effect.html.

"Legal Medicine may be": FGL, *Yankee Yarns* manuscript.

Magrath at Harvard: Letter from George Burgess Magrath to Edward H. Bradford, August 19, 1918, CHM.

"It is my desire": Letter from FGL to A. Lawrence Lowell, April 30, 1931, CHM.

"Your wishes will be": Letter from A. Lawrence Lowell to FGL, May 4, 1931, CHM.

Lee asked for Lowell's complicity: Letter from FGL to A. Lawrence Lowell, September 29, 1931, CHM.

"He really does not": Letter from A. Lawrence Lowell to FGL, December 10, 1931, CHM.

"I am not sure": Letter from Oscar Schultz to FGL, June 23, 1933, GHM.

"Our fight is going": Letter from Oscar Schultz to FGL, February 7, 1934, GHM.

Annual meeting of the AMA: Letter from Oscar Schultz to FGL, May 26, 1933, GHM.

"I have this morning": Letter from FGL to James Bryant Conant, March 24, 1934, CHM.

"The donor of money": Letter from David Edsall to J. Howard Mueller, April 9,

1934, CHM.

Magrath Library opening: "Mrs. Lee and President Conant Are Speakers at Opening of Library," *Harvard Crimson,* May 25, 1934.

Magrath introduced Lee to Gregg: Letter from George Burgess Magrath to Alan Gregg, January 25, 1935, RAC.

Lee sought Gregg's assistance: Alan Gregg diary, March 14, 1935, RAC.

Lee's proposal for the Department of Legal Medicine: Letter from FGL to Alan Gregg, March 30, 1935, RAC.

"Told her we were interested": Alan Gregg diary, March 14, 1935, RAC.

"The next time she comes": Memo from Alan Gregg to Robert A. Lambert, April 19, 1943, RAC.

New York University Department of Legal Medicine: Milton Helpern, "Development of Department of Legal Medicine at New York University," *New York State Journal of Medicine* 72, no. 7 (April 1, 1972): 831–833.

Gifts to her daughters: Letter from FGL to Frances Martin and Martha Batchelder, January 29, 1934, GHM.

"George seemed very pleasant": Letter from Roger Lee to FGL, November 1, 1935, GHM.

"Our reports about George": Letter from Roger Lee to FGL, June 5, 1937, GHM.

Magrath's pension: Memorandum, CSB, February 12, 1937, CHM.

"Without bringing her into": CSB, "Memorandum of a conference with Mrs. Lee on February 12, 1937," CHM.

"I think some action": Memorandum, CSB, February 12, 1937, CHM.

"A Medico-legal Library": Letter from Reid Hunt to David Edsall, April 30, 1934, CHM.

"I am loath to ask": Letter from FGL to James Bryant Conant, August 13, 1934, CHM.

"Since receiving your letter": Letter from FGL to James Bryant Conant, September 7, 1934, CHM.

Origins of the FBI: "Timeline," Federal Bureau of Investigation, accessed November 16, 2018, https://www.fbi.gov/history/timeline.

FBI authority over kidnapping: "Timeline."

Hoover fired all the female agents: "Timeline"; Winifred R. Poster, "Cybersecurity Needs Women," *Nature,* March 26, 2018, https://www.nature.com/articles/d41586-018-03327-w.

Lee described her plans to Hoover: H. H. Clegg, "Memorandum for the

Director," May 16, 1935, FBI; Mary Elizabeth Power, "Policewoman Wins Honors in Field of Legal Medicine," *Wilmington Journal,* June 16, 1955, 45.

"This lady is interested": L. C. Schilder, "Memorandum for Mr. Edwards," May 16, 1936, FBI.

The Glessners deeded their home: Al Chase, "Architects Vote to Turn Back Glessner Home," *Chicago Tribune,* June 16, 1937, 27; William Tyre, personal communication, 2018.

"Was considered one of": Judith Cass, "Monday Class in Reading to Hold Reunion," *Chicago Tribune,* April 2, 1936.

Property returned: Chase, "Architects."

"If Dr. Magrath is to write": Letter from FGL to Sidney Burwell, December 13, 1935, GHM.

7: The Three-Legged Stool

Lee's gifts to Harvard: Letter from FGL to CSB, May 23, 1936, GHM.

Lee's ultimatum: Alan Gregg diary, October 18, 1938, RAC.

Burwell convened a committee: Minutes of the first meeting of the Committee to Consider the Future of Legal Medicine in Harvard University, April 13, 1936, CHM.

"It is my unfortunate luck": Letter from S. Burt Wolbach to Alan Gregg, April 8, 1936, RAC.

Searching for Magrath's successor: Minutes of the second meeting of the Committee on Legal Medicine, December 11, 1936, RAC.

"I was third man": Alan Moritz, interview by Mary Daly, November 18, 1983, Case Western Reserve University Archive.

"There were several schools": Alan Moritz interview.

"I knew little or nothing": Alan Moritz interview.

"The more I have": Letter from ARM to CSB, May 24, 1937, CHM.

"Last summer I had": Letter from ARM to CSB, December 7, 1937, CHM.

"I have forced myself": Letter from ARM to Burt Wolbach, August 2, 1938, CHM.

"My greatest problem to date": Draft letter from ARM to FGL, undated, CHM.

"I had a letter": Letter from FGL to ARM, November 18, 1938, CHM.

"Without wishing to be arbitrary": Letter from FGL to CSB, December 16, 1937, CHM.

"She approved of the idea": CSB, "Memorandum of a conversation with Mrs. Lee concerning the situation in Legal Medicine," June 15, 1937, CHM.

World's Fair: Letter from FGL to ARM, November 15, 1938, CHM.

Lee reached out to Dr. Gonzales: Letter from FGL to Thomas Gonzales, November 4, 1938, GHM.

Gonzales on planned exhibits: Letter from Thomas Gonzales to FGL, November 7, 1939, GHM.

"I am anxious that": Letter from ARM to FGL, December 6, 1938, CHM.

"She suggests various methods": CSB, "Note on a conversation with Mrs. Lee regarding the future of the Department of Legal Medicine," December 9, 1939, CHM.

"That's the way to go": "Like a Lion Resting."

"Since you saw him": Letter from FGL to ARM, December 20, 1938, CHM.

"I read voraciously for weeks": Letter from FGL to George Burgess Magrath, undated, GHM.

Lee's book: FGL, "An Anatomography in Picture, Verse and Music" (unpublished manuscript, ca. 1929–1938), GHM.

"A coined word": Letter from FGL to George Burgess Magrath, undated, GHM.

"Although our work for": Letter from Parker Glass to FGL, May 17, 1939, GHM.

"This was the official number": Letter from FGL to ARM, January 10, 1939, CHM.

"It is a good time": Letter from FGL to CSB, December 20, 1938, CHM.

Lee's suggestions of a statewide system: CSB, "Memorandum of conversation with Mrs. Lee," October 3, 1938, CHM.

Massachusetts didn't adopt a statewide system: Randy Hanzlick and Debra Combs, "Medical Examiner and Coroner Systems: History and trends," *Journal of the American Medical Association* 279, no. 11 (March 18, 1998): 870–874.

"Poisoning is very common": ARM, "Confidential Report on the Status of Forensic Medicine in Great Britain, Europe and Egypt (1938–1939)," 1940, CHM.

"I had a very": Letter from ARM to CSB, April 6, 1939, CHM.

"My experience to date": Letter from ARM to S. B. Wolbach, August 2, 1938, CHM.

"I would like to": Letter from FGL to ARM, September 18, 1939, CHM.

"I am firmly convinced": Letter from FGL to ARM, September 27, 1939, CHM.

Lee's suggestion that Moritz write an article: Letter from FGL to ARM, April 22, 1942, CHM.

"I know of no": Letter from ARM to FGL, January 8, 1940, CHM.

Afternoon tea for department opening: Invitation to tea in honor of FGL, CHM.

"I'm still thinking of": Letter from FGL to CSB, February 15, 1940, CHM.

Department funding: Harvard Medical School, "First Annual Report of the Department of Legal Medicine, January 1, 1940–December 31, 1940," CHM.

The department's first fellows: Harvard Medical School, "First Annual Report."

"I can see one": Letter from ARM to CSB, July 30, 1938, CHM.

Conflicts with local police: Metro-Goldwyn-Mayer, *Murder at Harvard* treatment, September 17, 1948, CHM.

"Dr. Rosen, medical examiner": Teletype message, July 31, 1940, accompanying letter from Alan Moritz to Leonard Spigelgass, November 9, 1948, CHM.

Irene Perry case: "Girl, 22, Trussed and Slain," *Boston Globe,* August 1, 1940, 1; MGM, *Murder at Harvard;* "Examination of the Body of Irene Perry, Dartmouth, Massachusetts, 7/31/1940," Division of Laboratories, Department of Legal Medicine, Harvard Medical School, 40–139, CHM.

Conference outline: FGL, "Basic Scheme for a Series of Medico-Legal Conferences Biennial or Annual," May 17, 1940, CHM.

Conference suggestions: FGL, "Suggestions

for a Medico-Legal Conference to Be Held in Boston in October 1940," May 17, 1940, CHM.

Medical Society recommendations: "Physicians Rap System of Coroners," *Philadelphia Inquirer,* October 3, 1940, 21.

"I cannot impress upon": Letter from P. J. Zisch to J. W. Battershall, May 20, 1940, CHM.

"It seems to me": Letter from FGL to CSB, August 9, 1940, CHM.

"Of all men connected": Letter from FGL to Timothy Leary, August 9, 1940, CHM.

"In my opinion": Letter from Timothy Leary to FGL, August 14, 1940, CHM.

"I judge from your letter": Letter from FGL to William Wadsworth, October 28, 1940, CHM.

First year faculty: Harvard Medical School, "First Annual Report."

8: Captain Lee

Lee's dream of a centralized medical examiner's office: Based in part on untitled brief written by FGL at the suggestion of Roger Lee, March 7, 1939, CHM.

Dr. Roger Lee asked for plan: Letter from Roger Lee to CSB, March 10, 1939, GHM.

Lee's medical concerns: Letter from Roger Lee to FGL, June 21, 1939, GHM.

"I emphatically believe that": Letter from Roger Lee to FGL, June 27, 1939, GHM.

The Cocoanut Grove fire: Paul Benzaquin, *Holocaust! The Shocking Story of the Boston Cocoanut Grove Fire* (New York: Henry Holt and Co., 1959); "The Story of the Cocoanut Grove Fire," Boston Fire Historical Society, accessed October 17, 2017, https://bostonfirehistory.org/the-story-of-the-cocoanut-grove-fire/.

"Among the victims": Letter from ARM to FGL, January 9, 1943, CHM.

Lee's generosity: Letter from FGL to CSB, July 12, 1940, GHM; letter from CSB to FGL, April 7, 1941, GHM.

The Glessners' piano: "Music in the Mansion, Part 1: The Glessners' Piano," *Story of a House* (blog), April 4, 2011, http://www.glessnerhouse.org/story-of-a-house/2011/04/music-in-mansion-part-1-glessners-piano.html.

"I do not play": Letter from FGL to Roger Lee, September 12, 1942, GHM.

"You may be interested": Letter from FGL to ARM, November 9, 1942, GHM.

Lee's questions for Moritz: Typed list of questions asked of Moritz on November 20, 1942, FGL, January 5, 1943, CHM.

"I hope you can": Letter from FGL to ARM, January 5, 1943, CHM.

"One of the things": Letter from CSB to Jerome D. Greene, March 10, 1943, CHM.

"It will be recalled": Letter from CSB to Jerome D. Greene, February 23, 1943, CHM.

"This title would": Letter from Alan Moritz to FGL, February 19, 1943, CHM.

"I shall do my best": Letter from FGL to CSB, March 21, 1943, CHM.

"Not to be printed": Joseph S. Lichty, "Memorandum for Dr. Burwell," March 10, 1943, CHM.

Lee not identified in medical school catalog: Letter from CSB to FGL, March 20, 1943, CHM.

Dental records: FGL, "Plan for Unification of Dental Records for Dental Identification," February 16, 1942, CHM.

Dental study: FGL, "Plans for a Dental Project," February 16, 1942, CHM.

Medical examiners in 1944: Alan R. Moritz, Edward R. Cunniffe, J. W. Holloway, and Harrison S. Maitland, "Report of Committee to Study the Relationship of Medicine and Law," *Journal of the American Medical Association* 125, no. 8 (June 24, 1944): 577–583.

"During his first two years": Note on visit with Sidney Burwell, Alan Gregg diary, February 2, 1942, RAC.

Improved laws in some states: Letter from FGL to Joseph Shallot, July 28, 1948, GHM.

Restrictions on medical examiners: Moritz et al., "Report of Committee."

Coroners in Maryland: Goldfarb, "Death Investigation in Maryland."

Lee's speaking engagements: Based on correspondence at GHM.

Lee in Virginia: Letter from FGL to ARM, March 20, 1943, CHM.

Lee's suggestions in Virginia: "Comments and Recommendations Submitted by Mrs. Lee on Suggestions for a Medical Examiner System for the State of Virginia," undated, GHM.

Changes in Washington, DC: David Brinkley, *Washington Goes to War* (New York: Knopf, 1988).

"Believing yours to be": Letter from FGL to Fulton Lewis Jr., September 29, 1943, GHM.

"I cannot too strongly": Letter from FGL to Sherman Adams, February 9, 1945, GHM.

Lee appointed consulting deputy coroner: Letter from Cook County coroner

A. L. Brodie to FGL, December 18, 1941, GHM.

She singled out Oscar Schultz: Letter from FGL to ARM, May 6, 1942, CHM.

Oklahoma law: "Murder-Clue Team Set Here," *Daily Oklahoman,* November 16, 1945, 1.

"I earnestly hope that": Letter from FGL to W. F. Keller, November 9, 1944, GHM.

Oklahoma City agreement: "Murder-Clue Team Set Here."

"I've fallen completely under": Letter from FGL to Charles Woodson, April 20, 1946, GHM.

Colonel Ralph Caswell: "Much Progress in Fingerprint Library for NH," *Portsmouth Herald,* February 27, 1936, 3; Brian Nelson Burford, New Hampshire State archivist, personal communication, 2018.

Caswell on State Liquor Commission: "Around the Town," *Nashua Telegraph,* November 25, 1961.

"general police power": Commission from Lee, 1943.

"This was not an honorary post": Earl Banner, "She Invested a Fortune in Police, Entertained Them Royally at the Ritz," *Boston Globe,* February 4, 1962, 46-A.

Lee on medicolegal investigators: FGL, "The Department of Legal Medicine: Its

Functions and Purposes," July 13, 1947, CHM.

"An alarming possibility occurs": Letter from FGL to CSB, April 29, 1944, CHM.

9: In a Nutshell

"Five years ago": ARM, "The Status of the Department of Legal Medicine of Harvard Medical School After Five Years of Its Existence: Report to the Dean," May 15, 1944, CHM.

Increased gifts to the department: Letter from CSB to FGL, January 28, 1944, CHM; Letter from FGL to CSB, June 23, 1944, CHM.

Lee's thoughts on the School of Business: "Mrs. Frances G. Lee — lunch," Alan Gregg diary, April 16, 1947, RAC.

"In a word" and following quotes: FGL, "Suggestions for a Police Course," October 19, 1942, CHM.

"The matter of providing": FGL, handwritten note, undated, GHM.

"It has been found": FGL, "Dolls as a Teaching Tool," undated, GHM.

"Why not let me make models": FGL, *Yankee Yarns* manuscript, GHM.

"I have some special work": Letter from FGL to Ralph Mosher, June 9, 1943, GHM.

"If you will send": Letter from Ralph Mosher to FGL, June 11, 1943, GHM.

"The work I want": Letter from FGL to Ralph Mosher, July 8, 1943, GHM.

"In the original": Letter from FGL to ARM, August 21, 1945, CHM.

Trying to purchase tools during the war: Letter from Sears Roebuck and Co. to FGL, August 3, 1943, GHM.

Form PD-1A: Application for Preference Rating, September 3, 1943, GHM.

Trying to acquire a saw and motor: Letter from FGL to Union Twitchell, Irving & Casson-A. H. Davenport Co., April 21, 1943, GHM.

Replacement of a truck part: Letter from C. E. Dolham, parts department, International Harvester Company, to FGL, July 15, 1942, GHM.

"We are in the midst": Letter from FGL to C. E. Dolham, July 20, 1942, GHM.

"The package containing the wire": Letter from FGL to A. J. Monroe, January 7, 1944, GHM.

Quarter-inch brass hinges: Letter from Union Twitchell to FGL, January 6, 1944, GHM.

"Lucite is on priority": Letter from Union Twitchell to FGL, July 13, 1943, GHM.

"I shall be very glad": Letter from FGL to

Union Twitchell, July 14, 1943, GHM.

Whiskey bottles: Letter from Alynn Shilling, National Distillers Products Corporation, to FGL, October 19, 1944, GHM.

"I have never seen": Letter from FGL to W. B. Douglas, February 26, 1946, GHM.

"The most difficult matter": FGL, "Dolls as a Teaching Tool."

"Most of the furniture": FGL, "Nutshell Studies of Unexplained Death, Notes and Comments: Foreword," undated, CHM.

"I found myself constantly": Letter from FGL to ARM, August 21, 1945, CHM.

"I have in prospect": Letter from FGL to ARM, January 5, 1944, CHM.

"Believing firmly that the": FGL, "Legal Medicine at Harvard," *Journal of Criminal Justice and Police Science* 42, no. 5 (Winter 1952): 674–678.

Student reports on the Nutshells: FGL, undated manuscript about Department of Legal Medicine, CHM.

"It must be understood": FGL, undated manuscript about Department of Legal Medicine, CHM.

"The students should be warned": FGL, "Nutshell Studies of Unexplained Death."

The purposes of HAPS: Harvard Associates in Police Science Articles of Incorporation, January 8, 1963, GHM.

"These were wonderful affairs": Earl Banner, "She Invested a Fortune in Police, Entertained Them Royally at Ritz," *Boston Globe,* February 4, 1962, A46.

"There is no place": Handwritten note on back of photograph, undated, GHM.

"I am making arrangements": Letter from FGL to CSB, May 29, 1945, CHM.

"I dislike to attach conditions": Letter from FGL to CSB, July 30, 1945, CHM.

"Expressed the opinion that": CSB, "Memorandum of talk with Mrs. Lee on March 27, 1945," CHM.

10: Murder at Harvard

Lee felt that Fisher was capable: Letter from FGL to C. W. Woodson, August 5, 1946, GHM; letter from FGL to C. W. Woodson, September 20, 1946, GHM.

Department of Legal Medicine at Medical College of Virginia: Mary A Giunta, "A History of the Department of Legal Medicine at Medical College of Virginia" (master's thesis, University of Richmond, 1966).

"As for my 'complete anonymity' ": Letter from FGL to ARM, July 12, 1946, CHM.

"LIFE is still very": Letter from Jeff Wylie to FGL, March 7, 1946, GHM.

The Nutshells national debut: *Life* magazine, June 3, 1946.

"The Coroner, an undertaker": Letter from R. F. Borkenstein to FGL, April 21, 1948, GHM.

Knowledge from the seminar: Martin, "How Murderers Beat the Law."

"I thought you had": Martin, "How Murderers Beat the Law."

Homicide seminar, April 1947: William Gilman, "Murder at Harvard," *Los Angeles Times,* January 25, 1948, F4.

Arnette and the Texas City disaster: Martin, "How Murderers Beat the Law."

Texas City disaster casualties: Hugh W. Stephens, *The Texas City Disaster, 1947* (Austin: University of Texas Press, 1997), 100.

Eighteen fellows in 1947: Letter from Richard Ford to Alan Gregg, July 19, 1949, CHM.

Medical examiners replacing coroners: Martin, "How Murderers Beat the Law."

State laws influenced: "Annual Report, July 1, 1947, to June 30, 1948," Department of Legal Medicine, CHM.

University programs started: "Annual Report."

"She thinks [Moritz's] heart": Alan Gregg diary, April 16, 1947, RAC.

Attendance by 1949: Martin, "How Murderers Beat the Law."

"Why should Harvard Medical School": Letter from George Minot to CSB, September 24, 1945, CHM.

"We were informed by": Lucy Boland, "A Few Days at Harvard Seminar," *VOX Cop,* Connecticut State Police, June 1950.

"Few of the States": Boland, "A Few Days."

"We feel that": Letter from Samuel Marx to FGL, February 9, 1948, GHM.

"I have listened": Letter from FGL to James R. Nunn, December 7, 1944, GHM.

Dr. LeMoyne Snyder: "Biographical Note," LeMoyne Snyder papers, Michigan State University Archives, accessed December 20, 2018, http://archives.msu.edu/findaid/ua10-3-97.html.

"Your remarks made me feel": Letter from LeMoyne Snyder to FGL, July 19, 1944, Michigan State University Archives.

"I thought it over": Minutes of Harvard Associates in Police Science meeting, undated, GHM.

"He was the most interested": Meeting minutes, HAPS board, 1949, GHM.

"Your stories are formulaic": Erle Stanley Gardner, "A Wonderful Woman," *Boston Globe,* February 4, 1962, 1.

"I just can't believe": Minutes of Harvard Associates in Police Science second annual meeting, February 10, 1949, GHM.

"A perfectionist in every sense": Gardner, "A Wonderful Woman."

"This book was written": Erle Stanley Gardner, *The Case of the Dubious Bridegroom* (New York: William Morrow & Co., 1949).

Gardner autographed the first copy: Letter from Erle Stanley Gardner to FGL, December 21, 1948, GHM.

"I want to have it photographically reduced": Letter from FGL to Thayer Hobson, May 19, 1949, GHM.

"A book in which": Letter from Erle Stanley Gardner to FGL, December 21, 1948, GHM.

"A lively correspondence": Letter from FGL to ARM, January 19, 1949, GHM.

"Taking the wrong attitude": Letter from FGL to Charles W. Woodwon, March 8, 1949, GHM.

Gardner attended a second homicide seminar: " 'Perry Mason' Goes to Harvard with Police," *Boston Globe,* May 1, 1949, C1.

Meeting with Maryland Post Mortem Examiners Commission: B. Taylor, "The Case of the Outspoken Medical Examiner, or an Exclusive Journal Interview with

Russell S. Fisher, MD, Chief Medical Examiner of the State of Maryland," *Maryland State Medical Journal* 26, no. 3 (March 1977): 59–69.

Lee recommended Fisher: Letter from FGL to Huntington Williams, July 5, 1949, GHM.

Fisher appointed: "Dr. R. S. Fisher Assumes Post as Examiner," *Baltimore Sun,* September 2, 1949.

Ultimate vision for the Maryland Office of the Chief Medical Examiner: Letter from Huntington Williams to FGL, September 2, 1949, GHM.

"I am reluctant": Letter from Alan Moritz to Miss Mills, January 7, 1947, CHM.

"Our belief is": MGM, *Murder at Harvard.*

"I am of the opinion": Letter from CSB to Edward Reynolds, January 10, 1949, CHM.

"Mrs. Lee has": MGM, *Murder at Harvard.*

Lee asked to write article for *Scientific Monthly:* Letter from Gladys Keener to FGL, May 31, 1949, GHM.

"I would like to": Letter from FGL to Gladys Keener, July 14, 1949, GHM.

"Members of the faculty": Minutes of the Harvard Associates in Police Science Second Annual Meeting, February 10, 1949, GHM.

"I am not unmindful": Letter from ARM to FGL, January 31, 1949, CHM.

11: The Decline and Falls

"We will be sunk": Letter from FGL to Roger Lee, February 28, 1949, GHM.

Dr. Richard Ford: *Harvard Law Record,* undated, CHM.

"The more I see": Letter from FGL to Roger Lee, February 28, 1949, GHM.

"During the past ten years": Letter from ARM to CSB, May 11, 1949, CHM.

"Lurid or otherwise offensive": Letter from Edward Reynolds to Lowe's Inc., June 13, 1949, CHM.

Mystery Street filming locations: "Mystery Street," Internet Movie Database, accessed December 28, 2018, https://www.imdb.com/title/tt0042771.

MGM payment to Harvard: Letter from ARM to Richard Ford, September 2, 1949, CHM; letter from ARM to Richard Ford, December 12, 1949, CHM.

"Mrs. Lee has asked me": Letter from Richard Ford to George P. Berry, December 14, 1949, CHM.

"There is more science": Metro-Goldwyn-Mayer, "*Mystery Street* Reviews," undated, CHM.

480

"I must confess that it is a mystery": Letter from FGL to Richard Ford, January 31, 1951, CHM.

"I must confess that I am greatly disappointed": Letter from FGL to Alan Gregg, January 31, 1951, RAC.

Harvard limiting attendance at seminars: Memo from SAC, Richmond, to J. Edgar Hoover, December 21, 1950, FBI.

"In my opinion": Letter from FGL to Alan Gregg, January 31, 1951, RAC; letter from Alan Gregg to FGL, February 16, 1951, RAC.

"Although no models": Letter from FGL to Allan B. Hussander, February 27, 1951, GHM.

"Captain Frances G. Lee": Erle Stanley Gardner, *The Court of Last Resort* (New York: William Sloane Associates, 1952).

"I have had to restrain": Letter from FGL to Francis I. McGarraghy and others, June 5, 1951, GHM.

"In desperation, I am writing": Letter from Margaret Roth to FGL, November 9, 1948, GHM.

"Dear Lady": Unsigned letter to FGL, undated, GHM.

Automotive Safety Association: Letter from Frank D. Miller to FGL, January 27, 1946, GHM.

Entrepreneur from Long Beach: Letter from Arthur W. Stevens to FGL, January 29, 1948, GHM.

"He has read of": Letter from John Crocker Jr. to FGL, February 9, 1955, GHM.

"While I am entirely sympathetic": Letter from FGL to John Crocker Jr., February 18, 1955, GHM.

"This appears to be": Letter from FGL to Mrs. Edwin B. Wright, October 25, 1949, GHM.

"Each member of the Advisory Board": Letter from FGL to Francis I. McGarraghy and others, June 5, 1951, GHM.

"It seems to me": Letter from FGL to Francis I. McGarraghy and others, June 5, 1951, GHM.

"We had not been visiting": Lee News, September 10, 1957, GHM.

Lee's visit to the FBI: Telegram from J. Edgar Hoover to FGL, November 20, 1951, FBI.

"When informed of Mr. Hoover's absence": Office of Director memo, December 21, 1951, FBI.

"No salary from Harvard": Letter from George P. Berry to David W. Bailey, June 16, 1954, CHM.

"I have talked again": Letter from David W.

Bailey to George P. Berry, June 25, 1954, CHM.

"You will agree with me": Letter from George P. Berry to Richard Ford, July 6, 1954, CHM.

"So you may have": Letter from George P. Berry to David W. Bailey, February 17, 1955, CHM.

Woodson's inquiry to the FBI: Teletype from FBI Richmond to Director, FBI, and SAC, Boston, February 2, 1955, FBI.

"This reception reportedly cost": Office memorandum from SAC, Boston, to Director, FBI, September 19, 1955, FBI.

"No derogatory info": Teletype from Boston Field Office to Director, FBI, February 2, 1956.

"I've been fighting": Lee News, October 7, 1957, GHM.

"The cocktail hour": Lee News, August 17, 1958, GHM.

"As I sit quietly": Lee and Lee, *Family Reunion,* 411.

"The most serious damage": Letter from Parker Glass to FGL, February 17, 1961, CHM.

12: Postmortem

Lee's funeral: *Lee News,* February 5, 1962, GHM.

"Mrs. Lee was unquestionably": Banner, "She Invested a Fortune."

"She was the only person": Mary Murray O'Brien, " 'Murder Unrecognized' Tops Harvard Seminar on Crime," *Boston Globe,* November 19, 1950, C36.

"She was . . . my personal friend": Gardner, "A Wonderful Woman."

Honorary degrees: "Quartet Receives Honorary Degrees from N.E. College," *Portsmouth Herald,* July 26, 1956; *Lee News,* May 13, 1958, GHM.

Honorary positions: William Tyre, personal communication, 2019.

Committee report on Department of Legal Medicine: "The Ad Hoc Committee Report," *Corpus Delicti: The Doctor as Detective,* Center for the History of Medicine at Countway Library, accessed December 5, 2018, http://collections.countway .harvard.edu/onview/exhibits/show/corpus -delicti/ad-hoc-committee-report.

Department of Legal Medicine ceased operations: "The End of Legal Medicine," *Corpus Delicti: The Doctor as Detective,* Center for the History of Medicine at

Countway Library, accessed December 5, 2018, http://collections.countway.harvard.edu/onview/exhibits/show/corpus-delicti/ad-hoc-committee-report/end-of-legal-medicine.

Law and Medicine Center at Case Western Reserve University: Jentzen, *Death Investigation in America*, 76–77.

Five thousand undetected homicides every year: "How to Get Away with Murder," *True*, July 1958, 48–101.

Murder of Marilyn Reese Sheppard: Douglas O. Linder, "Dr. Sam Sheppard Trials: An Account," Famous Trials (website), accessed November 24, 2018, http://www.famous-trials.com/sam-sheppard/2-sheppard; "Sheppard Murder Case," Encyclopedia of Cleveland, accessed November 24, 2018, https://case.edu/ech/articles/s/sheppard-murder-case; Sam Sheppard, *Endure and Conquer: My 12-Year Fight for Vindication* (Cleveland: World Publishing Co., 1966); James Neff, *The Wrong Man: The Final Verdict on the Dr. Sam Sheppard Murder Case* (New York: Random House, 2001).

Death of Richard Ford: "Dr. Richard Ford, 55, a Suicide; Witness in Many Murder Trials," *New York Times*, August 4, 1970, https://www.nytimes.com/1970/08/04/

archives/dr-richard-ford-55-a-suicide
-witness-in-many-murder-trials.html.

Donation of The Rocks: "History of The Rocks," The Rocks (website), accessed December 16, 2018, http://therocks.org/history.php.

Highway historical marker: "New NH Historical Marker Honors 'Mother of Forensic Science,' " New Hampshire Department of Cultural Resources press release, October 22, 2018, https://www.nh.gov/nhculture/mediaroom/2018/francesglessnerlee_marker.htm.

Prairie Avenue residence: "The House," Glessner House museum (website), accessed December 6, 2018, https://www.glessnerhouse.org/the-house/; William Tyre, personal communication, 2018.

"There are two minor items": Letter from Parker Glass to Dorothy Hartel, May 9, 1969, Maryland Office of the Chief Medical Examiner.

"Troubled by the implication": Letter from Steven A. Abreu to Scott Keller and Gary Childs, Harvard Associates in Police Science, October 17, 2017.

Death investigation systems today: Randy Hanzlick, "An Overview of Medical Examiner/Coroner Systems in the United States" (PowerPoint presentation prepared for National Academies: Forensic Science Needs Committee, undated), accessed April 9, 2019, https://sites.nationalacad emies.org/cs/groups/pgasite/documents/ webpage/pga_049924.pdf; Randy Hanzlick, "The Conversion of Coroner Systems to Medical Examiner Systems in the United States," *American Journal of Forensic Medicine and Pathology* 28, no. 4 (December 2007): 279–283.

Medical examiner and coroners in Illinois: "Medical Examiner," Cook County Government website, accessed November 22, 2018, https://www.cookcountyil.gov/ agency/medical-examiner; "Coroners Roster," Illinois Coroners and Medical Examiners Association, accessed November 22, 2018, https://www.coronersilli nois.org/coroners-roster; "Illinois Coroner/Medical Examiner Laws," Centers for Disease Control, January 1, 2014, https://www.cdc.gov/phlp/publications/ coroner/illinois.html.

Charleston dual system: K. A. Collins, "Charleston, South Carolina: Reversion from a Medical Examiner/Coroner Dual System to a Coroner System," *Academic Forensic Pathology* 4, no. 1 (2014): 60–64.

Not enough forensic pathologists: K. A. Collins, "The Future of the Forensic Pathology Workforce," *Academic Forensic Pathology* 5, no. 4 (2015): 526–533.

Current numbers: Denise McNally, executive director, National Association of Medical Examiners, personal communication, 2018.

Only 62 percent of cases referred: "Medical Examiners and Coroners' Offices, 2004," U.S. Department of Justice, Bureau of Justice Statistics, June 2007.

Absence of essential tools: Hanzlick, "Overview."

Hotel room deaths from carbon monoxide poisoning: "Health Department Issues Statement about CO Deaths in Hotel," WVTV, June 9, 2013, http://www.wbtv.com/story/22541035/health-department-issues-statement-about-co-deaths-in-hotel/.

DNA used to exonerate: "DNA exonerations in the United States," Innocence Project, accessed December 28, 2018, https://www.innocenceproject.org/dna-exonerations-in-the-united-states/.

Problems with DNA evidence: Matthew Shaer, "The False Promise of DNA Testing," *Atlantic,* June 2016, https://www.theatlantic.com/magazine/archive/2016/06/a-reasonable-doubt/480747/; Pamela

Colloff, "Texas Panel Faults Lab Chemist in Bryan Case for 'Overstating Findings' and Inadequate DNA Analysis," Propublica, October 8, 2018, https://www .propublica.org/article/texas-panel-faults -lab-chemist-in-bryan-case-for-overstated -findings-and-inadequate-dna-analysis; Greg Hampikian, "The Dangers of DNA Testing," *New York Times,* September 21, 2018, https://www.nytimes.com/2018/09/ 21/opinion/the-dangers-of-dna-testing .html.

FURTHER READING AND RESOURCES

Museums

Glessner House museum
1800 S. Prairie Avenue
Chicago, IL 60616
312-326-1480
glessnerhouse.org
info@glessnerhouse.org

The Rocks
4 Christmas Lane
Bethlehem, NH 03574
603-444-6228
therocks.org
info@therocks.org

Multimedia

Of Dolls and Murder (2012, Susan Marks director)
Murder in a Nutshell (in production, Susan

Marks director)

Mystery Street (1950, John Sturges director)

Professional Organizations

National Association of Medical Examiners (http://thename.org)

American Board of Medicolegal Death Investigators (https://www.abmdi.org/)

International Association of Coroners and Medical Examiners (https://www.theiacme .com)

National Institute of Standards and Technology Forensic Science Standards Board (https://www.nist.gov/topics/forensic -science/forensic-science-standards-board)

Scientific Working Group for Medicolegal Death Investigation (https://www.swgmdi .org/)

American Academy of Forensic Science (https://www.aafs.org)

Harvard Associates in Police Science (https://harvardpolicescience.org/)

Reports and Papers

Centers for Disease Control and Prevention. *Coroner/Medical Examiner Laws, by State.* Atlanta, GA: Centers for Disease Control and Prevention, 2016. https://

www.cdc.gov/phlp/publications/topic/
coroner.html.

Centers for Disease Control and Prevention. *Death Investigation Systems.* Atlanta, GA: Centers for Disease Control and Prevention, 2015. https://www.cdc.gov/phlp/publications/coroner/death.html.

Centers for Disease Control and Prevention. *Investigations and Autopsies.* Atlanta, GA: Centers for Disease Control and Prevention, 2015. https://www.cdc.gov/phlp/publications/coroner/investigations.html.

Collins, K. A. "The Future of the Forensic Pathology Workforce." *Academic Forensic Pathology* 5, no. 4 (2015): 526–33.

Committee on Identifying the Needs of the Forensic Sciences Community, National Research Council. *Strengthening Forensic Science in the United States: A Path Forward* Washington, DC: National Research Council, 2009. www.ncjrs.gov/pdffiles1/nij/grants/228091.pdf.

Hanzlick, Randy. "The Conversion of Coroner Systems to Medical Examiner Systems in the United States." *American Journal of Forensic Medicine and Pathology* 28, no. 4 (December 2007): 279–83.

Hanzlick, Randy, and D. Combs. "Medical Examiner and Coroner Systems." *Journal* of the *American Medical Association* 279, no. 11 (March 18, 1998): 870–74.

Hanzlick, Randy. *An Overview of Medical Examiner/Coroner Systems in the United States* Washington, DC: National Academies: Forensic Science Needs Committee. https://sites.nationalacademies.org/cs/groups/pgasite/documents/webpage/pga_049924.pdf.

Hickman, Matthew J., Kristen A. Hughes, and Kevin J. Strom. *Bureau of Justice Statistics Special Report: Medical Examiners and Coroners' Offices, 2004.* Washington, D.C.: U.S. Department of Justice Bureau of Justice Statistics, 2007. https://www.bjs.gov/content/pub/pdf/meco04.pdf.

Institute of Medicine (US) Committee for the Workshop on the Medicolegal Death Investigation System. *Medicolegal Death Investigation System: Workshop Summary.* Washington, D.C.: National Academies Press, 2003. https://www.ncbi.nlm.nih.gov/books/NBK221919/.

National Institute of Justice. *Death Investigation: A Guide for the Scene Investigator.* Washington, DC: National Institute of Justice, June 2011. https://www.ncjrs.gov/pdffiles1/nij/234457.pdf.

National Institute of Justice. *Status and*

Needs of Forensic Science Service Providers: A Report to Congress. Washington, DC: National Institute of Justice, 2004. https://www.ncjrs.gov/pdffiles1/nij/213420.pdf.

Schultz, Oscar T., and Edmund Morris Morgan. *The Coroner and the Medical Examiner.* Bulletin No. 64. Washington, DC: National Research Council of the National Academy of Sciences, 1928.

Legal Medicine and the Nutshell Studies

Eckert, Jack (curator). "Corpus Delicti: The Doctor as Detective." Center for the History of Medicine at Countway Library, 2016. https://collections.countway.harvard.edu/onview/exhibits/show/corpus-delicti.

"Inside the 'Nutshell Studies of Unexplained Death' — 360 VR." Smithsonian American Art Museum. https://americanart.si.edu/exhibitions/nutshells/inside.

May Botz, Corinne. *The Nutshell Studies of Unexplained Death.* New York: Monacelli Press, 2004.

"The Nutshell Studies." 99 Percent Invisible podcast, episode 165, May 19, 2015. http://99percentinvisible.org/episode/the-nutshell-studies.

Works by Medical Examiners and Coroners

Baden, Michael. *Unnatural Death: Confessions of a Medical Examiner.* New York: Random House, 1989.

Bass, William, and Jon Jefferson. *Death's Acre: Inside the Legendary Forensic Lab the Body Farm Where the Dead Do Tell Tales.* New York: G.P. Putnam's Sons, 2003.

Bateson, John. *The Education of a Coroner: Lessons in Investigating Death.* New York: Scribner, 2017.

Blum, Deborah. *The Poisoner's Handbook: Murder and the Birth of Forensic Medicine in Jazz Age New York.* New York: Penguin Press, 2010.

Cataldie, Louis. *Coroner's Journal: Forensics and the Art of Stalking Death.* New York: Berkley Books, 2007.

Cumberland, Gary. *My Life with Death: Memoirs of a Journeyman Medical Examiner.* Bloomington, IN: Xlibris, 2015.

DiMaio, Vincent J. M., and Ron Franscell. *Morgue: A Life in Death.* New York: St. Martin's Press, 2016.

Last Week Tonight with John Oliver. "Death Investigations." HBO, May 19, 2019. https://youtu.be/hnoMsftQPY8.

Maples, William R., and Michael Browning. *Dead Men Do Tell Tales: The Strange and Fascinating Cases of a Forensic Anthropologist.* New York: Broadway Books, 1995.

McCrery, Nigel. *Silent Witnesses: A History of Forensic Science.* London: Random House, 2013.

Melinek, Judith, and T. J. Mitchell. *Working Stiff: Two Years, 262 Bodies, and the Making of a Medical Examiner.* New York: Scribner, 2014.

Noguchi, Thomas T., and Joseph DiMona. *Coroner.* New York: Simon and Schuster, 1983.

Ribowsky, Shiya, and Tom Shachtman. *Dead Center: Behind the Scenes at the World's Largest Medical Examiner's Office.* New York: William Morrow, 2006.

Zugibe, Frederick, and David L. Carroll. *Dissecting Death: Secrets of a Medical Examiner.* New York: Broadway Books, 2005.

Other Books

Boos, William F. *The Poisoner's Trail.* New York: Hale, Cushman & Flint, 1939.

Frankfurter, Felix. *The Case of Sacco and Vanzetti: A Critical Analysis for Lawyers and Laymen.* Buffalo, NY: Little, Brown & Co., 1927.

Gardner, Erle Stanley. *The Court of Last Resort.* New York: William Sloane Associates, 1952.

Jentzen, Jeffrey. *Death Investigation in America.* Cambridge, MA: Harvard University Press, 2009.

Larson, Erik. *Devil in the White City: Murder, Magic, and Madness at the Fair That Changed America.* New York: Crown, 2003.

Puleo, Stephen. *Dark Tide: The Great Boston Molasses Flood of 1919.* Boston: Beacon Press, 2003.

Spears, Timothy B. *Chicago Dreaming: Midwesterners and the City, 1871–1919.* University of Chicago Press, 2005.

Tejada, Susan. *In Search of Sacco and Vanzetti: Double Lives, Troubled Times, and the Massachusetts Murder Case That Shook the World.* Boston: Northeastern University Press, 2012.

Tyre, William H. *Chicago's Historic Prairie Avenue.* Charleston, SC: Arcadia Publishing, 2008.

Watson, Bruce. *Sacco and Vanzetti: The Men, the Murders, and the Judgment of Mankind.* New York: Viking Adult 2007.

ACKNOWLEDGMENTS

The undertaking of a project like this isn't done alone. One name is on the cover, but many people were involved to make this happen. Some provided feedback or encouragement, while others helped in more substantial ways. I am thankful for all of it.

Several individuals shared documents and other material produced in the course of their own work. I am particularly grateful to documentary filmmakers Susan Marks and Virginia Ryker and curator Katie Gagnon for their generosity.

This book could not have been completed without the cooperation and assistance of William Tyre, executive director and curator of the Glessner House museum. Tyre allowed exclusive access to the Glessner papers, without which this book would not be possible, and patiently answered countless questions. During my time at the museum, Gwen Carrion was graciously

499

welcoming. I also enjoyed meeting Kathy Cunningham, who shared her enthusiasm for the Glessners. Tyre and the museum's interns have done commendable work to document the lives of the Glessner family and bring that material to the public. Joan Stinton and Cray Kennedy organized and cataloged Frances Glessner Lee's papers. The museum's blog, *Story of a House,* has been an invaluable resource and is fascinating reading about life during Prairie Avenue's heyday.

Dominic Hall, Jack Eckert, and Jessica Murphy of the Center for the History of Medicine in the Francis A. Countway Library of Medicine at Harvard were helpful and accommodating during my research. Eckert curated an online exhibit, *Corpus Delicti: The Doctor as Detective,* that is very informative.

I am indebted to the staff at the Renwick Gallery of the Smithsonian American Art Museum, especially conservator Ariel O'Çonnor, who revealed so much that was previously unknown about the Nutshell Studies. O'Connor was assisted by Gregory Bailey, Constance Stromberg, and Haddon Dean. I also want to thank Nora Atkinson, Scott Rosenfeld, Dave DeAnna, Sean White, and many others for their work on the exhibition of the Nutshell Studies.

I'm grateful for the assistance of New Hampshire State Archivist Brian Nelson Burford, Helen Conger of Case Western University Archives, Lee Hiltzik of the Rockefeller Archive Center, Dale Wilkins of the Temecula Valley Museum, Clare Brown of the Bethlehem Heritage Society, Nigel Manley of The Rocks, Sandra L. Fox of the Navy Department Library, Denise McNally of the National Association of Medical Examiners, Jane Warren of the American Board of Pathology, Cheryl Irmiter of the Institute of Medicine of Chicago, Harvard Associates in Police Science, the Maryland Medico-Legal Foundation, and Dr. Kim Collins. Stacy Dorsey and Sruti Basu provided editorial assistance. Thanks also to my brother, David Goldfarb, for feedback and advice.

It's been an honor to befriend many members of the Glessner/ Lee family: John Maxim Lee, Percy Lee Langstaff, Lee M. Langstaff, Virginia Lee, Gail Batchelder, Paula Batchelder, Liz Carter, and many others. Getting to know the wonderful extended Glessner/Lee family has been an unexpected reward.

I'm grateful for the support and encouragement of many friends and colleagues:

Elizabeth Evitts Dickinson, Kathy and Ed Rusen, Sarah Archibald, Dave Mastric, Nick Kolakowski, Tim Friend, Katie Horton, Meg Fairfax Fielding, Maria Stainer, David Rivers, Risa Reyes, Ernie Gambone, Larry Goldfarb, Rafael Alvarez, and the members of the Aging Newspaperman's Club and the Ladies Auxiliary.

It's my privilege to work with a group of people who rarely receive public recognition for the important tasks they perform. They are dedicated professionals, good people interested in nothing but the truth and the best interests of decedents. Each has, in their way, shaped and informed my understanding of forensic science.

Drs. Mary Ripple, Pamela Southall, Zabiullah Ali, Carol Allan, Russell Alexander, Patricia Aronica, Melissa Brassell, Stephanie Dean, Pamela Ferreira, Theodore King, Ling Li, J. Laron Locke, John Stash, Jack Titus, and Donna Vincenti. Dr. Nikki Mourtzinos deserves special thanks for answering questions about forensic pathology.

I learned a lot on the job from Det. Sgt. Edward Wilson of the Baltimore City Police Department. Wilson is among the most proficient and skilled fingerprinters in the country. Genuine, decent, always good with a story, Wilson personifies the everyday dedication at the OCME.

Special thank you for all the help from Eleanor Thomas, who has coordinated the Francis Glessner Lee Seminar in Homicide Investigation for many years. I am particularly grateful for the friendship and assistance of Jerry Dziecichowicz, who assigns the Nutshell Studies during the homicide seminar and keeps the secret solutions under lock and key.

I wish to thank the secretaries and clerks who picked up the slack in my absences: Amber Conway, Sandra Dornon, Tiffinney Green, Marlene Groom, Angela Jones, Sharon Robinson, and Coriann Self. Especially Linda Thomas, who always has my back.

Forensic investigators past and present have been close colleagues. They are serious, well-trained, and dedicated professionals who have taught me a lot. Kristine Carder, Randolph Dailey, Dawn Epperson, Bethany Miller, Melinda FitzGerald, David Foehner, Stacy Groft, Aaron Hearn, Saundra Hensley, Stephanie Kimmel, Christina Rzepecki Leonard, Gray Maggard, Courtney Manzo, Anthony McCaffity, Joseph Mullin, Brittany Munro, Keith Opher,

Charlotte Rose Noranbrook, Stephanie Rollins, Bryant Smith, and Kimberly Winston. People who work in the toxicology and histology labs include Abraham Tsadik, Saffia Ahmed-Sakinedzad, Andra Poston, Xiang Zhang, Cindy Chapman, and Angela Dean.

The hardest working and most underpaid at the medical examiner's office are the autopsy technicians. Autopsy techs don't get thanked often enough for the job that they do, so let me thank them: Mario Alston, Darrolyn Butler, Ricardo Diggs, Larry Hardy, Leroy Jones, Curtis Jordan, Jessika Logan, Robert Mills, Mozelle Osborne, and Raymond Zimmerman.

Also: Tom Brown, Mike Eagle, Rebecca Jufer Phipps, Dawn Zulauf, Donnell McCollough, Brian Tannenbaum, William Spencer-Strong, Dr. Juan Troncoso, William Rodriguez, Dr. Warren Tewes, Craig Robinson, Barbara Haughey, Samara Simmorins, Ricky Jacobson, David Koch, Stoney Burke, and Dustin Saulsbury. Tim Bittner deserves special mention for his assistance bringing the Nutshell Studies back home after the Renwick Gallery exhibit, and Albert Kaniasty for being a fan.

I am grateful for the support of my boss, Dr. David R. Fowler. Every day at work is a seminar. I have learned much from Dr. Fowler about forensic science, governance and the law, integrity in the search for truth, running a busy forensic medical center at the top of its game, and many other things. I can't thank him enough for allowing me the flexibility to pursue this project and for taking the time to answer questions and provide information and resources. Dr. Fowler is the best boss anybody could hope for.

I'm fortunate to be represented by Tamar Rydzinski, who worked with me very patiently until I got it right. She is a fantastic agent, and I am grateful to UMBC friend Bryan Denson for the introduction. I owe a debt of gratitude to Sourcebooks editor Anna Michaels, who helped shape and improve the story immensely.

Most of all, I am deeply appreciative for the support and love of my family. My wife, Bridgett, has been a patient listener and provided key insights to the material. This book represents a sacrifice for the entire family — meals and events missed, nights away from home, hours spent at the keyboard. I couldn't have done this without their understanding and patience, and their commitment to having Lee's story told. This is from all of us.

ABOUT THE AUTHOR

Bruce Goldfarb is an award-winning writer who specializes in science, medicine, and health care and has written for national and local newspapers, magazines, and web publications. He works as an executive assistant for the chief medical examiner for the state of Maryland, where he maintains Frances Glessner Lee's Nutshell Studies of Unexplained Death. Bruce lives in Baltimore, Maryland.

The employees of Thorndike Press hope you have enjoyed this Large Print book. All our Thorndike, Wheeler, and Kennebec Large Print titles are designed for easy reading, and all our books are made to last. Other Thorndike Press Large Print books are available at your library, through selected bookstores, or directly from us.

For information about titles, please call:
(800) 223-1244

or visit our website at:
gale.com/thorndike

To share your comments, please write:

Publisher
Thorndike Press
10 Water St., Suite 310
Waterville, ME 04901